D0496643

Jonathon Green is a lexicographer, that is ⸍⸍⸍ specialising in slang, about which he has been ⸍⸍⸍⸍⸍ ⸍⸍⸍ aries. ⸍⸍⸍⸍⸍ ⸍⸍⸍⸍⸍ ⸍⸍⸍ ⸍⸍⸍⸍ He has ⸍⸍ written histories of lexicography and of slang. After working on his university newspaper he joined the London 'underground press' in 1969, working for most of the then available titles, such as *Friends*, *IT* and *Oz*. He has been publishing books since the mid-1970s, spending the next decade putting together a number of dictionaries of quotations, before he moved into what remains his primary interest, slang. Jonathon's slang work has reached its climax, but he trusts not its end, with the publication in 2010 of *Green's Dictionary of Slang*, a three-volume, 6,200-page dictionary 'on historical principles' offering some 110,000 words and phrases, backed up by around 410,000 citations or usage examples. The book covers all anglophone countries and its timeline stretches from around 1500 up to the present day. An online version, which is regularly updated, was launched in 2016. For those who prefer something less academic, he published the *Chambers Slang Dictionary*, a single volume book, in 2008.

Website: http://jonathongreen.co.uk
The Dabbler: http://thedabbler.co.uk/ (as Mister Slang)
Twitter: @misterslang
The Timelines of Slang: http://thetimelinesofslang.tumblr.com/
Green's Dictionary of Slang - Online is available at
https://greensdictofslang.com.
All the words included in *Stories of Slang* are listed there, with full definitions and etymologies, and can be accessed for free.

800 659 009

Also by Jonathon Green

Green's Dictionary of Slang (also online)
Language! 500 Years of the Vulgar Tongue
Odd Job Man: Some Confessions of a Slang Lexicographer
Chambers Slang Dictionary

The Stories of Slang

JONATHON GREEN

ROBINSON

ROBINSON

First published in Great Britain in 2017 by Robinson

1 3 5 7 9 10 8 6 4 2

Copyright © Jonathon Green, 2017

The moral right of the author has been asserted.

All rights reserved.
No part of this publication may be reproduced, stored in a retrieval system, or transmitted, in
any form, or by any means, without the prior permission in writing of the publisher, nor be
otherwise circulated in any form of binding or cover other than that in which it is published and
without a similar condition including this condition being imposed on the subsequent purchaser.

A CIP catalogue record for this book
is available from the British Library.

ISBN: 978-1-47213-966-5

Typeset in Adobe Garamond Pro by Hewer Text UK Ltd, Edinburgh
Printed and bound in Great Britain by Clays Ltd, St Ives plc

Papers used by Robinson are from well-managed forests and other responsible sources.

Robinson
An imprint of
Little, Brown Book Group
Carmelite House
50 Victoria Embankment
London EC4Y 0DZ

An Hachette UK Company
www.hachette.co.uk

www.littlebrown.co.uk

Contents

Introduction

A SK ANYONE, SLANG is all about fucking. Fucking and rhymes. Words and phrases for sex and the human giblets with which we do it, and that much-loved but somewhat tired phenomenon: rhyming slang, which however valid its mid-nineteenth-century origins, has long since become more of an intermittently amusing sideshow than part of the mainstream slang vocabulary.

I have written extensively about them both, and while they will undoubtedly push their way in here, the purpose of what follows is to take a look at what we might call slang's reserve team. It is a good reserve team, members jostling to reach the heights and quite capable of stepping up, but as I suggest, not always what people immediately think of when they say 'slang'. But there are 130,000 words and phrases in my database, and even if around 10,000 are in some way linked to sex, that leaves room for quite a number more. It's time, I suggest, to give these 'understudies' their own show.

I have divided the material into simple sections: people, places and things, plus language itself. Within those groups we shall meet doctors and the pox, foreigners and their funny food, life in the big city (slang's necessary partner in crime), anecdotes and catchphrases, slang's version of a mystery tour, the language of pulp fiction and of UK slang's current cutting edge, Multicultural London English, and among other things some of those body parts that remain vital even if they are not obviously required for the *old in-and-out* (much popularised in *Clockwork Orange* but actually used since 1635). I have moved a little outside the mainstream to include a selection of catchphrases, often pretty slangy, too.

Look at the slang vocabulary: this is not a feel-good environment. The compassionate, the empathetic, the kind of heart need not enter here. In a world where aggression – one-to-one, international, screaming from the foetid underside of social media – is the go-to emotion, slang, never one to mind its language, seems the go-to way of speech.

Slang is an unsafe space. It has no time for political correctness, none for true belief. Neither is it that pious product of Victorian muscular Christianity, Mrs Do-As-You-Would-Be-Done-By, nor does it turn the other cheek, other, perhaps than shifting a buttock all the better to deliver a noisome fart. Racist and nationalist, all-purpose-sexist, variously phobic, if it lacks micro-aggressions then it is because such piffling teases in turn lack sufficient antagonism. It is contemptuous of the special snowflakes and their identity politics and if it tosses snowballs, they are lined with stones. It is filled with stereotypes – how else to define the necessary 'other' against whom it aims its weaponry – but it lays down no laws, no diktats, no ukases. It is neither naive nor optimistic, it does not demand that things be otherwise, it knows too much. It is, in other words, real. Too real?

So some complain, but slang, with its emphasis on sex, drugs and at least in a figurative sense, all the self-indulgences that can be labelled rock 'n' roll, represents its users not as they should be, but how they are. But as the comedian Lenny Bruce noted;

everybody wants what should be, but what should be does not exist. There is only what is. Slang is. Call me a cynic, but to me slang paints a picture that shows ourselves at our most human. Which doesn't, unfortunately, mean nice. Slang is an equal-opportunity vilifier. Look at those words: to steal from the political philosopher Thomas Hobbes, who was talking about human beings, nasty, brutish and short.

Let us not get too gloomy. Slang may suit the times but it also defies them. Unlike the demagogue it does not lie. It lives to deflate pomposity. It's subversive, mocking, in short, it takes the piss. Critics of the great American essayist H.L. Mencken, eviscerator of every brand of his countrymen's infinite worship of charlatanry – read him now, his heyday was the 1920s, but all Trump is there – denounced him for lacking 'the sentiment of reverence'. Slang follows suit and always did.

Like us, slang saves itself through a love of humour and a capacity for wit. It may be somewhat dark-hued humour, and the wit a little cruel, but the aim holds true; you gotta laugh. It is my intent that via the overview that follows, there will at least be moments when you shall.

So what are slang's stories? They work on two levels; the *theme* and the *etymology*. The stories that slang tells itself, one might say, and those that lie behind the words and phrases that make up its vocabulary. To put it another way: the general and the specific. The intention of what follows is to take a look at both.

Compared with standard English, slang covers a narrow waterfront – it offers a few slogans, most of them sexual, but doesn't philosophise; it doesn't ponder abstracts, preferring the hard-edged concrete. On the other hand it digs deep: its primary themes number less than thirty, but it mines them for every possibility. As offered in the *OED,* standard English offers 102 synonyms for 'have sexual intercourse' and of these seventy-two 'fess up with their label 'slang'. Slang itself offers 1,600 more, though in fairness, since such is the way of a good deal of slang, this in turn has a certain circularity since many will play with standard words to achieve its seditious and counter-linguistic effect.

So what do we have? Five thousand terms for *criminals,* four-and-a-half for *drinking* and *drunks,* and four thousand for *drugs.* Three thousand for *women* (almost invariably considered negatively or at best congratulated only on their sexual allure), twenty-five hundred *fools,* twenty-two hundred *men* (of various descriptions, not invariably, but often self-aggrandising). Twelve hundred *homosexuals* and another twelve hundred *whores,* a round thousand *police.* There are seventeen hundred terms for *fucking* (plus 240 for *oral sex,* 180 for *anal* and sixty-five for *STDs*), fourteen hundred apiece for *penises* and *vaginas,* six hundred and fifty for the *anus* and *buttocks,* three hundred and fifty for *promiscuity.* And on it goes: *death* and *dying,* 831; *violence* and *assault* 728 and outright *murder* 521; *madness* 776; *shitting* and *pissing* 540; *ugly* 279; *fat* 247; *vomiting* 219. Will that do?

As for etymology, those stories are offered by the words themselves. In truth the bulk of the slang vocabulary is based on standard origins. Often the pleasure is in the manipulation of those well-known words for manipulation's sake – playing, punning, tweaking, twisting, turning inside out and round about. *Dog,* for instance, is good for two hundred-plus reinterpretations. Such playfulness, I like to think, is another very human trait. But while there are tales to tell, and my aim is to tell them when they are on offer, they are not always to be trusted. We may have chapter and verse for *sweet Fanny Adams* but only a selection of theories for *Betty Martin* (she of *all my eye and . . .*). And even when the slang collectors believe they've nailed a given story, they are not invariably trusted, given the Internet's open-all-areas access and disdain paraded by what Mencken would have termed 'the plain people' for 'experts', who at all costs must not be seen as knowing 'better'. Who needs 'truth' when you've got popular etymology. *Fuck* from *fornicate under command of the king*, *shit* from *store high in transit*, *nitty-gritty* as the detritus of a slave-ship hold . . . that sort of thing.

With all that in mind *Stories of Slang* makes no claims for narrative, let alone plot (other than, being slang, there will be no *happy endings*, other than the – literally – tacky pun enshrined in that phrase). This is not *The* Story of Slang, of which I have written elsewhere and which might be seen as a lengthy and never-to-be-finished race in which the hare-like coiners and users try to keep ahead of the slow-but-steady linguists and lexicographers. What you have here is far more random (in the standard sense). The exploration of some of the themes that are listed above, and of the individual words and phrases they have, and continue to throw up. If that offers something of an *olla podrida*, even a *gallimaufry*, so be it. No one ever pretended it wasn't a messy world.

Carry on Barding, or,
Much Ado About Pistol's Cock

THE NATURE OF slang – seditious, obscene, impertinent, too often lacking, we have to admit, the supposedly necessary seriousness of tone and depth of topic – means that many of its keenest users are not rated among the lit. crit. pantheon. That isn't to condemn them to mere hackery. But in the end, however much we revel in Seth Morgan, Helen Green van Campen, such best-sellers as George Ade or Irvine Welsh, and others who run glorious riot with the lexis, there just aren't that many superstars. Not a good career move? Low on creative writing sinecures. Yet for all those who opt to steer clear, some of the giants do nod in slang's direction.

Thus the greatest of them all, Shakespeare, uses, at my count, just over five hundred 'slang' terms, of which 277 are currently the first recorded use of a given term. Among these are *every mother's son*, *fat-headed*, *heifer* (for woman), *pickers and stealers* (hands), *small beer* (insignificant matters), *what the dickens*, and many more.

The Bard (which naming seems to have been made first by the actor David Garrick in 1769) is not alone.

There is Dickens, for instance. No one then or possibly even now could claim to know London as did he, and that meant knowing its language as well. Slang, in context, gives authenticity and Dickens was happy to draw on it. So too did such contemporaries as Harrison Ainsworth or Edward Lytton, but where they seemed to have the dictionary in one hand and the quill in the other, hunting and pecking for juicy syllables, with Dickens the seams never show.

The slang in, say, *Oliver Twist*, is one more way in which the novelist displays his mastery of the environment. Fagin the *fence*, Bill Sikes the *swell mobsman*, the Artful Dodger, that *downy cove* (though not Nancy, who for all her actual profession – a whore, and not a very classy one; the world would have called her a *tuppenny uprighter* – is female and as such sacrosanct and speaks standard English) are all imbued with cant, the language of the professional criminal. One does not ring a bell but *jerks the tinkler*, the handkerchiefs the gang steals from juvenile *kinchins* (i.e. German *kindchen*, a child) are *fogles* (from Italian *foglia*, a leaf or French slang *fouille*, a pocket), and Fagin, hoping for a *lagging* (from *lag*, to carry away, in this case in the form of transportation to Australia) will end his days *scragged* (from *scrag*, the neck), or hanged on the gallows erected outside the *Stone Jug* (a *jug* that contains people rather than liquids), Newgate jail.

Moving forward, no one could have been more loving of slang, and so wondrously productive in his use of it than P.G. Wodehouse, whose one hundred-plus books provide nearly 1,500 examples. *Browsing and sluicing* (eating and drinking), *soup and fish* (a dinner jacket), *ranny-gazoo* (perhaps from dialect *ranny*, rash and French slang *gazouiller*, to sing), 'rum goings on', and *oojah-cum-spiff* (*oojah* defeats research, *spiff* means first-rate), exactly as required. The fact that Wodehouse blithely intermingled these Edwardianisms with such modern American terms as *bump off*, *chucker-out* and *four-flusher* (from poker) merely ups the humorous ante.

Another example: James Joyce. It may come as a surprise to find that *Ulysses*, a book often cited as the greatest novel ever written and as such rated as somewhat serious, is a contender for slang stardom, but so it is. Joyce, always a connoisseur of language, was as keen on slang as the rest of the dictionary and his *magnum opus* has nearly a thousand slang terms. For a book that is celebrated for the recreation of a single day, 16 June, 1904, Joyce is splendidly all-encompassing in his borrowings. There is rogue's language from 1560 and Kiplingesque soldiers from the Raj, alongside stage Irishmen, English toffs and so much more.

However, as the chapter title should have made clear, what we are discussing here is Shakespeare. So let us do so.

This, for instance, is Shakespeare:

Hamlet: Lady, shall I lie in your lap?
Ophelia: No, my lord.
Hamlet: I mean, my head upon your lap?
Ophelia: Ay, my lord.
Hamlet: Do you think I meant country matters?
Ophelia: I think nothing, my lord.
Hamlet: That's a fair thought to lie between maids' legs.
Ophelia: What is, my lord?
Hamlet: Nothing.

> W. Shakespeare *The Tragedy of Hamlet,*
> *Prince of Denmark* c. 1600

This is definitely not:

Dr. Kenneth Soaper (Kenneth Williams): It has been my
experience that once young people sample the delights of

country life and the wonders of nature they just can't get
enough of it.
Miss Haggerd (Hattie Jacques): Exactly.
Dr. Kenneth Soaper: Well I was thinking of the girls . . .
Miss Haggerd: So was I.
Dr. Kenneth Soaper: Exactly.

T. Rothwell *Carry on Camping or*
Let Sleeping Bags Lie 1972

Definitely not? Are we sure? It is tempting to ascribe the latter
scene to the former, what the lit. crit. world calls intertextuality
and what the less guarded among us might see as plagiarism.
Not so, and it would be to traduce Talbot Rothwell, the ex-pilot
turned *Carry On* scriptwriter, who surely picked up his double
entendres in the wartime RAF messes of which he was doubtless
an adornment, rather than from scanning the Bard. In any case,
the point is the reverse. Not that *Carry On* films jam an elbow
into your ribs, removing it only to jab it back even harder, but
that Shakespeare, that epitome of 'literature' was already there so
long before.

'Pistol's cock is up and flashing fire will follow.' Is that the late
Frankie Howerd drawing an insinuating breath? Or maybe
Kenneth Williams. But in fact it's Shakespeare, in *Henry V*
(c.1600). And do not be fooled, Britain's most celebrated citizen
knew exactly whereof he spoke. Shakespeare is awash with double
(and even single) entendres, a veritable *Carry On* . . . of his era.

Nudge-nudgery has always lain at the heart of British humour.
Playing with words is central to slang, and even if not (quite)
everything is smut, the double entendre is ever-present. The jolly
rustics spouting low humour have a time-honoured place in
theatre; indeed the first ever recordings of slang in French are in

thirteenth-century passion plays, in which the rib-ticklers are delivered in the very shadow of the cross. Chaucer too can offer piety, but, typically in *The Miller's Tale*, he also gives us plenty of bawdy. But *Hamlet* is hardly a laff riot, and Hamlet's double entendres – *lap*: vagina, *c*(o)*untry* matters, and *nothing*, again the vagina, which Francis Grose in his 1785 slang dictionary defines thus '( )', i.e. 'nothing' – are delivered reflectively, and shortly after he briefs the Players on the delivery of their play within a play. It is one of Shakespeare's many great speeches, and there are no rustics here, no nudges either.

The double entendres, however, are inescapable and Shakespeare, for all his elevation to literature's Parnassus, has no desire to run away. Take *Romeo and Juliet*, another that gets listed among the tragedies. 'O, that she were / An open et-caetera, thou a poperin pear!' Nothing, one can be assured, to do with fruit, though it does suggest what elsewhere he describes as *plucking*. Any more than is his use of *fig*. As for *et-caetera*, the usual belief is that this too means the vagina, but it may in fact be a printer's oversight rather than a playwright's smut: sometimes what we see is really what we get. (On the other hand there is *Henry IV* Pt 2 and 'Come we to full points here, and are etceteras nothings?' where *point* is surely the penis, and as seen above, *nothing* its partner in pleasure.)

Nor is an *aunt* a relation, a *nunnery* remotely religious (even if it is populated by *nuns*, not to mention an *abbess*): we are in the world of brothels and sex-work; nor are the *low countries* (or indeed the *netherlands*) even vaguely Dutch but what modernity, coyly, terms *down there*. And as for that bizarre image of copulation: *groping for trout in a peculiar river* . . . The play also offers *bauble* for penis, *bird's-nest* for pubic hair and *salt-fish* for vagina (an early example of the many terms that equate the woman or her genitals with the water-borne species), as well as the once widely used *sir-reverence* for excrement, which led to Grose's 1796 definition of *reverence*: 'an ancient custom which obliges any person easing himself near the highway or foot-path, on the word *reverence* being given to him by a passenger, to take off his hat with his teeth, and without moving from his station to throw it over his head, by which it frequently falls into the excrement . . .'

Shakespeare uses *hare-finder*, to mean a womaniser (*hair*, as in pubic) and in *Love's Labour's Lost* (1595) he plays on *Ajax*, both Greek hero and a *jakes*, i.e. a 'close-stool' or water-closet. The pun was behind Sir John Harington's squib *The Metamorphosis of Ajax* (1596), a plea for the introduction of the water-closet, the supposed coarseness of which so displeased Queen Elizabeth I that its author was temporarily banned from court.

Shakespeare's works are full of crime, often at the highest level, but unlike most of the sixteenth-century writers to whom one has to look for early examples of the counter-language, he has no examples of cant (the formal term for criminal jargon). Such fellow-playwrights as Thomas Dekker or Shakespeare's enemy Robert Greene may have harnessed script-writing with pamphlets on what the latter called *coney-catching*, i.e. confidence trickery, but he did not. Shakespeare's five hundred slang terms cover a good deal of ground, but the primary focus – far more so than that of the pamphleteers – deals in slang's favourite topic: sex. The penis, the vagina and the intercourse between them; a minor deviation for the buttocks and a good many prostitutes. Still, there are very few of what modernity categorises as 'obscenities'; a list – by necessity short – would include *foutra* (i.e. fuck) in 'a foutra for', *cock* for penis, but only as a double entendre, *come*, to achieve orgasm, *hole* for vagina, and *piss* as both noun and verb – and piss, around 1600, was hardly slang. The double entendre, surrounded by pretty penetrable context, is far more likely: *juggle* or *occupy* for intercourse, *plum-tree* or *medlar* for vagina, *sword* or *weapon* for penis.

Intercourse itself is *it*, *nibbling*, *tick-tack* ('an old variety of backgammon, played on a board with holes along the edge, in which pegs were placed for scoring' *OED*), *night-work* and *stair-* or *trunk-work*, which last suggest clandestine or casual sex. A *diver* is a man 'on the job'. To have sex is predictably a man's occupation. Only *put a man in one's belly*, *shake a man's back* and *spin off* or *cleave the pin* (to bring a man to orgasm) take the female position (and even these are determined by the male point of view). Otherwise there is the usual 'man hits woman' aggression of slang's couplings: *board*, *charge* (from *sharge*, to attack), *foin* (i.e. stab) and *stab* itself, *horse* and *mount* (both precursors of *ride*), *plough*, *pluck*, *leap* (and *take a leap in the dark*), *thump*, *tumble*, *vault*, *work* and *top*. *Tread* and *tup* borrow from animals, the first from poultry, the second rams and ewes. Otherwise there are the slightly euphemistic *do the deed* (i.e. 'of darkness'), *do it*, *flesh it*, *have*, *bed*, *put it to*, *sluice* and *taste*. More elaborate are *play at cherry pit* (not the *cherry* of virginity, which other than a one-off in 1700 is a twentieth-century creation) but the pit or pip that lies within a fruit, *board a land carrack* (literally a coasting vessel, here a woman, usually a whore), *make the beast with two backs* (with its satanic overtones) and *grope for trout in a peculiar river*, which predates the use of *trout* as a woman, and again links to the many uses of *fish* for both the woman and her vagina.

That same vagina can be her *beef* (which also serves for the penis, and elsewhere, as does *meat*, for the entire body, irrespective of gender), *breach* (i.e. hole), *buckler* (a small shield, and set against his *sword*), *eye* (expanded in the nineteenth century to the *eye that weeps most when pleased*), *fountain* ('of love'), *buggle-bo* (otherwise a demon), *hell* (taken from the dictionary-maker John Florio who used it in 1598 to translate *Valle di Acheronte*, 'a womans priuie parts or gheare', and which refers to the river Acheron, supposedly leading to the underworld), *Netherlands* (a pun on *low countries*, though Shakespeare only uses that for the buttocks), *lap, nest, ring, medlar* (*tree*) (as a fruit nicknamed *open arse*), *orchard* and *plum-tree, petticoat, placket, rose* and, sounding more like something from John Cleland's infinitely euphemistic but highly pornographic *Memoirs of a Woman of Pleasure* (1749), *Venus's glove*.

If sex is violence, then the penis is made to dole it out: the *lance, pike, pistol, poking-stick, poll axe, sword, weapon*. Meanwhile, as well as *beef*, edibles include *carrot, poperin pear* (i.e. Poperinghe, in west Flanders, plus a supposed pun on 'pop her in'), and *potato-finger*. The *bauble*, otherwise a *jewel*, suggests the later *family jewels*, while *kicky-wicky* (from French *quelque chose*, something) is yet another euphemism, and a less boastful image than all that weaponry. So too *pillicock*, which evokes *cock*, but elsewhere means a fool. Otherwise there are the classic *cock* and *prick*, the *pen*, the *tail* (multi-purposed as vagina and buttocks) and the *tool*.

Finally, for flesh, the buttocks, which are variously *arse, bum, tail* and such jocular or punning uses as *catastrophe, holland, low countries* and *wind instrument*.

There are neutral women in Shakespeare but they are rare: *fro* (from Dutch), *hen, petticoat, she*. Otherwise there are two choices. The first portrays the woman as overly independent (or as Shakespeare would put it *robustious*), and thus a problem; a line from *The Merry Wives of Windsor* gives a good selection:

'Out of my door, you witch, you rag, you baggage, you polecat, you ronyon!' Only *ramp*, from rampant, is missing. Or, independent again, she is what the era termed *light* (i.e. easily pushed onto her back) or *easy*: the *doxy*, the *wench* and the *baggage* (originally a camp-follower – a woman who follows the military – but more commonly found in such combinations as *saucy baggage* or *sly baggage*; there may also be links to French *bagasse*, a prostitute, a wanton). Then there is *ling*, another woman = fish image, and summed up in the coarse mid-nineteenth-century song 'The Maid & The Fishmonger': Then the girl shoved her hand 'neath her clothes in a shot, / And rubbed it about on a certain sweet spot; / Then, blushing so sweetly, as you may suppose, / She put her hand up to the fishmonger's nose. / The fishmonger smelt it, and cried with delight, 'I know what you want, by the smell, now, all right, / 'Twas a good thought of yours, recollection to bring; I'll tell you directly – you wanted some ling'.

Usually she is simply a whore and the *hold-door trade*, and its attendant brothels supply the largest chunk of Shakespeare's non-standard lexis. There is, inevitably an overlap between *lightness* and commerce. Such as baggage and doxy can go either way. Other *gamesters* (the precursor of *on the game*), include the *Barbary hen*, *boiled stuff* (from the sweating tub in which she battled the pox), *bona roba* (literally 'a fine dress') and *loose-bodied gown* (like the contemporary synonym *white apron*, this was fashion as a badge of office), *carrion*, *flirt-gill*, *skainsmate* (a mystery word: perhaps from the dialect *skain*, a dagger; thus a figurative penis; or a *skein* of thread or wool, and thus related to the 'sewing' imagery of intercourse), *Galloway nag* (a strong, small horse), *daughter of the game*, *green goose* (a young girl, soon to be a whore) and the punning *guinea hen* (an expensive girl), *hackney* (the *hackney horse*, a run-of-the-mill horse, i.e. not a warhorse or hunter, which was used for everyday riding and thus the sort of horse available for hire), *hare* (playing on *hair*, presumably pubic, but also the stereotyped image of rabbits or hares as sexy beasts and possibly on *puss*, a hare and *cat*, a woman), *heifer*, *hobby horse* (which is 'ridden'), *jay* (a bird noted for its noisiness and bright colouring), *laced mutton* (the lacing is that of stays or corsets, embellishing a young, or disguising an ageing, figure), *ladybird*, *light o'love* (playing on *light* but also referencing on a popular dance), *Maid Marian* (the morris-dancing tradition of having that character played by a local prostitute), *mermaid* (who lured men, usually sailors, to their doom), *open-arse*, *pagan*, *punk*, *puzzle* (from dialect *puzzle*, a slut and beyond that French *pucelle*, a virgin; the reference is to young girls, especially when fresh from the country, who presented themselves as virgins, however inaccurately, and thus demanded higher prices), *quail* (a supposedly amorous bird), *stallion*, *drab*, *trader*, *trull* (from German), and the punning *wagtail*.

Brothels were primarily houses: *house* itself, the *hot-house* (both hot as sexy and hot as venereally diseased), the *house of profession*, *house of resort*, *house of sale*, *leaping house*, *victualling-house* (a pimp was a *victualler* although *eat*, as in fellate, was still far distant) and *naughty house*. Two examples deal not with the whole house but its design: a *red lattice* and the *manor of picked hatch*. A red lattice or grate was a popular tavern sign and thence, if the tavern was thus inclined, could also indicate a brothel; at one time an actual Red Lattice inn stood at Butcher's Row, off the Strand. A *picked*, properly *piked hatch* was a half-door, topped by spikes so as to prevent anyone climbing over. Again it denoted a brothel and the original such address was a tavern-cum-brothel in Clerkenwell (either in Turnmill or Turnbull Street – recalled by Falstaff as a favourite stamping ground – or slightly further north in a nest of alleyways off Old Street). Shakespeare also mentions the *suburbs*. Literally 'beneath the city', such early suburbs – Holborn, Wapping, Mile End, Bermondsey, Clerkenwell – may have become parts of central London but, in the sixteenth and seventeenth centuries, they were beyond the City and its walls, and, as such, were home to various 'stink' industries – tanning, leper hospitals, playhouses and brothels. And most notoriously the last. Thus a whore could be an *aunt of the suburbs*, a *suburb wench*, a *suburban strumpet*, a *sixpenny suburb-sinnet* and a *suburb lady*, while the world of prostitution was the *suburban trade*.

Slang's default gender is male. In slang terms, Shakespeare's default male type is the fool. He offers *asshead*, *beetlehead* (from *beetle*, a large hammer), *block*, *calf*, *calf's-head*, *goat* (also a lecher), *hobby horse* (its wooden head), *jack*, *jolthead*, *jolterhead*, *logger-head* (a *logger* being anything heavy and solid), *loon*, *nit*, *noddy* and *woodcock*. *Lubber*, the basis of the nautical *land-lubber*, a landsman or incompetent sailor, comes either from Old French *lobeor*, a swindler or parasite, and beyond that *lober*, to deceive, to sponge upon or to mock. The clumsiness implicit in the nautical use implies a further link to standard English *lob*, a country bumpkin, ultimately from a variety of Germanic forms all meaning heavy or clumsy. To be stupid is to be *clay-brained*, *knotty-headed* or *loggerheaded*.

Shakespeare uses all these and much else that in my book qualifies as slang too. But there's the rub. Can we really talk about 'slang' before the eighteenth century? The first dictionary that might be seen as including 'civilian' alongside criminal slang, appeared only in 1698. The word itself doesn't come on stream in the context of language till 1756 (there are a few adjectival references that equate slang with 'corrupt' twenty years earlier) so what do we do with all those terms plucked from the Bard and which have long since settled into the slang dictionaries? Can we define a lexis as slang in a world where slang does not yet exist? Is it just groundling talk? The street's unfettered alternative to what by 1600 was established as the early modern version of Standard English and as such toff-speak?

That these terms would in time enter the slang dictionaries is unarguable. But we must still ask: at the time that they were used, can they be classified as 'slang'? Is that what Shakespeare was using, consciously or not? They certainly fit the bill; they focus on slang's obsessions: parts of the body, sexuality, defecation, misogyny, insults and they are voiced by the lower classes of society: vulgar people and their vulgar tongue. If they are not yet labelled as slang, then it's hard to know where else to put them.

There is so much we cannot know. Where did Shakespeare find his slang words and phrases? He seems to have drawn on John Florio's Italian-English dictionary *The Worlde of Wordes* (1598), which among much else translated *Fottere* [. . .] to iape, to sard, to fucke, to swive, to occupy; the lexicographer and the playwright overlap on seventeen occasions. He has fifteen terms in common with Chaucer's *Canterbury Tales* of 1386 (mainly sex and defecation) and thirteen with the *Gesta Grayorum*, the record of a Christmas entertainment performed in 1594, and among several other authors some seventy-six with Robert Greene, a rival playwright (and author of pamphlets on 'coney-catching' or confidence trickery) who christened his contemporary 'an vpstart Crow, beautified with our feathers, that with his *Tygers hart wrapt in a Players hyde*, supposes he is as well able to bombast out a blanke verse as the best of you: and being an absolute *Iohannes factotum*, is in his owne conceit the onely Shake-scene in a countrey.'

Nor do we know to what extent these ludic winks and nudges had the gallery roaring. The groundlings may have heard nothing much beyond their own conversation thrown back to them. The sexual references may have passed without comment. The parallel with *Carry On* movies may be semantic rather than social.

What we do know is whatever they may have felt up in the gods, those in the dress circle would become less tolerant. Other than certain 'classic' works of out-and-out, purpose-written porn, the works of Shakespeare have been more often expurgated than those of any other English-language author except Chaucer.

The expurgations were not initially based on sex but on politics. Whole speeches rather than single, 'dirty' words. The first example came via Elizabeth I, who found the passage in *Richard II* in which the king is deposed so infuriating that she had it cut from all performances and it was only restored after her death. The next recorded expurgation of Shakespeare was carried out by Sir William D'Avenant, who held a monopoly of licensed plays in London, in 1660. In what was basically a sop to Puritan interests, he trimmed seven of the plays with the general intention 'that they may be reformed of prophanes and ribaldry'. Up to the nineteenth century, most censorship had the same justification: the authorities, especially the royal family, must not be mocked. Nor should the national playwright display anything that diminished his own dignity. Thus one expurgator removed the gravediggers from Hamlet: such low comedy disgraced so great a play. Paradoxically, Shakespeare was made if anything more ribald, as in Dryden's version of *The Tempest* in which Miranda is given a sexier twin sister, Dorinda.

This changed in 1807 when one Thomas Bowdler, a former physician, now country gentleman resident on the Isle of Wight and a herald of the grim moralism that evangelical Christianity would trumpet half a century on, took it upon himself to censor Shakespeare's works of 'everything that can raise a blush on the cheek of modesty', in effect about 10 per cent of Shakespeare's text. The book, initially created by his sister Henrietta Maria (Harriet) Bowdler, was entitled *The Family Shakespeare*. The Bowdlers' timing was perfect, and much embraced by the newly powerful evangelistic world. The word *bowdlerise*, a synonym for censoring on moral grounds (another synonym, since 1627, was *castrate*) is first recorded in 1836.

Profanity was verboten: 'God!' invariably became 'Heaven!', 'Jesu!' was simply dropped. The religious preferences were distinctly evangelical; Catholic susceptibilities were not soothed and oaths such as 'Marry!' (Mary) and ''Sblood!' (God's blood) were left intact. What mattered most was irreverence: no vestige of humour at God's expense was spared. Bowdler slashed *Romeo and Juliet* (the over-earthy Nurse practically disappeared), *King Lear* and *Henry IV, Part 2*. *Measure for Measure* defeated him and had to be printed with a warning, so hard was it to cut, as was *Othello,* which he stated was 'unfortunately little suited to family reading' and suggested that it be transferred 'from the parlour to the cabinet'. The Bowdlers had launched a minor industry. By 1850 there were seven rival expurgated Shakespeares; by 1900 there were nearly fifty. Not until 1916, when he was finally debunked in the *English Review,* did Bowdler's version of Shakespeare lose its authority.

Shakespeare, then, takes his place among the great slangsters. But let us not forget the *Carry On* stars with whom at least his humour seems to be running down similar lines. It is a truism that low comedians yearn to play the tragic greats. Sid James, of course, did play Marc Antony, albeit in *Carry On Cleo* (Kenneth

Williams was Julius Caesar.) It may be, however, that we have it arse about face. Hamlet, had he but known, might have shone as Sir Sidney Ruff-Diamond or the Rumpo Kid.

So exit, if not pursued by a bear, but by yet more double entendres.

> Malvolio: By my life, this is my lady's hand: these be her very C's, her U's, and her T's; and thus makes she her great P's.
>
> Shakespeare Twelfth Night (1600)

> Stuart Farquhar (Kenneth Williams): Please, Miss Plunkett, you're squashing my itinerary.
> Moira Plunkett (Gail Grainger): Oh, I'm terribly sorry. I keep on forgetting what a big girl I am now.
> Stuart Farquhar: Quite, shall we get them out now?
> Moira Plunkett: Why, Mr Farquhar!
> Stuart Farquhar: The people for the coach, I mean.
> Moira Plunkett: Oh, those. Yes, of course.
>
> Rothwell Carry On Abroad 1972

Plus ça bleedin' *change*, eh.

Pugilism: The Noble Art of Milling

THERE IS NO way round this. If slang has little or nothing of one aspect of humanity, affection, it offers an excess of its antithesis: violence. If anything, it offers too much. Murder, manslaughter, stabbing, slashing, garrotting, whipping, mugging, judicial execution, simple beating. Compared to these legions rape, to one's relief, is relatively overlooked other than when performed by modernity's gangs; yet we should not be too optimistic: perhaps macho, misogynistic slang simply failed to acknowledge the concept.

But all these, barring the violence that doubles as court-ordered punishment – though where would that be without crime aforethought? – are the products of villainy. They stand beyond the moral pale. One brand of violence does, however, gain acceptance, or does so on the whole. Boxing, originally known as prize-fighting: two men (or thus it was until recently), at first bare-knuckled and relatively free-form with a heavy larding of wrestling thrown in, later gloved and subject to a set of rules created by Oscar Wilde's persecutor the Marquis of Queensberry, bound by the 'square circle', limited in time, attended by seconds, judged by a referee. So let us focus on sanctioned slogging. The prize-ring. The 'Sweet Science' as first Pierce Egan and later the writer A.J. Liebling called it. The Manly Art.

The language that went with it was extensive, the 'manly tongue', one might suggest.

The proper name for that language was *flash* and its definitions were open to suggestion. *The Life and Character of Moll King* (1747) explained that 'This Flash, as it is called, is talking in Cant Terms, very much us'd among Rakes and Town Ladies.' Grose, from 1785, defined 'FLASH LINGO' as 'the canting or slang language'. By 1789 in George Parker's *Life's Painter*, it is lumped together with slang and cant: the reader is advised that 'The explanation of the Cant, Flash and Slang terms [. . .] gives at one view, a perfect knowledge of the artifices, combinations, modes and habits of those invaders of our property, our safety and our lives, who have a language quite unintelligible to any but themselves.' Finally, in its last incarnation, laid down in W.T. Moncrieff's 1821 play *Tom and Jerry* (the dramatic version of Pierce Egan's *Life in London*) the man-about-town Corinthian Tom pronounces that, 'Flash, my young friend, or slang, as others call it, is the classical language of the Holy Land; in other words, St. Giles's Greek [. . .] a species of cant in which the knowing ones conceal their roguery from the flats.'

What united all of these was that if the vocabulary still dealt with the same old themes, a new factor had joined the game: unlike cant, associated with lower-class villains, flash, bringing together the upper and lower orders, indicated that slang had become fashionable. Flash dealt with some of the same topics as cant – typically money, drink, criminal types and their schemes – but its use did not automatically brand one as a criminal. To use flash was to be in the know; it was, logically, to be *flash to*, which we might call 'on the ball'.

It's all about 'knowingness'. Here's another definition, from the three-times transported James Hardy Vaux, who had appended a 'New and Comprehensive Vocabulary of the Flash Language' to his *Memoirs*, first published in 1812 and thus creating Australia's first ever dictionary, of any sort. As a noun flash could be 'the cant language used by the *family*' i.e. the underworld (a term that long predates its attachment to the US Mafia), and that 'a person who affects any peculiar habit, as swearing, dressing a particular habit, taking snuff, *&c.*, merely to be taken notice, is said to do it *out of flash*'; it is the adjectival use that clearly crosses classes. 'FLASH, to be *flash* to any matter or meaning, is to understand or comprehend it, and is synonymous with being *fly*, *down*, or *awake*.' *Woke* as we put it now.

The term *prize-fighter* dates back to the seventeenth century, when it seems to have been used only historically, and with reference to gladiators. It takes on a modern use with the rise, around 1800, of the *Fancy*, described by Robert Southey as 'the Amateurs of Boxing'. The Fancy comprised the boxers (*fancy coves*) themselves, plus the fans (*fancy blokes*): sporting gents of one degree of respectability or another, bookmakers (*commissioners* or *legs*, which equated the bookie with a blackleg or racecourse swindler whose name came from the black-topped boots such swindlers favoured) of equal variety, plus anyone who was up for the trek to some distant field where beadles and bailiffs (*body-snatchers*, *bums*, *shoulder-clappers*) – empowered to halt such illegal festivities – feared to tread. The fights went on for scores of rounds. The Queen of Marksbury, as various fistic practitioners have malapropised him, had yet to rule. And like any self-respecting coterie, there was a language.

Prize-fighting was a perfect complement to flash. It was not wholly illegal – although beadles and bailiffs would attempt to curtail matches if they could. Its fans, known as *the Fancy*, were a socially mixed group that brought together the fighters themselves, their professional handlers, a collection of more or less honest bookmakers, a range of noble supporters, and anyone – in and out of the underworld – who appreciated 'the Manly Art'. Writing 'Tom Crib's Memorial to Congress' (1819), his satirical account of that year's congress of Aix-la-Chapelle, Byron's friend Tom Moore – 'passing from the Academy of Plato to that of Mr Jackson—now indulging in Attic flashes with Aristophanes, and now studying Flash in the Attics of Cock Court' – signed himself 'One of the Fancy'. Keeping in the boxing mode, he cast the diplomatic encounter as 'The Grand Set-to between Long Sandy and Georgy the Porpus' (i.e. Tsar Alexander and King George IV). Among its flash-filled verses were such as this:

> Neat milling this Round – what with clouts on the nob,
> Home hits in the bread-basket, clicks in the gob,
> And plumps in the daylights, a prettier treat
> Between two Johnny Raws 'tis not easy to meet.

His preface gave a mini-glossary and the verses were properly footnoted.

A year later there appeared *The Fancy* or 'The Poetical Remains of the late Peter Corcoran', which pseudonym masked John Hamilton Reynolds (1794–1852), poet, satirist, critic and playwright, and friend of Keats. The hero is a young poet, whose growing obsession with prize-fighting takes over from his writing, his job as a lawyer and his sweetheart who, seeing him with a pair of black eyes, breaks off the relationship. In the end Corcoran, whose 'memoirs' are filled with flash, dies of brain fever. His cranium, it is noted, has an unusually large organ of combativeness.

Boxing was also seen as the one cross-class sport in which a gentleman could indulge. As 'Mr Thornton' puts it in *A Bachelor of Arts* (1800) 'A young man, fresh from school or college, can be but little in want of Latin or Greek; but, what he is in want of is, knowledge of the world—that acquaintance with life and its usages which is essential for entering into society. My son, for instance, ought to be perfectly master of riding, fencing, and shooting; he should even learn to box, for do we not meet with imposing toll keepers and insolent cabmen at every turning? And as he can't call them out, he should be able to knock them down.' To what extent gentlemen faced off against impudent proles is unknown, other than in the popular 'sport' of boxing a charley – overturning a watchman in his box – but the principle was there.

Not everyone appreciated this socially transgressive world. The US writer Washington Irving's 'Buckthorne: the Young Man of Great Expectations' in his *Tales of a Traveller* (1824) was unimpressed: 'I know it is the opinion of many sages [. . .] that the noble science of boxing keeps up the bull-dog courage of the nation; and far be it from me to decry the advantage of becoming a nation of bull-dogs; but I now saw clearly that it was calculated to keep up the breed of English ruffian. "What is the Fives Court [London's leading boxing school]," said I to myself [. . .] "but a college of scoundrelism, where every bully ruffian in the land may gain a fellowship? What is the slang language of The Fancy but a jargon by which fools and knaves commune and understand each other, and enjoy a kind of superiority over the uninitiated? What is a boxing-match but an arena, where the noble and the illustrious are jostled into familiarity with the infamous and the vulgar? What, in fact, is the Fancy itself, but a chain of easy communication, extending from the peer down to the pickpocket, through the medium of which a man of rank may find he has shaken hands, at three removes, with the murderer on the gibbet?"' His assessment may have been spot-on, but what the priggish Yankee missed was the appeal of the Fancy to both noble and vulgar. Not to mention its slangy language.

Slangwise these were fistiana's glory days. Not till the 1930s, which offered such Palookaville pleasures as *the tanker*, who *takes a dive* or *goes in the water* (a *tank* being a swimming pool), the *umbrella*, who 'folds up', and *the tomato can*, who is 'easily crushed', did the *smackers*, *soccers* and *bruisers* offer so many synonyms.

The big word was *mill*. *Milling* had already meant any form of beating or thrashing but now it meant prize-fighting – with bare knuckles – and a fight could be a *milling-bout* or a *milling-match*. *Mill* itself meant a fight. Thus 'An Amateur' (actually the slang collector John Badcock), tells in *Real Life in London* (1821) how 'There was a most excellent mill at Moulsey Hurst [a cricket ground near the Thames and later the Hurst Park racecourse] on Thursday last, between the *Gas-light man*, who appears to be a *game chicken*, and a prime *hammerer*—he can give and take with any man—and Oliver—*Gas* beat him hollow, it was all Lombard-street to a china orange.' (There was an original Game Chicken – the bare-knuckle champion Henry 'Hen' Pierce who had died in 1809). The *milling-cove* or *milling kiddy* was a boxer, and the *milling-panney* (from *panny*, a house) the place where the fight took place. There was a seeming variation: *milvader*, to box and thus *milvadering*, the fight. But there was no link: it came from Scottish *milvad*: a blow.

The boxers (*buffers*) seemed to be built on different lines. Nothing as simple as a head: there was the *nob*, the *attic*, the *knowledge box*, the *top-loft*, the *brain canister* and *upper crust* (fifty years before it began referring to a somewhat different variety of nob). Eyes were *ogles, peepers, daylights* and *day-openers*; teeth were *ivories, domino boxes* and *grinders*; the stomach, that alluring target, was a *bread-bag, bread-basket* or *bread-room*, a *tripe-shop* or a *victualling office* (Australia opted for *tuckerbox*); the nose a *bowsprit, smeller, sneezer, sniffler* or *snifter, snuff box* or *bag* or *sensitive plant*; the ribs were *palings*. The arms were *props*. The fist, one's most vital appendage, was the *mitt* or *mitten*, the *hard dumpling*, the *famble*, the *daddle, bunch* or *box of fives, mauler* or *mauley* or the *prop*. It was also the *auctioneer*: it 'knocked things down'.

Knocking down was of course the point. One used nothing so prosaic as a jab, hook or uppercut. Blows could be *nobbers* or *headachers* (to the head), *mufflers* (to the mouth), *facers* (to the face), *props* (uppercuts) and *chippers* (jabs). A simple blow was a *fib*, which gave *fibbing gloak*, the boxer (*gloak* being a variant on *bloke*) and *fibbing*, the 'noble art' itself. As explained by the great boxing journalist Pierce Egan in his *Book of Sports* (1832): to fib was 'technical, in the P[rize]R[ing], to *hammer* your opponent repeatedly in close quarters; and to get no return for the compliment you are bestowing on him'. It could also be *pepper*, and the boxer was a *pepperer*. There were *staggerers* and *tellers* (which 'told' on one's stamina) and the *gaslighter* which presumably put out one's lights. The knockout punch was a *burster*, a *clicker* (which also meant the fighter), a *doser*, a *finisher*, a *full stop*, a *settler*, a *stopper* and a *turfer* or *sender* (both of which sent one *to the grass*). Suffering dizziness after a blow was *shooting stars*. Other punches included the *plump*, the *bung* (usually 'in the eye') the *buster*, the *click*, the *culp* (going back to Latin's *colaphus*, a box on the ear), the deceptively mild *poke*, the *toucher, dig, dab* (thus *dab the paint*, to jab) or *dub* (especially as *dub o' the hick*, a blow on the head), the *milvad*, the *mill*, the *stoter* (from Dutch *stooten*, to knock, to push), the *teaser*, the *ticket*, the *rattler* (presumably aimed at the teeth though it just might undermine a fighter's composure), the *walloper*, the *whiffle* and the *whistycastor*.

It was all very detailed, though that may have stemmed from the boxing writers' need to hold their readers' attention. The *belly-go-firster* or *-fister* was a blow to the stomach, especially one given with no warning, or at the start of a fight. A punch to the eye was an *ogler*, *winker* or *blinder* and to *bung up an eye* was to blacken it. Black eyes were *peepers in mourning*. The *brisketer* or *brisket-cut* was launched at the chest. The *flytrapper*, *chatterer*, *muffler*, *munzer* (from *muns*, the face) and *muzzler* targeted the mouth, the *cheeker* the cheek and the *facer*, *conker*, *chop* or *chopper* the face (*chops* had meant the face since 1577). The *throttle* hurt the throat, the *bellier* or *bellowser* the stomach (and the phrase *bellows to mend* was applied to a man who was running out of wind), the *rib-tickler* or *-bender* or *ribber* savaged the ribs. Blows to the head included the *topper*, *nutcracker* (*nutcrackers* themselves were fists), *header*, *jobber*, *topper*, *nodyer* (from Australia) and *nope* (from northern dialect *nawp*, *noup*, *nope*, a blow and ultimately a supposed Scandinavian verb *nawpe*, to strike down). The nose attracted *smellers*, *sneezers*, *snorters*, *nosegays*, *nosers*, *nosenders* and *snufflers*. Finally the ear was assailed with *luggers* (from *lug*), *buckhorses* (in honour of the pugilist Buckhorse, real name John Smith, who, for a small charge, allowed people to hit him hard on the side of the head), and the *whisterclyster*, *whisticaster* or *whisterpoop*. Whister meant a whisper, clyster an enema and cast to throw.

The product of all of this was blood. Or *claret*. Of all the Fancy's favourite terms this is perhaps the sole survivor. One could *claret* one's opponent or *tap their claret*, i.e. draw their blood; and the first such blow was the *claret-christening*; the nose was the *claret-jug, claret-cask* or *claret-spout*. To make it bleed was to *tap a judy* which played on *judy*, a woman, and the blood that flowed when she was deflowered.

Modern boxing is more likely to provide imagery than slang: *out for the count, beat someone to the punch, saved by the bell,* or *chuck, throw* or *toss in the sponge* or *towel,* itself already in use in the mid-nineteenth century. The last great exponent of language in the world of boxing was Muhammad Ali, but his delivery was all his own work.

Tom Moore's friend Lord Byron was a great fan. He was a regular at the training sessions offered by John Jackson (1769–1845), an ex-prizefighter (champion from 1795–1803) who taught Byron and a number of his friends. The aristocratic poet termed him his 'old friend and corporeal pastor and master' and noted in his 'Hints from Horace' that 'men unpractised in exchanging knocks / Must go to Jackson ere they dare to box.' It was a quintessential flash relationship: the lord and the butcher's son turned publican, united no doubt in language as much as in friendship.

Byron was an aristocrat and a renowned if controversial poet, but the Fancy's true laureate was less socially distinguished. If prize-fighting and its language has a story over and beyond those who actually battled out the bouts it is that of its chronicler-in-chief, Pierce Egan (1772–1849). As John Camden Hotten put it, writing the introduction to his 1869 reprint of Egan's 'novel' *Life in London* (1821) 'In his particular line, he was the greatest man in England. [. . .] His peculiar phraseology, and his superior knowledge of the business, soon rendered him eminent beyond all rivalry and competition. He was flattered

and petted by pugilists and peers: his patronage and counte-
nance were sought for by all who considered the road to a
prize-fight the road to reputation and honor. Sixty years ago, his
presence was understood to convey respectability on any meet-
ing convened for the furtherance of bull-baiting, cock-fighting,
cudgelling, wrestling, boxing, and all that comes within the
category of "manly sports".' Egan's 'peculiar phraseology' would
make him the father of every sportswriter who, perhaps unconsciously, has adopted his heightened style as a blueprint for their
own.

Egan was born in Ireland but at some stage moved to the
London suburbs, where he would spend his life. By 1812 he had
established himself as the country's leading 'reporter of sporting
events', which at the time meant mainly prize-fights and horse-
races. As A.J. Liebling, his spiritual if not actual successor, put it
over a century later, 'Egan [. . .] belonged to London, and no
man has ever presented a more enthusiastic picture of all aspects
of its life except the genteel. He was a hack journalist, a song
writer, and conductor of puff-sheets and, I am inclined to
suspect, a shake-down man.' Most important for Liebling, who
wrote for the *New Yorker* on boxing among much else, was that
'In 1812 he got out the first paperbound instalment of *Boxiana;
or Sketches of Ancient and Modern Pugilism; from the days of
Brougham and Slack to the Heroes of the Present Milling Aera.*' The
journal lasted until 1828, its fifth volume, and established its
editor as the foremost authority on what in the fourth volume
(1824) was termed 'the Sweet Science of Bruising' which Sweet
Science 130 years on gave Liebling a title for his collected boxing
pieces.

Egan's journal mixed round-by-round reports of fights with
biographies of those who fought them, but as Liebling notes, as

well as these unsurpassed technical skills what Egan achieved was to portray the links that held together the Fancy – its 'trulls and lushes, toffs and toddlers' – and its world of flash. 'He also saw the ring as a juicy chunk of English life, in no way separable from the rest. His accounts of the extra-annular lives of the Heroes, coal-heavers, watermen, and butchers' boys, are a panorama of low, dirty, happy, brutal, sentimental Regency England that you'll never get from Jane Austen. The fighter's relations with their patrons, the Swells, present that curious pattern of good fellowship and snobbery, not mutually exclusive, that has always existed between Gentleman and Player in England.'

Like Tom Moore's satire, *Boxiana* was a showcase of 'Fancy slang'. But by its nature it was restricted to the topic in hand. Seven years after the launch of his boxing journal Egan achieved a best-seller that packed in even more flash, and proclaimed itself as a very Bible of Fancy goings-on, both high and low. Pugilistic poetry was now cropping up in magazines such as *Blackwood's Edinburgh Magazine*, which also serialised Egan's work and stated that 'The man who has not read *Boxiana* is ignorant of the power of the English language.'

In 1821 he announced the publication of a regular journal – *Life in London* – to appear monthly at a shilling a time. It was to be illustrated by George Cruikshank (1792–1878), who had succeeded Hogarth and Rowlandson as London's leading satirist of urban life. The journal was dedicated to the King, George IV, who at one time had received Egan at court. The first edition of *Life in London* 'or, the Day and Night Scenes of Jerry Hawthorn, esq., and his elegant friend, Corinthian Tom, accompanied by Bob Logic, the Oxonian, in their rambles and Sprees through the Metropolis' appeared on 15 July.

Egan's creation was an enormous, instant success, with its

circulation mounting every month. Pirate versions appeared, featuring such figures as 'Bob Tallyho', 'Dick Wildfire' and the like. Print-makers speedily knocked off cuts featuring the various 'stars' and the real-life public flocked to the 'sporting' addresses that Egan had his heroes frequent. There was a translation into French. At least six plays were based on Egan's characters, contributing to yet more sales. One of these was exported to America, launching the 'Tom and Jerry' craze there. The version created by William Moncrieff, whose knowledge of London and of its slang equalled Egan's, was cited, not without justification, as 'The Beggar's Opera of its day'. Moncrieff (1794–1857) was one of contemporary London's most successful dramatists and theatrical managers. His production of *Tom and Jerry, or, Life in London* ran continuously at the Adelphi Theatre for two seasons; it was Moncrieff as much as Egan who, as the original *DNB* had it 'introduced slang into the drawing room'. Some theatrical versions (of 1822 and 1823) felt it worth offering audiences a small glossary, mainly derived from the footnotes in Egan's prose original. In all, Egan suggested in his follow-up *The Finish to the Adventures of Tom, Jerry and Logic* (1830) some sixty-five works were created on the back of his own. And added that, 'We have been pirated, COPIED, traduced; but, unfortunately, not ENRICHED.'

'We' had also come to epitomise a whole world. The adjectival use of *tom and jerry* lasted into the mid-century. Young men went on 'Tom-and-Jerry frolics', which usually featured the picking of drunken fights and the destruction of property, and in 1853, in Robert Surtees' *Mr Sponge's Sporting Tour*, the story of a plausible con-man among the hunting set, the ageing rake Mr Puffington, ever-assuring his friends that, like Corinthian Tom, he could show them 'Life', can be found reminiscing and '[t]elling how Deuceace and he floored a Charley, or Blueun and he pitched a snob out of the boxes into the pit. This was in the old Tom-and-Jerry days, when fisticuffs were the fashion.' There were *tom-and-jerry shops*, which were cheap, rough taverns, *tom-and-jerry gangs* of rowdy, hedonistic young men, and a verb use which mean to go out on a spree. By 1840 the names had come to christen a highly spiced punch, still being served up by Damon Runyon in 'Dancing Dan's Christmas' a century later. It was adopted by London costermongers to mean a cherry in rhyming slang.

Life in London appeared until 1828, when Egan closed it down. The journal was incorporated into the sporting magazine *Bell's Life*, which would last until in 1886, it too was bought up, by the *Sporting Times*. Egan's prose style was incorporated as well, and it was seemingly still popular thirty years on. When, during his freshman term at Oxford, set c.1850, the fictional 'Mr Verdant Green' tries some genteel prize-fighting, it ends, as do most of his sporting efforts, in disappointment: in 'the sporting slang of Tintinnabulum's Life [. . .] his claret had been repeatedly tapped, his bread-basket walked into, his day-lights darkened, his ivories rattled, his nozzle barked, his whisker-bed napped heavily, his kissing-trap countered, his ribs roasted, his nut spanked, and his whole person put into chancery, stung, bruised, fibbed, propped, fiddled, slogged, and otherwise ill-treated.' It was all getting a bit stale, and would be gone in another decade, but journalists had to earn their pennies per line and the readers definitely expected something a little livelier than 'A hit B'.

If slang, or rather flash, did manage to reach the essentially female arena of the drawing room, it would have appeared only in a very few, and most likely those of the better class of brothel.

Flash remained a male delight. And a raffish one. Egan uses it in many of his London scenes, but they are invariably those where our heroes encounter the low end of the city's life. Indeed sophisticate Tom is constantly warning country Jerry to mind his language when voyaging amongst 'the Roses, Pinks and Tulips, the flowers of Society'. It is when they visit All Max, the East End gin shop, and encounter such members of the 'flash part of mankind' as Bob the Coal-Whipper and Black Sal that the racy slang comes out; in the fashionable West End club Almacks, 'we must mind our P.'s and Q.s'. Not merely that but the trio arrange a fail-safe, a murmur of 'lethe' (Greek for forgetfulness) if any of them are heard to fall from social grace. As Tom says, 'Indeed, if it were possible to call to your aid the waters of lethe, to cleanse your pericranium of all ideas of "the slang" for a night, upon entering those regions of refinement, [. . .] it would be highly advantageous towards your attraction.' Code-switching is not a modern invention.

In 1823 Egan consolidated his role as a leading purveyor of flash with his revision of Francis Grose's *Classical Dictionary of the Vulgar Tongue*. It is effectively the dictionary's fourth legitimate edition although as Julie Coleman points out, Egan's direct source was the pirated *Lexicon Balatronicum* of 1811. Egan's Grose, as it is generally known, embellished its predecessor with the inclusion of a variety of mainly sporting Regency slang. He also cuts the 'coarse and broad expressions' and 'neglected no opportunity of excluding indelicate phrases [. . .] nor of softening down others which Grose had allowed and notes the way that some slang terminology, typically *rum* – once a positive term, but by 1820 generally the reverse – had altered its sense. At the same time he hoped that in sum that his efforts work 'to improve, and not to degrade mankind; to remove ignorance, and put the unwary on their guard; to rouse the sleepy, and to keep them awake; to render those persons who are a little up, more fly: and to cause every one to be down to those tricks, manoeuvres and impositions practised in life, which daily cross the paths of both young and old.' Among the headwords he excluded was the linguistic sense of slang (he defines it only as meaning fetters and as the verb to cheat), which Grose had listed, although at flash, defined as 'knowing' he offers *patter flash* 'to speak the slang language'.

Perhaps Egan's most original contribution was the eleven-page 'Biographical Sketch of Francis Grose, Esq.' The sources for this have vanished, and it has come to be queried by modern researchers, but the picture he paints of the bonhomous, rotund lexicographer making his nightly tours of London's taverns and rookeries is undeniably appealing.

Jack's a Lad: All Aboard the Oggin

GIVEN SLANG'S HARD-WIRED identification with all things urban, it's paradoxical, at least at first glance, how much the sea has come to register on its coinages. But there it is, and not just by chance.

The best incubators for slang are nailed down and shut tight. Inward-looking and forced together willy-nilly. What John Camden Hotten termed 'the congregating together of people [. . .] the result of crowding, and excitement, and artificial life'. The old slang collector-cum-purveyor of S&M porn was thinking cities but they're not exclusive. An external threat may help. War is the obvious one; '14–'18 produced a vast increase in the slang vocabulary, but there are alternatives. Worlds that are similarly closed and which generate their own languages. Among them is that of the sea, which naturally means ships and they in turn mean sailors. The influence of the sea on slang is thus worth more than just a glance.

This is not navy slang – properly known (if not that often) as *altumal*, and possibly from Latin's *altum mare*, the deep sea – which is a whole other thing, but the crossover from the watery world to the innately citified one of the counter-language. We must, sadly, sidestep such onboard characterisations as *jemmy ducks*, who looked after the poultry, *jack dusty*, the stores assistant (the 'dust' being flour) and *jack nastyface*, the cook's number two. Gone too must be *Jimmy Round*, a Frenchman (from *je me rends*, I surrender, and attributed to the Napoleonic Wars).

There are, for starters, the words that mean sailor. There are twenty-three *jacks* in slang which probably makes it the biggest creator of homonyms in the lexis but only one counts here: the one that abbreviates *jack tar*, which refers to the old habit of smearing your breeches with that sticky, liquid-repellent substance in a primitive effort at waterproofing. (He also comes as *jackie*, *john* and *jackshite*.) The image also gave *tarpaulin* (plus *tar* and *tarry-breeks* or *tarry-jacket*), which implied a man who had quite literally got his hands dirty learning the job and hadn't merely got there through connections.

Breeks began as white and his jacket as blue and thus the *blue-jacket*; he roamed the sea, which gave *lagger* and *lag-cull* (both from *lag*, water) and was thus piscine: the *scaly fish* (who was tough), the *otter* and the *sea-crab* (which may have reflected a well-known ballad featuring the crab, a chamberpot, and the suggestion that one had best look within before squatting). He went shoeless which gave *flatfoot*, obsessively washed down the decks, thus *swab* and *swab-jockey*, and allegedly spat to excess, the *gob* (from *gob*, a clot of slimy substance). He often fought the French but still borrowed their *matelot*, though spelled it *matlow*. As Village People fans will recall, the sailor is a popular gay sex-object and usually twinned with something one might *eat*. Known as *sea-food* he was also a *blueberry pie*, *lobster pot*, *sea pussy* and, specifying his penis, a piece of *salt water taffy* (the UK's *rock*).

The sea itself tends to rhyming slang: *housemaid's knee*, *coffee and tea*, *River Lea*, plus the *briny*, and the jokily miniaturising *puddle*, *pond* and *ditch*. Sailors, meanwhile, opt for *oggin* (which in terms of sailing, one *flogs*). The *oggin*, as a selection of its many literary appearances makes clear, is large, deep, wet, and while a necessary given for the naval personnel who coined the term, seems to suggest greater duty than pleasure. Safe on land the lubber may extol it, the sailor merely falls in and does not invariably emerge. One thing unites them: ignorance of its origins. The etymology of the word, that is.

One belief is that sailors, universally unable to pronounce 'ocean', called it 'oggin'. This is a calumny and may surely be dismissed. Wilfred Granville, in his 1949 collection of *Sea Slang* suggests an abbreviation of *hogwash*, which started off life meaning brewery swill, which was fed to the pigs, and thence bad beer or wine (and indeed tea) and in time, and figuratively, nonsense. The *OED*, as of 2004, rejects this but a link remains, however tenuous one might feel it. Hogwash can mean drink; one of the slang terms for the sea is *the drink*. A *noggin* is a drink (and before that a small drinking vessel). Oxford's suggestion, therefore, is of a play on *noggin*, altered to *oggin* by metanalysis (the same phenomenon that once saw words such as *nangry*, and *nanger*, not to mention the Sansrkit *nāraṅga* which via Arabic *naranj* and Italian *narancia*, gives English *orange*).

Which is where, absent alternative theories, it must be left. All that remains is a song. The tune will be self-evident:

> If the skipper fell into the oggin,
> If the skipper fell into the sea,
> If the skipper fell into the oggin,
> He'd get sod-all lifebelt from me.

But enough with water. Let us turn to alcohol. Not especially as drunk by *jack ashore*, a compound that has illumined all manner of self-indulgence ever since its appearance around 1860, but in slang's cheerful borrowing of seaborne imagery to denote that happy state wherein one is *all at sea*.

There is the basic: *drunk as a sailor*, or *as a Gosport fiddler*, which pays tribute to the Royal Navy base. The wind plays its role: *breezy*, a *few sheets in the wind*, a *sheet in the wind's eye*, *hulled between wind and water*, *in the wind*, *under the wind*, *listing to starboard*, *shaking cloth in the wind*, *shot between* (or *betwixt*) *wind and water*, *three sheets before the breeze*, *three sheets in the wind*, *three sheets over* and *three sheets spread*. *Sheets*, by the way, are not as might seem logical, sails, but ropes. The term comes from Old English *scéat*, a corner, and thence the corner of a sail and ultimately the rope that secures that corner. The unsecured sheet, blowing in the wind, weaves in the air like the drunk swaying down a road. Meanwhile *hull* means to drift with no sails spread.

The terms can be neutral, even optimistic: *aboard* (*of the grog*), *afloat*, *all sails set*, *well under way* and *under full sail*. They can, logically enough, note the pervasive dampness of both liquor and the sea: *damp*, *awash*, *capsized*, *decks-awash*, *drenched*, *floating*, *under the tide*, *half the bay over* or *over the bay* or *dam*, *over the plimsoll* (*line*), that physical line that denotes the limit of safe loading, *slewed*, *soaked*, *submerged*, *torpedoed*, *waterlogged*, and *wrecked*. The popular *half seas over* may suit the list, but there are suggestions that Dutch *op-zee zober*, 'foreign strong beer' is the actual root.

Other nautical origins can be found in terms such as *block and block*, *castaway*, *foggy*, *round the horn*, *top-shackled*, *taking in cargo*, *needing a reef taken in*, *Lloyd's List* (i.e. *pissed*), *steamed up*, *stoked*, *bungs up*, *waving a flag of defiance* and the punning *tight as a clam's* (or *crab's*, *fish's* or *oyster's*) *arse*. *Grog*, always a naval staple with its roots in standard English *grogram*, 'a coarse fabric of silk, of mohair and wool, or of these mixed with silk' (*OED*) and the coat of such stuff as worn by Admiral Vernon, known as 'Old Grog' from his having ordered the navy's rum to be diluted with water, gives *groggified*.

Finally, a bunch of *admirals*, taken from a mid-seventeenth-century lexicon of drinking, *The Eighth Liberal Science*. *Admiral of the blue*, a publican or innkeeper (his traditional blue apron); *admiral of the red*, a heavy drinker (as well as the colour of wine, the term may also refer to the drunkard's red nose) and *admiral of the narrow seas* (playing on *narrow seas*, the British Channel or Irish Sea) a drunkard who vomits over his neighbour at table. In 1796 Francis Grose noted an expanded version: *vice-admiral* (*of the narrow seas*) 'A drunken man that pisses under the table into his companions' shoes.'

The girls came off the streets of London after the Street Offences Act of 1959 and their disppearance has done nothing for slang coinage. The Ratcliff Highway, London Docklands' homegrown Sodom and Gomorrah, whose taverns and tarts saw for as many seafarers as ever did the ocean, has long since fallen silent. The ubiquitous *ho* may be accurate, albeit bereft of a few letters, but it hardly sets the juices flowing. It was not always thus and the sea, given jack's recreational partialities, played its part. All too aware of her dubious allure he called her a *land pirate* (usually a highwayman) but that didn't hold him back. Not for nothing are ships invariably 'she'.

There are the basic ships: the *schooner*, the *pinnace*, the *privateer* and the *land carrack*. All these are relatively lightweight in terms of tonnage and punnage too (the larger *battleship* is invariably old, plain and dismissed as unalluring): *light*, as in unable to keep her heels on the ground, is an old term for a 'loose woman'.

The *tilt-boat,* playing with tilt as in falling over, sustains the idea. Then we meet the *light frigate,* double-punning both on her 'sailing' the streets and on the term *frig,* from Latin *fricare,* to rub and meaning both to have sex and to *jerk off,* oneself or a client. The frigate comes in two flavours; the *frigate well-rigged,* who is neatly, fashionably dressed, and the *frigate on fire,* a specimen of *hot stuff* who is suffering some form of STD. Best, though rarely avoided, she can also be a *fireship.*

Setting aside rhyming slang's *boat and oar, barge,* which suggests a certain embonpoint, and *scupper,* into which one tosses unwanted waste (thus linking to the use of *crud, muck, scum* and *slime* for semen), we find *hooker,* undoubtedly one of prostitution's leading synonyms and productive of a variety of back-stories. Popular etymology suggests the denizens of *Corlear's Hook,* known as *The Hook,* a red-light area on the New York City waterfront. There is also the city's use of *hooker,* a tug that cruised to pick up incoming schooners off Sandy Hook and the sailor's affectionate nickname, hooker, for any vessel. The link to Corlear's Hook is sanctified by Bartlett's *Dictionary of Americanisms* (1859), which defines *hooker* as 'a resident of The Hook, i.e. a strumpet, a sailor's trull'. On the other hand the memoirs of the ex-madam Nell Kimball stated: 'The moniker hooker came about in the Civil War . . . General Joe Hooker, a handsome figure of a man, was a real quif-hunter, and he spent a lot of time in the houses of the redlight district, so that people began to call the district Hooker's Division.' Sounds good? Yes, but the term is thirty years older. In the end, like much slang, the origin is probably a tweak of standard English, in this case *hook,* to catch, to lure, to entice, but with strong reinforcement from both the New York City location and the sailor's nickname.

But monetary exchange is not mandatory. Looking back at

some of the sea-based novels produced around 1800, focused on what was still an unreformed Navy, the punning on naval jargon reaches near *Carry On* proportions.

The components of the ship herself, or the old *bitch* as she is sometimes termed, are a ready source. The *cat-head*, for instance, is officially a protruding spar that keeps the anchor away from the superstructure. There are two: one per side. The *bow*, we know, is the front of the ship and the *stern* its antithesis. *The Post Captain, or, the Wooden Walls Well Manned*, written in 1805 and as such the first of these works, gives us dialogues such as these; 'Faith, Hurricane, our lady passenger is a fine girl. She has a good pair of cat-heads!' 'Yes, sir, she is nice and bluff about the bows.' (Though her stern goes unremarked.)

Later we also find this: the Captain is speaking to the 1st Lieutenant, about to go below to sleep with his wife (women, 'legitimate' or otherwise, being far from invisible onboard in this era): 'Mr Hurricane . . . bear a hand and get your anchor a cock-bill.' 'It already hangs by the stopper. My shank-painter is let go; and I have roused up a good range of cable on deck.' 'Then let go the anchor.' How the knowledgeable must have sniggered. Not only the *anchor*, which phallically dangles, there is the *bob-stay*, 'a rope which holds the bowsprit to the stem'. Captain Grose (of the militia not the navy), writing twenty years earlier, has noted that the word had been grabbed by slang to denote 'the frenum of a man's yard'. Now it is the Captain's turn for connubial pleasures: 'Come, Cassandra [. . .] let us descend and turn in. If I don't ease my laniard I shall carry away my bob-stay.'

Moving beyond specifics there is a good deal more. In literary terms sailors were one of first occupational groups to be attributed a distinctive speech-style. Smollett's *Roderick Random* offers Lieutenant Tom Bowling, described as 'a scoundrel of a seaman [. . .] who has deserted and turned thief'. This is backed up lexically, and Bowling offers such as *rigg'd*, for dressed, *shake cloth in the wind*, for hurry up and *don't lag astern you dog*'. Slang owes the sea a good deal.

Other terms include these: to be *adrift*, *loose* and *turned adrift*, all mean to be discharged from work; to *bring your arse to anchor*, sit down; *bring someone to their bearings*, to bring them to their senses; *cant a slug into your bread room*, have a drink; *fin*, an arm; *pump ship*, to urinate; *smash*, mashed potatoes as originally served alongside a leg of mutton; *floating academy*, the prison hulks; *nip-cheese*, a miser was first of all a ship's purser; *deadlights*, the eyes; *shipshape*, *keelhaul*.

Nor by any means is it all sex, though *splice*, to marry, is of course based on seaborne imagery. And *toplights* are brought down from the masthead to stand for human eyes. *Jonathan*, for an American vessel, usually refers to any United States native (though originally a New Englander) and fits in the taxonomy of *John Bull*, *Lewis Frog* and the rest. (Its opposite number *lime-juicer*, thence *limey*, appears c. 1850.) *Crappo*, from *crapaud*, a toad, is a Frenchman (substituting for the usual *frog* which during the Napoleonic wars still seemed to refer primarily to the Dutch). The *galoot*, which is seen as *echt* 'Wild West' and meaning an awkward fool, began life afloat and meant a marine (the awkwardness implicit in his being ultimately a lubberly soldier). The etymology is lost but there are suggestions of the intensifier *ker-*, and Scots *loot*, a lout. The deliberate mispronunciation *ossifer* seems also to have originated on board. *Lubber* seems to come from old French *lobeor*, a swindler or parasite and of course leads to *land-lubber*, a landsman or incompetent sailor. The clumsiness implicit in the nautical use implies a further link to *lob*, a country bumpkin.

Some parts are more versatile than others. The buttocks can be the *beam-ends*, the *fantail*, the *keel*, the *poop* or the *stern*. Certain bits of kit are popular. Beyond the literary double entendres above, *anchor* ranges wide. Setting aside *anchor and chain*, like *ball and chain* a wife, the noun means variously a pick-axe; a reprieve or temporary suspension of a sentence; brakes and thus *drop*, *put on* or *slam on the anchors*; a stickpin; thus *anchor and prop*, a stickpin with a safety catch that anchors it to the tie; one's home, one's address; a younger relation or other small child who 'holds one back' from social life. In phrases, *to bring oneself to an anchor* was to sit down; *to drag one's anchor*, to go slowly or to idle, though the simple *drop anchor* means to defecate. *To swallow the anchor* means both to stop doing something and to give oneself up to the police. Meanwhile *to drop anchor in bum bay* refers to that portion of Churchill's summary of naval traditions – rum, sodomy and the lash – that dealt in neither drunkenness nor flagellation.

Let us conclude with food. Here we do step on board, but some things are just too tasty to miss. Sailor's food irresistible? Only lexically.

Rations came down to two words: biscuits and beef (though any meat that could be salted, e.g. pork, served muster). The first were of tooth-snapping solidity, the second was salted and not to be confused with what modern America terms corned beef (from the corns of salt used in its curing) and reaches its acme when paired with a bagel. The first were known as *hard tack*, the second as *salt junk*. The *hard* was self-evident; *tack* comes either from another piece of self-description, standard English *tack*, a quality of binding or solidity (and is thus linked to *tacky*, sticky), or from the pleasingly nautical *tackle*, which in this context is generic for food. Bread, which would be brown (and not only because of its inevitable population of weevils) was *tommy* or *soft tommy* (soft that is in comparison to the biscuits), which was a poor pun on *Tommy Brown*. If you soaked your hard tack in water and baked it with fat and molasses, it became *dandyfunk*, *daddyfunk* or *dunderfunk* and may represent a mixture of *dandy*, a sloop, and *funk*, a stench, though the link is unexplained. *Salt junk* (plus *old* or *tough junk*), which was dried and salted beef or pork (often the veteran of several voyages prior to being soaked and then eaten) played on the nautical jargon *junk*, old or second-rate cable or rope and possibly nodded to standard *junk*, a lump or chunk. The old rope imagery led naturally to a sailor staple: *rope-yarn stew*, from *rope-yarn*, properly used for twisting up into ropes. Alongside this was *twice-laid*, literally describing rope made from a selection of the best yarns of old rope, this dish was made of the salt-fish left from yesterday's dinner, and beaten up with potatoes or yams.

In time – such packaging was launched in 1847 – salt was replaced by tins. The meat, no longer stowed in casks down in the hold where the ship's rats had been able to take first helpings, now came pre-packed and blessed with a new name: *canned willie* (the US army, similarly provisioned, called it *corned bill*). Why willie? The obvious, coarse etymology doesn't stand up: that *willie* doesn't come on stream till the 1960s and this was established by the late nineteenth century. Canned willie remains mysterious. And, memoirs suggest, inedible.

It might, of course, have been eponymous: perhaps there was a hapless, anecdote-laden Willie. There certainly was a *Sweet Fanny Adams*, which does not only mean the landsman's dismissive 'nothing' but to sailors denoted tinned mutton. The blackly humorous nickname was based on the brutal murder and dismemberment of eight-year-old Fanny Adams, at Alton,

Hampshire, on 24 August 1867; the murderer, one Frederick Baker, was hanged at Winchester on Christmas Eve; 5,000 people watched the execution. There was also a real-life *Harriet Lane*, borrowed by the US Navy to mean chopped, tinned meat. In this case the reference was to Harriet Lane, the victim and wife of the murderer Henry Wainwright, executed 1875; coincidentally the USS *Harriet Lane*, launched 1857, was commanded by one Jonathan Wainwright, who was killed on board her during the US Civil War; the ship, however, was named for the niece of President James Buchanan. (The modern Navy offers a single anthropomorphism: *baby's head*, a steak and kidney pudding, in which the smooth pastry rises like a shiny infant head.)

It will not be surprising to find that the solution was stew. Lots of stew in various guises and with names to match. Aside from those already cited were those that, within context, were self-explanatory: *choke-dog* and *dog's body* leading the way. *Hishee-hashee* presumably went back to *hash*, itself meaning stew and rooted in French *hach*é, chopped. *Sea-pie* suggested fish, but not to initiates. As defined in Smyth's *Sailor's Word-book* (1867) it was a dish of meat and vegetables, etc. boiled together, with a crust of paste, or 'in layers between crusts, the number of which denominate it a two or three decker'. It was still being served in 1940s Borstals, as witnessed by a young Brendan Behan who recounted the bad boys' aphorism: 'Sea pie today, see fugh-all tomorrow'. It might also be called *blanket stew*, which applied to all stews that came with a pastry crust.

There was more. The unappetisingly named *slumgullion* or *slum* was defined by the slang collector as 'mean fish offal or other refuse', and even more gruesome, 'the watery refuse, mixed with blood and oil, which drains from blubber', but even sailors were not expected to consume that. *Loblolly* can be traced to the sixteenth century: it was a thick gruel, choked down by peasants as wells as sailors, and sometimes doubled as a simple medicine. The word may be no more than echoic; the sound of the thick gruel bubbling in a pot, alternatively, or maybe additionally, it reflects a dialect term *lob*, to bubble while boiling, especially of a thick substance like porridge and the Devonian *lolly*, broth, soup or other food boiled in a pot. On shore the word has also meant a country bumpkin, a weakling, a mudhole and a fat child (both in the US). The *loblolly boy* was a junior crew-member, irrespective of weight, who ran errands for his seniors.

Burgoo and *skillygalee*, are the equivalents of Scotland's porridge and Ireland's stirabout: in all cases oatmeal boiled in water. The former sailor and novelist Captain Marryat called it 'very wholesome'. More enterprising cooks threw in meat and veg. The literary publican Ned Ward, in 1704, cited it along with red herring and dried whiting as the Dutchman's favourite food and once picked up by landsmen in Kentucky, burgoo became the basis of nineteenth-century 'burgoo feasts'; British soldiers used it as a synonym for porridge. The roots lie in Arabic *burgul*, cooked, parched and cracked wheat. As for *skillygalee*, it defeats the etymologists, and reached a greater fame as the echt-workhouse/prison sludge, *skilly*, often paired with *toke*, i.e. bread. It was this that no doubt induced poor Oliver to make his celebrated request. Jack London described it as 'a fluid concoction of three quarts of oatmeal stirred into three buckets and a half of hot water', while a tramp told Orwell that it was 'A can o' hot water wid some bloody oatmeal at de bottom.' *Lob-dominion* – 'two buckets of water and an old shoe' – was equally tasteless, and equally disinclined to confess to an origin.

Some of these probably tasted good, or at least served to mask the basic ingredients, where lack of flavour was balanced

only by a garnish of unwanted species of insect life. One definitely didn't. This was *soup-and-bouilli*, thus characterised by
William Clark Russell in his lexicon of *Sailors' Language* (1883):
'Soup-and-bouilli [. . .] taking it all round, is the most disgust-
ing of the provisions served out to the merchant sailor. I have
known many a strong stomach, made food-proof by years of
pork eaten with molasses, and biscuit alive with worms, to be
utterly capsised by the mere smell of soup-and-bouilli. Jack
calls it "soap and bullion, one onion to a gallon of water," and
this fairly expresses the character of the nauseous compound.'
It is, however, the same *bouilli* that graces the traditional French
kitchen, pieces of beef being simmered with vegetables to
create a savoury stock, and that which lies behind *bully beef*,
itself a variation on canned willie. More palatable – surely –
was *pillau*, made of salt beef, fowl, rice, and onions, all cooked
together. Indeed it sounds almost too good for the tars, and
may have been officers only. It comes, just as does that featured
in your local Taj Mahal, from Persian *pulaw* and Hindi *pulāv*,
a dish of rice and meat.

There were relatively few sweets. To steal from Russell again,
'"Duff" means a large lump of flour and grease boiled in a bag;
"doughboys" – pronounced "doboys" the o broad – are the same
flour and grease in small lumps. Dough jehovahs are a Yankee
pudding, and worthy of the people who first taught the British
sailor to eat pork with treacle.' The cowboy's *dough god*, a form
of bread baked over an open fire (and thus kin to Australia's
damper) can't be that dissimilar.

Someone, of course, had to cook these savoury messes. The
cook was the *slushy*, a name that came from his perk, the selling
of *slush*, the refuse fat from boiled meat. The name, if not the
job, has been picked up in Australian shearing camps;

sometimes it means his assistant. The original *slush fund* was what he made from his enterprise. If he was not slushy, then he had another occupational title: *drainings*.

Like a small child, forcing down the vegetables to reach the chips, let us save the best till last. The best: so they do say, even if not often at the time. This is *lobscouse*, best known this side of the North Sea as *scouse* and as such generic for native Liverpudlians and their dialect. The cultural commentator Jonathan Meades explains that 'Lobscouse is labskaus in the Baltic, specifically in Schleswig Holstein, Lubeck, Hamburg, southern Denmark. It is beef and potato hash, the beef sometimes salted/corned. Unvinegared beetroot is sometimes added. It's often served with a matjes herring and a fried egg.' In his TV series *Magnetic North* (2008) he watched it being prepared: it looked like thick pink slurry but allegedly tasted just fine. The modern recipe seems somewhat more generous than the sailors' version, though that boasted salt meat, biscuits, potatoes, onions, and spices and must have been a good deal tastier than the usual mush.

The naming tradition has continued. An online list of 'Navy Scran' (from Scottish *scran*, 'food, provisions, victuals, especially inferior or scrappy food') notes these. *Adam and Eve on a raft*, eggs on toast, which has been used since the late nineteenth century in US short-order caffs; the addition of 'and wreck 'em', turns the eggs scrambled. There is *hammy cheesy eggy topsides*, a seaboard special, which may be a product of Far East pidgin; and there are such dubious delicacies as *labrador's arsehole* ('Sausage Roll – look at one end on and imagine'), *bollocks in blood* ('meatballs in tomato sauce') or *Satan's suppositories* ('Kidney Beans in Red Hot Chilli Con Carne sauce'). All are undoubtedly slangy, and such as *shit on a raft* ('kidneys on toast') are echoed elsewhere in America's *shit on a shingle* (chipped beef on toast, usually found in prisons or messhalls) but they are best left on board, even if it may be that former matlows bring them into civvy street.

No one, other than fiction's Popeye the Sailor-man, seemed to eat spinach.

Doctors & Nurses

BUTCHERS, BAKERS AND candlestick makers . . . other perhaps than clergymen (such as *bollockses*, *devil-drivers*, *tickle-texts*, *God-botherers*, *hymn-slingers*, *mumble-matins* and *pulpit-pounders*) and lawyers (among them *ambidexters*, *ambulance-chasers*, *pentitentiary agents*, *sons of prattlement* and *shysters*) and others whose uniform contains the *slabbering bib*, the job (at least the legitimate variety: from commercial sex alone slang can come up with 914 whores, 235 pimps, and 29 bawds) is not that well catered. Fair enough, slang is hardly the language of legitimacy, let alone employment.

There were a couple of formulas for job titles, both popular between the eighteenth and nineteenth centuries. There were *brothers*: among them a *brother of the blade*, a swordsman or soldier, of *the mawley* or *bunch of fives*, a prize-fighter, of *the brush*, both artist and housepainter, of *the sock and buskin*, an actor (a generic use of names for the low and high boots worn by classical Athenian actors), of *the quill*, a writer, of *the whip*, a coachman or cabbie (a *brother of the whip and spur* was a huntsman) and of *the bung*, a publican. Or there were *knights*: of *the grammar*, a teacher, *the hod*, a brickie, *the napkin*, a waiter, *the rainbow*, a footman (from his often colourful uniform), *the pigskin*, a jockey and *the satchel* a bookie. Brothers suggested the once powerful London guilds; not all knights were exactly 'employed' and many of the names suggest something of a joke: the *knight of the black jug* or of *the brush and moon* (a generic tavern sign) were topers, of *the elbow*, a card-sharp, of *the collar or halter*, a victim of the hangman, *the jemmy*, a burglar and *the pit*, a fan of cock-fighting.

One profession stands out (other perhaps than the hangman amongst whose fifty-plus synonyms are *Jack Ketch*, the *fluffing cull*, the *dancing master,* the *scragger* and *Nosey Bob*). We've enjoyed the drink, the drugs, the debauchery, so what we do we need? Yes. The doctor.

Slang's medical interventions are irreverent, but nothing like the stuff that the hospital professionals create themselves, the true jargon of the profession. The classic term is the mid-twentieth-century *gomer*: a patient who is whining and otherwise undesirable. This has rival origins, the best-known being 'get out of my emergency room'. Others include the 'Grand Old Man of the Emergency Room,' American TV's echt-incompetent *Gomer Pyle, gummer*, one whose toothless mouth chews on its gums and *gomeral*, an Irish term for lout. Such patients may well receive an *SFU 50* dose: this is the amount of a sedative or anti-anxiety medication that, in 50 per cent of the cases, causes a patient to 'shut the fuck up'.

There are many more. Among them the scalpel-happy *cowboy*, who operates first and thinks later; *plumbers*, urologists; *gas passers*, anaesthetists; and *flea*, an acronym for 'fucking little esoteric asshole' and applied to an intern. A child with a genetic or congenital condition is labeled *FLK* ('funny little kid'), while *frequent fliers* are those who turn up continuously at an emergency room, whether they need care or not. *Harpooning the whale* is to give an obese mother-to-be an epidural; mother herself is also known as *fluffy*. There is a *Hollywood code* (or *Slow Code*): rather than the rush to the dying patient so beloved of TV drama, this is the reverse: come what may the patient will not live and the doctor simply strolls in, goes through a variety of rote procedures but is really playing for time until he or she can declare the unfortunate individual dead. Those who die have been *discharged up* or *sent to the ECU* (the 'eternal care unit').

There is *watering the rose garden*, changing the drips on the geriatric ward. Finally, patients who exaggerate their symptoms, are *dying swans* (from the celebrated ballet) or *Camilles*, recalling the Dumas novel *La Dame Aux Camélias*, the highpoint of which is the heroine's protracted death.

These are slang, but localised, and unheard outside the ward or ER. (For those who want to pursue the lexis, I recommend the excellent http://messybeast.com/dragonqueen/medical-acronyms.htm

This has a vast list including vet-speak, e.g. *DSTO*: Dog Smarter Than Owner). But slang's own medical vocabulary is equally brusque, and the good bedside manner is not required.

Let us start, however, with *doctor* itself. The word multitasks, though its meanings are far from traditionally medicinal. Standard English doctor means to mix or to adulterate, and slang borrows it for a drink containing milk, water, rum and nutmeg, for alum, when used to adulterate food or drink (thus keep the doctor, to sell adulterated liquor), and for brown sherry, which is a mixture of sherry and wine, thus gaining its darker 'brown' tint. Then there are the more 'medicinal' uses: as a hangover cure, and as any form of alcohol used as a restorative. To *go to* (*see*) *the doctor* or *have a doctor's appointment* are euphemisms for having a drink. The equation of doctor with the final throw in a game of dice or ninepins presumably nods to the medico's appearance as life ends; he can also be the cook on an Australian sheep station (borrowed from the seaborne *doctor*, a shipboard cook, or New Zealand's whalers' *doctor*, a Maori slave used as a cook.)

The UK's Bingo (US Lotto), where the doctor means the number nine, provides various synonyms: the *doctor's shop* or *favourite* and *doctor's orders*. All go back to the military use of pill number nine, the most frequently prescribed medicine in the Field Medical Chest; there is also a reference to the nine months of pregnancy, after which one 'calls for the doctor'. The final noun use is gay, and refers to a man with a large penis: he gives you 'an injection'. The *doctor's curse* is a dose of calomel and the *doctor's loss* is one pound sterling (perhaps referring to a fee which he lost were the patient to die). Australia's *go* (*through*) or *look for the doctor* was a racing term wherein one rider and his mount move significantly ahead of the field; this was recycled for use beyond the racetrack as meaning to bet all one's money and after that to go full tilt at something or to commit oneself wholeheartedly. Used in the plural *doctors* were counterfeit coins or loaded dice. To *load the doctors* was to slip them into the game and to *put the doctors on* was to start using them.

Slang's default doctor is mendacious, cack-handed, greedy and preys gleefully on the gullible. This is the *quack*, a term that appears in the mid-seventeenth century and while one might have equated the 'quack' with verbosity of the high-pressure salesman, the term abbreviates *quacksalver*, a sixteenth-century term, which was borrowed from Dutch, where it meant one who cures with home remedies. The *snake-oil salesman* is similar, but much more recent (snake-oil was seemingly used in traditional Chinese medicine but its modern version – no snakes were ever harmed in its manufacture – was merchandised by a variety of twentieth-century charlatans). The quack toured the country, appearing at fairs and similar rural entertainments, usually accompanied by a couple of clowns. Such gurning, capering entertainers enjoyed a number of names. The *jack-pudding* and *pickle-herring* were stock figures (the latter, whose origins were in Holland and also served slang as a nickame for the Dutch, was usually accompanied by his broomstick), and as the *Supplement to the Memoirs of Mrs. Woffington, being the atchievements of a Pickle-Herring* (by 'Buttermilk Jack') put it in 1760, the celebrated actress 'well knew that a *Pickle-Herring* or *Jack-Pudding* gave more Joy to three Fourths of the World than the rolling Thunder of a SHAKESPEAR'. There was the *zany*, which slang borrowed as *sawney* and translated as 'laughing stock'. The name comes from Italian *commedia del arte*, where *zani* play servants and act as clowns. Finally the *merry-andrew*, usually found at London's annual Bartholemew Fair, which seems to commemorate the performer of a specific sideshow.

In 1785 Francis Grose could offer another name: the *crocus metallorum*, usually *crocus* or *croacus*. It meant either a doctor, fake or otherwise, or a beggar who posed as one. Originally an army term, the obvious root is a pun on *croak*, to die or kill, but this is so far first recorded at least twenty years later, and the *OED* suggests 'the Latinized surname of one Dr Helkiah Crooke, author of a *Description of the Body of Man*, 1615, *Instruments of Chirurgery*, 1631, etc . . .'. The assumption that 'Dr Crocus' was a quack adds a further possible link, to *hocus-pocus*, itself meaning variously a conjuror, a juggler or his tricks and drugged alcohol. For fairground workers crocus remains a doctor or a herbalist, even a self-proclaimed miracle-worker (in market use, where the word played on *crocus*, the flower, he was a fair-weather trader who only worked during the spring or summer). *Metallorum*, literally 'of metals' plays on the 'real' *crocus metallorum* or *crocus antimonii*, both of which are more or less impure oxysulphides of antimony, obtained by calcinations. Crocus produced a variety of spin-offs. The *crocus-chovey* was a chemist's shop or a doctor's consulting room (*chovey* continues to defeat all etymologies); the *crocus-pitcher* or *crocus worker* synonyms for the itinerant quack and the *crocussing rig* the job itself. *Crocus-tan* remains a hospital for Romanis.

Other quacks have included the *horse-leech* (used in standard English as a vet and assumed to be based on the use of blood-sucking leeches in medicine; however it is arguable that the meaning runs in the opposite direction, and it is the worm's function as a 'doctor' that gives it its own name). *Vet* itself has also been borrowed for human doctoring. There is the *med-* or *medicine-man* and the *medicine sharp, sharp* being an all-purpose and long-established – 1680 – adjective for a wide range of cheats, not merely card-hustlers. Similarly multi-purpose is America's *jackleg*, which applies to an incompetent, unskilled or unprincipled worker or professional person, especially a quack doctor, a corrupt lawyer or a hypocritical preacher. Where jack-leg originates is unknown: the current theory is a mix of *jack*, as in the given name and thus a generic for 'simple, common', and *leg* as a version of the earlier *blackleg*, a racecourse swindler. Perhaps fittingly, this does not inspire confidence.

If the quack was not selling a variety of distasteful, but almost certainly useless potions, then his stock-in-trade, bullshit aside, was pills. So too the legitimate physician. An early term for pills (usually large) was *bolus* and that, or *brother of the bolus*, meant a doctor or apothecary (a prototype pharmacist: the name goes back via French and German to Greek, where *apoteke* meant a store-house; the original apothecaries sold spices and preserves as well as drugs).

Modernity prefers the simple *pill* or *pills*, both of which mean a doctor, as do *pill-shooter, -slinger, -driver, -masher, -peddler, -pusher* and *-roller*. The pharmacist is a *pill-grinder* (from an era when pills were created in-house) or *pill-puncher*. The most recent iteration is the *pill mill*, a doctor's surgery, often in a run-down area, in which the bulk of prescriptions are written for drugs which are then sold in the street.

As well as giving out pills, there are other medical tasks. The *piss-prophet*, the *water scriger* (a possible corruption of *scriver*, a scribe) and a *knight of the pisspot* (also an apothecary), all reflect the useful role that an analysis of urine has long played in diagnosis. There is the *clyster-pipe* (from the standard *clyster-pipe*, a tube used to administer clysters, or enemas) and the *squirt* which draws on the use of *squirts* or syringes. Other apothecaries included the *mixum*, which was what he did, and the *gallipot*, properly a small earthen glazed pot, especially when used by apothecaries for ointments and medicines (the ultimate root is a pot that has been carried or imported in a galley). The *knight of the pestle* is another, especially one who prescribes for venereal diseases. (Francis Beaumont's 1607 play *The Knight of the Burning Pestle* played with that meaning, among those of other sexual double entendres.) More recently one finds the *needle man* (also a drug addict), a *needle pusher* and a *needle puncher*.

Dr Draw-fart is another itinerant quack. In standard English a chancre is a syphilitic lesion, but the *shanker mechanic* is just a doctor, the disease he treats is not necessarily an STD. Nor is the *twat-scourer* invariably focused on the vagina. A *baby-catcher* means a midwife as well as a doctor. Finally the US military *Band-Aid*, a brand-name equivalent to the UK Elastoplast, though the latter has failed to amuse slang.

If the simplest term of all is the abbreviation *doc*, then after quack, the best-known is probably *sawbones*. It must have been earlier, but the first recorded use is still from Dickens' *Pickwick Papers*: 'What! don't you know what a Sawbones is, Sir? [. . .] I thought everybody know'd as a Sawbones was a Surgeon.' There were, if later, *bone-juggler* and *cross-bones* and *bone butcher*. Which leads to Australia's *butch* and a number of other terms in which the physician's role is seen as promoting not so much cure but kill. There is *Dr Death*, a prison doctor; *007* who is 'licensed to kill', a *body-snatcher* or *corpse provider* (both of which usually refer to 'resurrection men') and the *cow-killer* who is barely safe with animals, let alone humans. As for *croaker*, a staple of noir fiction, there are no chronological problems here: the term which appears in 1859 could look back to *crocus*, but it could equally play on *croak*, to kill, recorded in 1812. It gives *croaker joint*, a hospital or surgery; *nut croaker*, a psychiatrist; a *croaker's chovey* was a pharmacy. A *stir croaker* was a second-rate, barely qualified doctor, assigned to prison work; he was also known as a *ford*, any generally antagonistic or unhelpful doctor and based on the perceived inferiority of a Ford automobile.

A few other terms include the rhyming *gamble and Proctor*, the punning *guinea pig* (like slang's lawyers its doctors are always focused on the fee, which was traditionally counted in aristocratic guineas rather than plebian pounds), the *cranker* (from German *krank*, sick) and a *med*.

Slang seems to have overlooked the nurse. Her earliest incarnation was a *gamp*, in memory of the fictional Sarah Gamp, created by Charles Dickens in *Martin Chuzzlewit* (1843–4). Otherwise we have the modern *candystriper*, Scotland's *milk woman* – a wet-nurse (thus the *green milk-woman*, one who has only recently given birth) and *needle queen*.

The references to bones, above, can also describe a surgeon, whose primary task seems to have been equated by slang with amputations. As well as those there are the *bone-bender, -breaker, -butcher, -carpenter* and *-chiseller*. He could always be simple *bones*. His other skills produced little better, e.g. *flesh tailor* or *lint-scraper* who was a junior surgeon and capable of nothing more sophisticated. A *pintle-smith* or *pintle-tagger* did not in fact focus strictly on the *pintle* or penis but was just one more hacker. The *-smith* suffix is as in blacksmith, the *tag* meant to stitch together. There was also the still mysterious *nimgimmer*, who specialised in STDs. Finally, suggesting an early disparity between doctors' and surgeon's fees, there was the crime of *clacking the doctor*, impersonating a doctor in order to rob a surgeon. *Clack* meaning chatter, referred to the spiel thus involved.

If, as noted, the *croaker* is a regular in noir fiction it is because he often pursues a lucrative sideline; the supplying of prescriptions for 'recreational' drugs, usually narcotics. Such a doctor *sails* ('close to the wind'), *turns* (against professional ethics) or *writes*, and is known as a *writing croaker* or an *author*. In the criminal reversal whereby *right* equals corruptible, he can also be a *right croaker*. The *hungry croaker* is equally amenable and, for whatever reason, is willing to prescribe drugs for any user who asks for them. A prescription is abbreviated as a *script*: it gives *script doctor*, another writer, and the modern *script mill*, a doctor's surgery where, for a price, one can obtain prescriptions for narcotics, painkillers or whatever hits the mark. The *ice-tong doctor* was usually employed elsewhere: as an illegal abortionist – absent proper forceps ice tongs were seen as a necessary tool of the trade – but he often compounded one crime with another and was happy to supply illegal drugs. Some doctors resisted: the junkies called them *poison. Dr. Feelgood* did not. Created by the blues pianist Piano Red (William Perryman) playing in 1962 as 'Dr Feelgood and the Interns', the original doctor focused strictly on sex. The doctor was all *size-freak*, setting out a minimum weight of '400 pounds' and instructing the girls 'If you don't weigh what I want, baby, don't bother to come around.' There were no drug references. By 1971, the other end of the Sixties, the meaning had changed. The doctor had become one who obliges patients, often showbusiness or entertainment celebrities, with amphetamines or narcotics, which, although the user has no real medical need for them, guarantee 'good feelings'. The term isn't used in the lyrics, but the Beatles 'Dr Robert' (1966) a real-life Harley Street dentist, fitted the bill.

Of course you have to ask first. The doctor, however *bent*, is not usually waving a prescription across the desk as you walk in. Something melodramatic is needed and slang notes several examples of the type: essentially a fake fit – allegedly brought on by the agonies of narcotics' withdrawal – after which the doctor, possibly quite amenable in the first place, has no choice but to reach for the prescription pad.

There is the *brodie*, which honours Steve Brodie, a 23-year-old New York saloon-keeper who on 23 July 1886 allegedly leaped some 45m (135ft) from the city's Brooklyn Bridge in order to win a $200 wager. He survived the fall and was scooped out of the East River by a friend in a small boat. He was subsequently charged by the police with attempted suicide. Whether he actually made the jump remains unproven (the witnesses, all of them his friends, claimed that he did, but the general consensus was that a dummy was tossed over the bridge and Brodie, hiding on shore, quickly swam underwater to the point where it had hit the river, in time to be 'rescued'). This scepticism is reflected in theatrical jargon: a brodie, a (much touted) flop. In drug terms, it simply means a fake. Other versions include the *circus*, a *figure-eight*, in which a fit is augmented by much tortured twisting of the body, the *twister*, which one *frames*, is similar, as is the *wing-ding*, which one *throws*. One who performs the latter is a *wing-dinger*.

Slang's dental surgery is small and to the point; all terms focus on the *tooth carpenter* or *snag-catcher*, sitting you down in his *tooth booth* or *house of pain* doing something unpleasant and nasty to your teeth. There is the anomalous and hard-to-understand *kindheart*, used around 1610–20, but this possible irony aside all else is barren.

All terms depend on parts of the mouth. There are the *fangs*, the teeth themselves, which give *fang-bandit, -carpenter, -hustler, -man, -lifter, -faker* and *Mr Fang*; plus *fang chovey* (from *cove*, a man) or *factory*, a dental surgery. There is a *gum-digger*, otherwise *-puncher, -smasher*, or *-tickler*. The *ivory-carpenter* or *ivory-snatcher*. The *jawsmith, jawbreaker* or *jawbone breaker, jawbone doctor, jawbuster* or *jaw puller*. Last the *tusk-hoister* or *tusk jerker*.

If the ice-tong doctor prefers to hide his gruesome kit, others of slang's abortionists are less squeamish. Not that any of the associated vocabulary lets you off the hook. Perhaps the least offensive is the *angel-maker*, borrowed from France's synonymous and equally euphemistic *faiseur d'anges*. Otherwise one has the *lock-picker*, the *rabbit-snatcher* and the *pin artist*. If the coat-hanger is mercifully absent, there are intimations in the grim collection around *scrape*: *scrape job, scraping* and *scrape out*. To procure an abortion is to *crack an egg*, to *hoover*, to *bring it away* and, in the Caribbean, to *throw away belly*. *Cemetery*, still in the West Indies, refers to a woman who has had (or is suspected of having had) an abortion. To *make a woman one* is the reverse of *fall in two*: to give birth, in this case the 'other' is no longer there. The seventeenth-century *stifle the squeaker* was baldly defined as to murder a child 'and throw it into a House of Office (i.e. a privy)'.

The ambulance, which slightly paradoxically comes from Latin *ambulans*, walking, but which came into use via the mobile hospitals invented during the Crimean War, makes its mark on slang. A *blood box* or *blood wagon*, a *bang box* (i.e. carrying those that have been 'banged'), a *bone cart* or *bone box*, a *fever cart*, a *butcher wagon* or *meat wagon* (that which takes corpses to the morgue was a *meat rack*, nodding to the lack of comforts – why bother – within). The *daffy chariot*, accompanied no doubt by men in white coats, take the unfortunate eccentric to the mental ward. Similar conveyances included the *green cart* (an Australianism and not necessarily green, but perhaps reflecting the institutional paintwork) and America's *cookie truck*, filled not with biscuits but *kooks*. At best it was a *bus* or the nicely punning *pick-me-up*. In New Zealand a St John's Ambulance man is a *Zambuck* or *Zambuk*, and comes from Zam-buk, a proprietary antiseptic ointment. As explained on the Zam-buk website, 'The word Zam-Buk originated in New Zealand, and was used to describe someone who administered first aid to wounded sportsmen.'

Ambulances tended to be white, though they've turned yellow these days. The *black maria* is almost always defined as a van taking prisoners either to the police station or a prison but there is at least one example (perhaps in error) that equates it with an ambulance. The earliest recorded use, 1835, is found in New York, although it was well established in London by the 1860s. Its obvious origin was in the colour of the van, but just who was Maria, and for that matter why? Suggestions include an abbreviation of slang's *married*, two or more prisoners chained together; a play on the *-ria* of Queen Victoria's name (which fails in the face of its origins in the US, although *V.R.* for Victoria Regina was inscribed on the British vans) and Ephraim Brewer's suggestion in the 1894 edition of his *Dictionary of Phrase and Fable* of a derivation from one Maria Lee, a Black madam of Boston, Mass. So large and fearsome was Ms Lee that she was regularly called upon by the local police to help them first arrest and then take criminals to prison.

Then of course we have the *ambulance-chaser*, defined less than amicably as a lawyer who specialises in representing the victims of street and other accidents, to whom he offers his services – often appearing at the victim's hospital bed to promise a substantial claim – which are accepted while the victim is still too shocked to make proper and rational arrangements. By extension the term suggests anyone who tries to benefit them-selves by another's disaster.

If the ambulance lacks much sympathy, its destination, the *hossie* or *hozzy*, doesn't improve matters. The hospital can be the *blood factory*, the *body shop*, the *bone factory*, *-house*, *-shop* or *boneyard* which, perhaps not coincidentally, can also mean a cemetery (as do the *bone* and *skull orchard*). The *butcher's shop* is hardly cheering, while *inside* otherwise refers to imprisonment. The *boogie* or *boogie house* may sound fun, but the boogie in question is not dancing, or not directly, but a term for syphilis and is rooted in the standard English *bougie*, 'a thin flexible surgical instrument made of waxed linen, india-rubber, metal, etc., for introduction into the passages of the body, for the purpose of exploration, dilatation, or medication' (*OED*); the tool was used in the treatment of STDs, although a proposed link to the notorious Tuskegee experiments, clandestinely inducing African-American prisoners with the disease, known in slang as *boogie*, cannot stand up: the term existed since at least 1926 and the experiments began only in 1932. A hospital specialising in gynaecology is the *cat's meat gaff: gaff* as in a place (originally Romani *gav*, a fair) plus a blackly humorous reference to the lungs and similar animal intestines that are used to feed cats and dogs. A *spike*, usually a workhouse or similar down-and-out's hostel, can be borrowed in Ireland for a maternity hospital, the emphasis being on its lack of physical comforts. *Laid up in lavender* means put aside or pawned, thus *in lavender* refers to life in a charity ward; the inference being that one has been wholly forgotten. Last, and long gone, is the 1940s Harlem slang, a *pad*, i.e. house, of *stitches*.

If slang's vision of a general hospital is bleak, that for a psychiatric institution, where patients are confined *over the blue wall*, is simply cruel. Using, in many cases, its mocking names for the mad, it simply adds some kind of place name, e.g. farm, house or factory, and takes things from there. Thus along with *farm* itself, we have *drool farm, ding farm, funny farm, cuckoo farm, happy farm, loony farm* and *nut farm*. The *banana farm* is in a tropical or semi-tropical country. *Factory* (or *foundry*) produces the *puzzle factory, cackle factory* (a *cackle tub*, however, is a pulpit or a dissenting chapel), a *cracker factory* or *cracker-box* (whose inmates have gone *crackers*), a *foolish factory*, a *giggle factory, funny factory, loony factory*, a *fruit* or *fruitcake factory* for the *fruitcakes* who are of course *nuts*, which in turn produces *nut factory* or *foundry*. The *rat factory* is Australian and stems from *ratty*, eccentric, which also offers *rat joint*, again a mental hospital, *get, have* or *go rats, give rats*, to drive someone mad, and *rattiness*. (To *have rats in the attic* or *garret* has origins in America.)

House is even more productive. Compounds include the *nut house*, *pipe-house*, *fit house* (a hospital for the criminally insane), *bat house* (from *bats in the belfry*), *big house* (usually a Federal prison), *birdhouse*, *brickhouse*, *crazy house*, *cuckoo house*, *dippy house*, *fool-fool house*, *foolish house* (which has also been used for a carnival's hall of mirrors sideshow), *franzy house* (from standard English *frenzy*, craziness and which can also mean a brothel), *funny house* (or *funny bin* or *funny place*), *giggle* or *giggley house*, *happy house* (or *home*), *itzy house*, *kooky* or *kookie house*, *loony house*, *monkey house*, *rathouse*, the US military's *red house*, *silly house*, *whacky house*, *booby house*, *buzzy house*, *potty house* (as in eccentric rather than commode) and *bughouse*.

The *bug*, a figurative insect which buzzes *in one's head* (or *brain*, *cotton* or *wig*), also gives the *bughouse fable*, an exaggerated story; the *bug ward* or *bughouse ward*, a psychiatric ward and *bughouser*, an asylum inmate. The *bug doctor* or *inspector* is a psychiatrist, and *bug juice* a sedative drug used for controlling violent or non-cooperative prisoners. Bug as a verb means to commit to a psychiatric institution, as does the almost humorous *drop a net on*.

The *boob* or *booby* is an inmate, which makes for the *boob box* and for one of the best-known terms: the *booby hatch*, or *hutch*, which underpins the simple idea of confinement with the once celebrated asylum at Colney Hatch near London, opened in 1851. (There is also the Royal Navy's *booby-hatch*, a large inverted box that covers a hatch, and intended to stop careless sailors from falling.) Synonymous are *booby box* or *booby cage* plus *squirrel cage*, *ranch*, *pen* or *tank*. There are also the *cranky hatch* and *canary hatch*, the *cuckoo academy* and *cuckoo's nest* (seemingly coined by Ken Kesey in his asylum-based 1962 novel *One Flew Over the Cuckoo's Nest*).

Nut means the head (since around 1790; before that it was the head of the penis) and a *nut* has meant an eccentric since 1908; *nuts* has meant crazy since 1840. Thus we have the *nut bin, box, college, hatch, hut, place, wing, house* and *hospital*. There are *nuttery* and *nutty house*. The *nut croaker* is a psychiatrist and at US college *nuts and sluts* is a course in abnormal psychology.

Still educational we find the *brain college*, the *academy* and *laughing academy* (plus *laughing farm* or *house*) and the *giggle* or *giggling academy* or *bin*. There is simple *bin*, plus the *buggy*, the *loony bin* (perhaps the best known term of all and possibly coined by P.G. Wodehouse who used it in 1909), *loony-boob, pen* and *roost*. Last of a long list: the *shrink klink*, which combines *shrink*, as in *head-shrinker* (plus *shrinker* and *shrinkette*) with *clink*, a prison, since 1515 when it was the name of an establishment in London.

Francis Grose, never loath to regale his readers with more than just simple definitions, and the size of whose dictionary entries sometimes rivalled that of his stomach, also offered the verb dowdy. To *dowdy* was to play a practical joke based on one's pretending to be mad, especially to have just escaped from one's keeper or from a psychiatric institution. As he explained, dowdy-ing was 'a local joke formerly practised at Salisbury, on large companies, or persons boasting of their courage. It was performed by one Pearce, who had the knack of personating madness, and who by the direction of some of the company, would burst into a room, in a most furious manner, as if just broke loose from his keeper, to the great terror of those not in the secret. Dowdying became so much the fashion of the place, that it was exhibited before His Royal Highness the Prince of Wales [. . .] Pearce obtained the name of Dowdy, from a song he used to sing, which had for burthen the words dow de dow.' You had, as they say, to be there.

Running these many institutions were the experts, usually psychiatrists (slang seems to have evolved nothing to describe the actual keepers). These were doctors and so named: the *head doctor* (or *head feeler* or *tripper*), the *loony doctor* (another Wodehouse coinage: in *Carry on Jeeves*, 1925), the *nut doctor*, *talk doctor* and *skull doctor*. Shrink aside, the tongue-twisted *trick cyclist* is popular while *wig-picker* and *sky artist* are less common.

Given slang's lack of respect for those who claim to follow the Hippocratic oath, perhaps we should conclude with those necessary figures who turn up to clear up the medical mess. The undertakers, practitioners of the *black job* or *black work*, and known as *black coats* (as were clergymen) and *black job masters*. *Undertaker*, while never slang, is itself a euphemism: what is this unspoken task that they *undertake* to do? Digging the grave gives *sod-buster*, as does *landbroker*. A coffin is a *wooden kimono*, as well as *wooden suit*, *uniform*, *doublet*, *surtout* and *ulster* (the last pair both terms for overcoats) and *wooden habeas* which puns on *habeas corpus*, a piece of legal Latin and a writ whereby an accused and jailed person must be brought before the court and the reason for their imprisonment justified; the literal translation is 'thou shalt have the body'. Thus the undertaker could be an *over-coat-maker* and a *wooden overcoat man*. He was a *gloomer*, from his professional misery, and, unflatteringly, a *meat-packer* (*meat* being the corpse), a *bone-snatcher*, a *ghoul*, a *death-*, *bug-* and *carrion hunter*. The *Memoirs of Sally Salisbury*, one of the great eighteenth-century courtesans, recount how Sally, infuriated at some aspect of a friend's funeral, 'flew at the poor Undertaker, hit him an unmerciful Box on the Ear, D--n you, said she, for a Whining Carrion-hunting Son of a Bitch!' There was also the *carrion-crow man* and the *raven*, both of them black and with a reputation for carrion-hunting of their own, and the phrase *cry pork* was to tell the undertaker that a funeral was in the offing; the term comes from the supposed similarity of *pork!* to a raven's cry.

That one more term for the undertaker was *body-snatcher* brings us to those who were interested in the body, even after the burial. Such *resurrectionists*, another grim and even blasphemous pun, and *all-night men* (when they plied their ghastly trade of disinterring the freshly buried) worked to supply hospitals with otherwise forbidden corpses. Specialists and their students needed something to practise on and other than a regular supply of freshly hanged criminals, until the Anatomy Act of 1832 legitimised the use of any corpse, digging up the recently dead was the only way. Sometimes, however, the *resurrection-men* proved a little over-enthusiastic. Such a zealous duo were the two Williams, Burke and Hare, a pair of Edinburgh villains who didn't bother to wait, but during 1828 murdered sixteen unfortunate victims so as to sell their corpses to the medical school for surgical dissection. Burke was hanged in 1829; Hare, who turned King's evidence, escaped the noose. Robert Louis Stevenson immortalised them in 'The Body Snatchers' (1884) while the noun *burker*, and verb *burke* are slang's memorial.

Sweety Darling:
Carrying the Torch for Love

I F SLANG HAS stories, then they are not to be found on those shelves marked 'romance'. Slang likes its four-letter words, but l-o-v-e does not qualify and when Cupid enters the picture then if there is a 'story' its definition is rarely more than the one that is a synonym for 'hoax' or 'trick' or even 'lie'. The truth is simple: if we are seeking hearts and flowers, we are foolishly misguided, for slang has no words for love.

The first thing we need to take on board is that while slang undoubtedly boasts the widest-ever-ranging vocabulary when it comes to sex and the bits and pieces that we need to accomplish it, love, that much fetishised emotion, doesn't come into the picture. Yes, the lexis does offer the odd, dare I suggest grudging acknowledgment: there is *love* as a noun, but that's far from emotional, and defined as any person or thing that is pleasant or attractive, e.g. *it's a real love*. There is love as in *love of a . . .* which is a term of praise kindred to *duck*, as in 'duck of . . .' and tends to apply to small children or else items of clothing: hats, dresses, although Walter, the narrator of that multi-volumed piece of Victorian porn *My Secret Life*, recalls how, on holiday, his hosts offered to 'get me a love of an Italian boy to bugger'.

But of the thirty-plus compounds that attend it, love has

quietly but comprehensively replaced itself by sex. Other than the whole humans implied in *love muffin* and *love machine*, it's all down to those bits and bobs. There are the penises; the *love truncheon, warrior, pump* (notably in Spinal Tap's epochal 'Lick My Love Pump'), *hammer, staff, stick, steak, bone, dart, gun* and *muscle*. (Not to mention *corporal love*, which fleshy non-com 'stands to attention'.) There are the vaginas: the *love box, canal, flesh, glove* (otherwise a condom), *hole, cabinet* and *shack* (another rock 'n' roller, by the B-52s). *Love hillocks* are the female breasts as are *love apples* (which can otherwise be testicles), *love button* the clitoris, *love-lips* the labia, *love grenades* or *spuds* the testicles, *love juice* or *custard*, semen, *love rug* the pubic hair and on it goes. *Love handles* (the idea being that one can hold on to them during sex) represent the excess flesh around a portly stomach that may be seen in a kinder light by those who appreciate the Rubenesque figure. There is the *love bug*, which in this context stands for VD rather than VW, as in Disney's twee Herbie. There is a moment's possibility in *love affair*, but inspection reveals that this is drug slang, and refers to a shot of heroin and cocaine mixed, and the *love letter*, showcasing slang's usual cynicism, is in fact a stone, as thrown maliciously at a human target.

Love's lexis is not all sexual. The *love drug*, plain and simple, is MDMA or Ecstasy, *love weed* marijuana and *pure love* LSD. *Love curls* were a hairstyle in which the hair is cut short and worn low over the forehead, *love-pot* a drunkard. And *for the love of Mike!* (which love-object can also be *Heaven! holy Buddha! Jupiter! Michael Angelo! Moses! Pete* (and *Alf*)*! Peter the hermit!* and *Polly Simpkins!*) is an exclamation of exasperation or surprise.

One can expand the search, but can one render the definitions more affectionate? No. *Love and kisses*, rhyming on 'the missus' at least suggests a tinge of harmony, but *love and marriage* is merely a carriage, while other rhymes offer *love and hate* (weight), *God-love-her* (one's mother) and *light of love* (a prison *gov*ernor), and never forget that this last, when un-rhymed, means a whore.

Last chance: definitions containing 'love', and excluding those that include 'affair'. Slang resists moderation and passion, even obsession, is the rule. There's the passionate lover who goes at the beloved *hot and heavy like a tailor's goose*. The *goose* being the iron used to perfect a fresh-sewn garment, a reference that not for the first time has one wondering about the back-story of a folk song, in this case 'dashing away with the smoothing iron'. Alternatively he may be a *bone-setter*, the force of his affections threatening to break the loved one's limbs, though there may be a pun on *bone*, the penis, too.

But *tender passion* (on stream from 1752)? Not much improvement here. Slang's list for 'being in love' includes such as *doing one's balls on, bughouse, busted on, collared on, dead set on, daffy, dippy, dotty, doughy, dropping one's ovaries* (a camp gay term, at least in South Africa), *fall for, have it for, hung up on, gone a million, nuts on, potty, snowed over, soft, spoons on, stuck on, going turtles on* ('turtle dove' = love), *whipped, whooped, wrapped* (i.e. *rapt*) and *yar*. Is it just me, or do others also fail to see much in the way of hearts and flowers? Half of them, after all, are synonyms for 'mad' and there are a few fools too. One that is not is *sugar on*, but that ushers in a whole new selection: what one might term 'sweet talk', a term that, as far as the love-making sense goes, seems to have appeared as recently as 1945, as part of a slang glossary entitled *Hepcats' Jive Talk*.

The obvious candidates are *sugar* and *sweet* and both enlisted as terms of endearment, but they are not alone. The equation of the loved one and the toothsome treat, one who is 'good enough to eat', is venerable. 'Thy lips, O my spouse, drop as the honeycomb: honey and milk are under thy tongue' declares the *Song of Solomon* around 200 BCE and the pattern has continued. *Honey*, with its combinations *honeychild*, *honey-chops*, *honey-dip*, *honey-baby*, *honey-pot* and *honey-bun* all arrive in the early twentieth century, as does *crumpet*. The equation seems unquenchable and endearments include *honey-bunch*, *honey-bunny* (used to grim effect in Tarantino's *Pulp Fiction*), *honeybugs*, *honeypie* and *honey-cunt*. Like sugar there are less appetising senses, notably the ironic: a *honey of* a mess is problematical; while *honey* can denote various bodily fluids, whether sexual or excretory – the latter best known in *honey cart*, used in various forms of public transport to describe a container for what an earlier world, equally euphemistic, termed *gold* (a substance that was removed by the *gold-finder*, otherwise known matily as *Tom Turdman*). The rival images combine in the eighteenth century's *it's all honey or all turd with them* said of those whose relationship fluctuates violently between amity and its antithesis.

Sweetie, *sweetie-pops*, *sweetycakes*, *sweetie-pie*, *sweet pea* and *sweet potato pie* are other modernisms. *Sweetmeat* is ambivalent: it can be a lover or a mistress but it can be, with knowing cyncism, an underage prostitute. *Cake* has been popular in the States for a century; *lollipop* has been common since 1850.

Tart is perhaps the most interesting. Now seen as a pejorative, other than in Australia and Liverpool where it remains neutral, it began life positively. The *Slang Dictionary* of 1859 explained; 'Tart, a term of approval applied by the London lower orders to a young woman for whom some affection is felt. The expression is not generally employed by the young men, unless the female is in "her best", with a coloured gown, red or blue shawl, and plenty of ribbons in her bonnet – in fact, made pretty all over, like the jam tarts in the swell bakers' shops.' (Beware, however, of compound tarts: rhyming slang is pervasive and the *raspberry, strawberry, cherry* and *treacle* varieties all mean farting.) When *tart* turned nasty is hard to nail down, though by 1889 the Portsmouth Evening News of 30 May could report that 'a Court of Law has decided it is libellous to call a girl a "tart".'

Moving on to the physically attractive, it's definitely more of the same. A pretty girl can be *jam, crumb, biscuit, pie, bun, raspberry, peach* (and the intensified *peacherino*) and *cupcake. Cheesecake*, a pin-up, appeared around 1930 (its male counterpart *beefcake* is slightly younger).

Other expressions of affection or approval include *dishy, tasty, fruity, scrumptious, flavour, slice* and *yummy*. Endearments have included a *banana*, a *basket of oranges* (a reference apparently to glittering nuggets of gold as well as fruit), one who is the *jammiest of the jam* or the *real raspberry jam*, a *bun, butter*, a *cutesie-pie*, a *dixie cup*, a *creamie*, a *pancake*, a *pastry*, and even a *penn'orth o' treacle*.

Sometimes sweet turns sickly and endearment turns to abuse. Such terms include *pieface, muffin, fruitcake, jellybean, jellyhead*, all of which suggest a certain 'softness', and *social doughnut hole*, in other words a human 'nothing'.

Those seeking solace in a bit of rom, with or without com, may be cheered to find that while slang's words for womaniser (*alley-cat, belswagger, chicken-butcher, jelly roller, lusty lawrence, poodle-faker* . . .) number 131, those for 'lover' rack up twenty more. Even in sneering slang cads and bounders are seemingly vanquished, in theory if nowhere else, by lurve.

Given slang's default position – the sneer – *goo-gooer* is probably the mot juste. That and *pash, sweet daddy* and *daddy-one, main man, duck, goodie, momma, boopsie, heart* and *last heartbeat*. The blues, all nudge-nudge and somewhat transparent double entendre went for *biscuit rollers*, *coffee grinders* and *ash-haulers*, which last comes from *haul someone's ashes*, where ashes meant *ass*, in its vagina definition. Bessie Smith celebrated those adept in the sexual side of *eating*: 'He's a deep-sea diver / with a stroke that can't go wrong, / He can touch bottom, and his wind holds out so long.' *Lemons* were of course, always up for *squeezing*.

There was the *carpet knight* who is also found as a *carpet-champion*, *carpet lover*, *carpet-monger*, *carpet squire* and *carpet warrior*. In all cases he preferred the boudoir where the only war was between the sexes over the harsher environs of the real-life battlefield. Like the *smoodger* (from *smoodge*, to kiss and cuddle), there is the *squeeze* who can be elevated to *main squeeze*. The *panorama* garbled paramour, and *pully-hawley* reverse engineered *play at pully-hawley*, another of those terms for intercourse that emphasised the sheer physicality of the act. A *torch* was carried and refers to lost or unrequited love: the 'light of love' is still burning, even if it is unreciprocated. The *flamer*, variously an admirer, lover or promiscuous woman, 'burnt brightly'. As for men, the *missionary man* was no more exciting than his position of choice, and what a girl needed was a *natural-born man*. What she probably got was *Jody*, otherwise *Joe the Grinder* (*Sancho* to Spanish speakers) who moved in when hubby or boyfriend had to be elsewhere, especially in wartime.

Names for the womaniser, the punning *cock of the game*, seem to advocate not especially procrastinated rape (a plot device that was once advised as a guarantor of fictional best-sellerdom). It's up and at her all the way: the *mutton-*, *hair-* or *fleece monger*, the *rump-* and *whiskersplitter*, the *bum-fighter* (who is not a sodomite: *bum* works for the vagina as well) and *quim-sticker*, the *buttonhole-worker*, *gulley-raker* and *tuft-hunter* (more usually discovered sucking up to a *tuft*, i.e. toff, from the distinguishing golden tassel on his university mortar-board), a *leg-* or *linen-lifter*. There is the *smock-soldier* and *feather-bed soldier*, the *parlour python* and the *lounge lizard*, the *meathound* (a carnivore only in the figurative sense) and the *jazzhound* (where *jazz* means intercourse, not music), the *dasher*, the *masher* and the *pieman* and *crumpet-man* and the *he-whore* (who may be *donkey-dicked*). In no case is there a sense of critique: this was slang-man's go-to position. No namby-pamby gender equality here.

It is hard, slang being what it is, to decide where to limit the list of what the lexis at least, defines as 'promiscuous' women. If one believes slang, most, even all women, other than those sidelined as mothers, nags or hags (and even *mother* is more likely to be a brothel-keeper), are seen as being *up for it*, and if in truth hope is ever-vanquished by experience, slang has no intention of telling. The line between a professional and an enthusiastic amateur is opaque: context helps a little, but not invariably. Those who slang tells us enjoy *more pricks than a second-hand dartboard* (not to mention a *pin-cushion*) may or may not opt for an income. There are 1000+ prostitutes to 170 promiscuous women, and forty-four who are labelled as both, but there is no system of checks. *Whore* is too random an insult to be very much believed. For our purposes let us forget them all. Instead, let us consider the mistress.

The point of the mistress is that she is not the wife. Thus the *backstreet wife* (her male equivalent being, when he's not a sodomite, a *backdoor man*), the *left-handed wife* (there is also a *left-handed bridegroom*), the *side-dish* and the *bit on the side*.

The long-vanished *loteby*, coined in the fourteenth century, was based on *lote*, to skulk or hide.

She could be a *rainbow*, from her taste in colourful, thus

arousing clothes (so too could be a whore) but she can equally be a *wife in water-colours*, a muted version of the actual spouse, presumably portrayed in garish oils. On the other hand, and contrasted with the excitements of adultery, the wife is a *cooler*, who 'cools one's passions' while the mistress 'heats them up'. The relationship is not acknowledged as serious: she's a *bit of nonsense* or a *gallimaufry*, which also works for her vagina and is properly defined as a stew that is made of random bits of food. Clothes may also underpin the *fancy piece* or *fancy bit*, though these may be a matter of 'a little of what you fancy'.

However independent the *grandes horizontales* of courtesan legend may have been, slang's mistress is, of course, at her lover's disposal. A *convenient* or *conveniency* (itself a convenient word, meaning not just mistress, but wife, prostitute, vagina, brothel – a *convenient house* – and lavatory). She is both a *comfortable importance*, and a *comfortable impudence*, especially when he takes her out in public and introduces her as his wife. Her lover cannot see her daily, and may not wish to, which makes her a *weekender*, or a *Saturday-to-Monday*, although these seem illogical since most married men are locked into domesticity at that time of the week.

She is, however could she not be, morally unacceptable. Thus the *blowen* (also a whore) which according to the nineteenth-century expert in matters Romani, George Borrow, comes from *beluñi*, 'a sister in debauchery', though Hotten brings in German's *bluhen*, bloom, and *buhlen*, sweetheart, but adds 'the street term . . . may mean one whose reputation has been "blown on", or damaged'. *Trug* or *trugmallion*, from Italian *trucca*, defined in 1598 as 'a fustian or rogish word for a trull, a whore, or a wench' is possibly cognate with standard English *truck*, to barter or exchange commodities.

She's a plaything, a *gamester* (her game being sex; when used of men the word means *stud*) and a *dolly*, which comes from *doll*, but may be linked to Italian's *dolce* and thus part of the stage/gay language Polari. She is quite simply a *toy*, which slang uses indiscriminately for penis, vagina, whore and mistress. One of her earliest incarnations was the *doxy*. She began life in the sixteenth century as the female companion of a variety of mendicant villains and soon embraced a less specific role as a mistress. If she survives, anachronistically, it is as a 'good-time gal'. Roots are debatable: possibly Dutch *docke*, a doll, possible standard English *dock*, a tail (and thus its various sexual meanings in slang) and possibly lowland Scots *doxie*, meaning lazy.

Her role is primarily sexual, which makes her an *underput* or *belly-piece*, both suggesting the missionary position, and a *pintle-bit* or *pintle-maid*, where *pintle* is the penis; the dismissive *bit* has been used for women, always in a sexual mode, since 1665, usually in compounds such as *bit of drapery*, of *muslin*, of *skin*, of *raspberry* and so on. *Bit of how's-your-father* is of course sex. The *buttered bun* (*butter* being semen and *bun* the vagina) was originally and remains a woman who has had intercourse with one man and is about to repeat this immediately with a new partner; she has also signified both mistress and prostitute. And if sex is *riding*, she can be a *mount*, a *mare* (a semi-positive use of a word that usually, and, nastily, denotes an older woman), or a *hobby horse*, not so much the children's toy, but a small horse who can be 'ridden' by all and sundry. The eighteenth-century *ligby* seems to come from *lig*, to lie down. Ironically, we assume, she is a *pure*. Yet like all women she is weak: a *frail*, and the *frail sisterhood* was one of many Victorian euphemisms for prostitutes. 'Frailty,' declared Shakespeare's Hamlet, though for once sidestepping entendres of any dimension, 'thy name is woman.'

Mystery Tour: Far Away Places

ONCE UPON A time, prior to the seventeenth century, there wasn't any difference between dictionaries and encyclopedias. The idea was that a good reference book offered all knowledge, or at least all sorts thereof, and why differentiate? The aim was to offer what Latin termed an *omnium gatherum*, a collection of all (knowledge). To an extent, notably in certain US dictionaries, this never went away, and they persisted in providing non-linguistic information, typically gazetteers of world geography, but such as Samuel Johnson or the *OED* decided otherwise. Dictionaries were about words, not wanderings.

Slang, cheerfully breaking most of the other lexicographical rules, breaks this too. It doesn't produce full-on gazetteers, but dig around, there's an encyclopedic side to slang. Mainly places, some real, some otherwise, and a few people, on just the same basis.

It's not exactly slang from day one but it's worth getting a little back-story. The idea of 'far, far away' first emerges in Latin's *Ultima Thule* – the land of Thule being supposedly six days' sail north of Britain and thus the northern limit of navigability; for Latin speakers that meant the Shetlands, while in 1771 Smollett, in *Humphrey Clinker*, equated it with the Orkneys or Hebrides.

Since then archaeologists have named Thule as a pre-historical Inuit culture, lasting from c.500–1400 and encompassing an area from Alaska to Greenland. Moving from the specific to the general brings the *back of beyond*, which concept has been recorded since 1816 (Walter Scott coined it for his novel *The Antiquary*, though he went further in time – talking of an old Roman camp – than he did in distance). In any case even if the use is no earlier the concept undoubtedly must be. The *OED* defines it as a 'humorous phrase' and the image, however contrary might be the reality, remains so.

Neither of those are slang, but there is no doubt about the *arsehole* (or *asshole*) *of the universe*, which is a place not so much distant but beyond acceptability. Alternative forms include the *arsehole of creation, of the world,* and the *bunghole of the universe.* The concept seems to have appeared in the mid-nineteenth century, but TripAdvisor followers might want to note the description of Holland as 'the Buttock of the world, full of veins and blood, but no bones in't' in *A Brief Character of the Low Countries* (1660) and Ned Ward's reference in 'A Trip to Jamaica' (1704) to 'The Dunghill of the Universe, the Refuge of the Whole creation, the Clippings of the Elements, a shameless Pile of Rubbish, confus'dly jumbl'd into an Emblem of the Chaos.' In 1946 Primo Levi, fresh from its horrors, used Latin to describe Auschwitz as *anus mundi*.

If you want mystery you want distance; faraway places, real or otherwise, have to be far away and it helps if one's local topography conjures up such imagery. Sadly, the UK isn't really much help here. Australia and America, big countries both, come up with the goods, but the UK doesn't cut it – John O'Groats and Lands End, Britain's famous extremes, are too parochial, just too close. Wales can't help: the root of 'Welsh' means 'unintelligible language' and thus 'foreigner' but Wales just isn't foreign enough. Only, perhaps, in its linguistic links to *rotwelsch*, Germany's name for its homegrown criminal cant: *rot* means red, which takes us to red hair, seen as stereotypically Jewish and therefore, another anti-semitic trope, symbolic of cunning. The whole, therefore, 'cunning talk'.

So the 'tight little island' remains just that. Getting away from it all is something for others, or at least for them to describe. The great deserts epitomise the lonely wasteland, and the Sahara, of course, boasts *Timbuktu*, the daddy of all such terms, first recorded in this sense in 1863. A settlement had existed since the Iron Age: the perception of isolation is purely Occidental.

Timbuktu is real. But it is, in every sense, an outlier. Australia, with its vast interior *never-never* (the outback was also *neverland*, before that was ceded to Peter Pan and Co.) is far more product-ive. It is, after all, also credited with the original use of the *middle of nowhere* (also known, but only locally, as the *red centre*). Never-never was first used in 1833 of the 'Never-never blacks' and there are regular examples from the 1860s onwards. The name gained wide popularity with the book *We of the Never-Never* (1908) by Jeannie Gunn, a memoir of her life on a cattle station in the Northern Territory. Despite the logic of the English term, it may in fact come from Comderoi *nievahvahs*, unoccupied land, although this equally may be pure coincidence (the suggestion appears in a book of 1857); on either count it precedes J.M. Barrie's coinage; another, perhaps one-off use, comes in Rolf Boldrewood's bushranging yarn *Robbery Under Arms* (1888), when a Native Australian character declares : 'I want to die and go up with him to the never-never country parson tell us about.'

There is a mix of real and fantastical among the names slang uses to epitomise the furthest of distances. *Nar Nar Goon* is an actual small town, with a population of 1,010 at last count, near Melbourne. The name supposedly means koala. *Bullamakanka* or *Bullabananka* has a tenuous link to Fiji *bullamacow*: bully beef, but it may be coincidence and there is no more such a township than there exists New Zealand's *Waikikamukau* which needs to be pronounced slowly, i.e. 'Why kick a moo-cow', the physical manifestation of which is limited to a meat-free restaurant in Brighton, Sussex. Similarly playful are the entirely fictional *Wheelyabarraback* ('wheel your barrow back') and *Bundiwallop* (which may play on the alcoholic 'wallop' delivered by 'Bundy', i.e. Bundaberg rum). The latter is also found as 'Bandywallop' (which was popularised by Australia's longest-running children's TV show *Mr Squiggle*, created by the puppeteer Norman Hetherington in 1959). We may also visit, at least in America, 'Y.U. Bum University' (better known as 'why, you bum, you') and 'Wassamatta U.', created for the Rocky & Bullwinkle cartoon series and which sounds, if properly pronounced, like a refugee from a Scorsese Mafia saga.

Oodnagalahbi has been twinned with real-life Oodnadatta: a small town in northern South Australia but the important syllable is the *galah*, both noisy bird and slang for fool. Slang's many-headed lexis of stupidity also underpins Australia's *Woop Woop*, otherwise found as *Upper Woop Woop*, *Oodnawoopwoop*, or *Wopwops*. The *woop* is a peasant, with that species' stereotypes. Both the human and the reduplicated metonym seem to have been born in the 1930s. There is *Bunyip flats*, name-checking the bunyip, a supposed monster that inhabits the country's deep and inaccessible heart. Australia has also given *Hay and Hell and Booligal*, anywhere hot and uncomfortable and popularised by 'Banjo' Patterson's eponymous poem. Hell is of the reader's own definition but Hay and Booligal are actual New South Wales communities. Patterson targeted Booligal: the others get off lightly:

> 'No doubt it suits them very well
> To say it's worse than Hay or Hell,
> But don't you heed their talk at all;
> Of course there's heat – no one denies –
> And sand and dust and stacks of flies,
> And rabbits too, at Booligal.'

Rabbits? Indeed. The First Fleet of 1788 brought rabbits as well as humans and by the 1890s they were serious, crop-ravaging vermin. A dingo fence had been completed in 1885; now the aim was to corral the bunnies. The fence was completed in 1907. The rabbits were undaunted (the deliberate introduction of the rabbit-focused disease myxomatosis proved more cruelly efficient) but the equation of the boundary and desolation in the phrase *beyond the rabbit-proof fence* was in place as soon as were the wire and palings. The contemporary *over the fence*, playing the abstract role, means beyond the bounds of taste.

Synonyms can be found in *back of Bourke*, celebrating a town in the extreme west of New South Wales which was the terminus of the railway line from Sydney and thus the start of the real Outback, and *beyond the black stump*, where the stump represents a symbolic marker that divides the 'civilised' world from the wastelands beyond; the antithesis is of course *this side of the black stump*. Actual black stumps, rendered thus by lightning or some other source of fire, crop up everywhere and they are useful as boundary markers or signposts. The symbolic version is recorded in 1882, though it is possible that this indicates a factual rather than figurative use. A popular etymology for the phrase cites a particular black stump at the Astro station near Blackall, Queensland, used in 1887 by surveyors involved in the mapping of outback Australia. Given that Blackall was some one thousand kilometres west of the state capital Brisbane, it was seen as the last stop before civilised life ran out. Still, the sense is that it was just one more among many.

Outside Australia one finds the Caribbean *behind the bananas* and *behind god's back*, meaning deep in the countryside and Ireland's *back of God-Speed*, a place so very far off that the positive reinforcement of one's wish of 'God-Speed' to a traveller will have faded away well before they arrive.

In New Zealand the backwoods are the *booai* or *booay* which originates either in the Maori *puhoi*: dull, slow, or *Puhoi*, a failed mid-nineteenth century utopian settlement. This gives *up the booai*: totally confused, absolutely wrong, of plans, ruined and of items wholly non-functional and adjacent perhaps to the canonical *shit creek*. (Though Booai too, allegedly, was a genuine settlement, not that far from Auckland.) Spelt Boohai, and here defined as 'a fictitious river', the phrase is also used to brush aside questions involving the word 'where?': the answerer explains that he is 'up the Boohai hunting pukeko with a long-handled shovel' (or 'a popgun').

America cuts, as ever, to the grosser aspects of the chase. *B.F.E.* and *B.F.A.* – 'butt fucking Egypt' or 'Africa' – stand for somewhere very far way. The place itself, coined by the military, is *Bumfuck, Egypt*, also known as *Bumblefuck, Egypt, Butt Fuck, Egypt* (and *West Buttfuck*), or, bowdlerised at least of its sodomy, as *Beyond Fucking Egypt*. What Captain Grose in his notes termed *arse-men* (the term would not actually enter print till the 1940s) and *invaders of the rear settlements* are not mandatory: there is no suggested reference to either City of the Plain and

Egypt seems to exist purely on grounds of assonance; *Bumfuck*, while sometimes set on foreign soil as befits an image of distance, can be found nearer CONUS, in Iowa, or Wyoming. Nor should *bugger's woods*, while defined as out of the way and unimportant, be confused with this group. This bugger is a *booger*, i.e. a bogeyman, and lurks in the woods. Nor need the distance be that great: the implication is simply of inaccessibility and inconvenience, be it of a parking lot or a restaurant.

America is also responsible for the seemingly obscene *Gobbler's Knob*, but like certain Australian towns, the actual place exists, in this case a small town best known for its hosting of the annual Groundhog Day ceremony. Not so much distant, but supposedly obscene are the two Pennsylvania towns of *Blue Ball* and *Intercourse*. Neither apparently had obscenity in mind at their founding – Blue Ball actually commemorated a tavern, the sign for which was a blue ball hanging from a post, and Intercourse, originally Cross Keys, noted the confluence of two main roads – but were notoriously used in 1962 by the US publisher Ralph Ginsberg as mailing addresses for his magazine *Eros*. All pretty puerile, but Ginsberg was still prosecuted for obscenity, and even the Supreme Court conceded the guilty verdict.

Other images of inaccessibility include *Doo-wah-diddy, High Street, China* and *West Hell*, which last is the antonym of the equally forlorn *East Jesus*. Black America offers its own subset. These include the nonsensical *B. Luther Hatchett* or *Beluthahatchie, Ginny Gall*, which refers back to the west African region of Guinea, and *Zar*, apparently eliding 'it's there'. The implication remains that of a place that is far away, unpleasant and culturally alien. Guinea, in addition, was the trading post for much of the slave trade.

Finally, a *hole in the wall*, which comes either from the holes in the walls of English debtor's prisons, through which the inmates could obtain supplies and money to alleviate their situation, or from the small shops and similar establishments found in the broad stone walls of fortified medieval cities. Hole in the wall, now usually an ATM, became a generic for anywhere tiny and tucked away, and often outside the law. There was a Wild West Hole in the Wall, named as such and an outlaw hideaway that provided a refuge for Butch Cassidy and the Sundance Kid and the real-life Wild Bunch. Perhaps least savoury was the Hole in the Wall on Water Street, NYC, where c. 1860 its proprietor Gallus Meg (a monstrous Englishwoman) bit the ears off ill-behaved customers and preserved her trophies in a pickle jar displayed behind the bar. Whether her nickname came from *gallows*, a Scots term for rascally and dissolute, and which slang adopted as a synonym for 'extreme' (often with overtones of violence) or whether she had the habit of wearing *galluses*, i.e. braces (US suspenders) is unknown. Both terms suggest hanging, whether for legal reasons or from the shoulders down.

Distance is evoked in a variety of dismissals, which put more than a little flesh on the bones of 'go away!'. There are *go to Jerusalem* and *to Jericho* which were presumably ways for the religiously inclined to avoid saying 'hell', but more dramatically, and devoid of superstitious self-censorhip was *go to hell Hull and Halifax*, which flourished around 1600. It is accompanied by the somewhat blasphemous but definitely heartfelt prayer, 'from hell Hull and Halifax Good Lord deliver us'. Halifax in this context referred to the Halifax Gibbet Law under which a prisoner was executed first and his or her guilt or innocence ascertained afterwards. That the execution was effected by a newfangled machine that in its operations prefigured the guillotine of the French Revolution and beyond did not offer much comfort. As to Hull, this referred to a one-time practice of executing villains by tying them at low tide to gibbets in the Humber estuary and awaiting the sea's fatal return.

Early modern criminals, at least in London, might benefit from sanctuary, a form of 'nowhere' that existed primarily in law. The bricks and mortar and the local streets were undoubtedly present, but for whatever reason, they were beyond legal grasp. The metropolis offered three: *Alsatia* (upper and lower), the *Bermudas* and, still thinking West Indies, the *Caribees*, *Cribbeys* or *Cribbey islands*.

The first, Alsatia, was divided into Higher Alsatia (Whitefriars in the City) and Lower Alsatia (around the Mint in Southwark). It took its slang nickname from Alsace-Lorraine, the marginal, disputed border area between France and Germany. Higher Alsatia, its earlier manifestation, was once the lands of the Whitefriars Monastery, extending from The Temple to Whitefriars Street and from Fleet Street to the Thames. After the Dissolution of the Monasteries the area went downhill, and as allowed by Elizabeth I and James I its inhabitants claimed exemption from jurisdiction of the City of London. As such the area became a centre of corruption, a refuge for villains and a no-man's-land for the law. The privileges were abolished in 1697, but it was decades before the old habits died out. It was sufficiently well-known for a hit play, Shadwell's *Squire of Alsatia*, to wow London in 1688. Its programme, much required, came with a forty-seven-page glossary of criminal terms. Walter Scott also used the zone as a backdrop for a chunk of his historical novel *The Fortunes of Nigel* (1822).

The 'West Indian' sanctuaries were less formalised, and smaller, but they still worked. The Bermudas were equally applied to Covent Garden and the transpontine Mint. Both provided warrens of hard-to-access alleyways and dense-packed hidden courts. The Cribbeys were Covent Garden only. Although the pun seems pretty definite, Captain Grose essayed another origin, at least for the Cribbeys: the term came 'perhaps from the houses built there being *cribbed* (stolen) out of the common way or passage.'

For devotedly urban slang anywhere beyond the concrete is too distant and the *sticks*, wherein live the *hicks*, represent many steps too far. If there is a hell on earth then it may well be a small town: certainly slang has plenty to offer, and none kindly. They can be found in **Cities: Smoke & Mirrors**.

Other examples of *Anytown, USA* include Superman's fictional, but emblematic *Smallville*, though Andy Hardy's hometown, Carvel, never attained generic status; nor does Grover's Corners, the eponymic 'star' of Thornton Wilder's play *Our Town* (1938). *Hoboken, Dubuque* and *Peoria* are all quite real: towns in respectively New Jersey, Iowa and Illinois. The former is best known for its association with Frank Sinatra, the next was cited by the *New Yorker*'s founding editor Harold Ross as that place, replete with its old ladies, for whom his magazine would not be edited, and finally the third is traditionally used as a demographic gauge of what will or will not appeal to America's great non-metropolitan public. 'Will it play in Peoria?' allegedly asked Groucho Marx, assessing a new vaudeville act, and the concept stuck. It remains the 'test market capital of the world'.

Podunk is another epitome of the American average, though for all its bricks-and-mortar reality – there are five instances of the name listed in American gazetteers and the word itself is established in the Algonquin language – it still suggests a certain unreality. The idea of Podunk as a settlement representative of the much-feted, if elusive 'real people' began in Samuel Griswold

Goodrich's 1840 book, *The Politician of Podunk*, which cites 'a small village of New York' around 1800. The modern use was popularised six years later in 'Letters from Podunk', published in the *Daily National Pilot* of Buffalo, NY. By 1869 Mark Twain could mention 'Podunk, wherever that may be' and get his laugh. Quite why Podunk, sometimes appended to 'university' to suggest some out-of-the-way and inferior seat of learning, has gained this image is unknown. None of the five towns are especially large, but this opprobrium seems unearned. It is perhaps the lumpish 'chunk' sound of the name (one thinks 'stick-in-the-mud'), and thus an equation between the onomatopoeia and the supposed 'lumpishness' of the small-town inhabitant.

Still on the American front, there's *Marlboro country*, which represents the kind of remote countryside once suggested by landscapes in advertisements for Marlboro cigarettes, and *Plumnelly*, which is often used in the context of a border between two states or other areas: 'plum out of Georgia and nelly out of Alabama'. In the version 'plum out of town and nelly out of this world' the inference is that wherever we're talking about, it's barely on the planet.

Australia and America stand for quantity when it comes to such terms, but they are not unique. One finds them elsewhere, for example in Ireland. Last of all, and based on the Irish 'Baile', that is, home or town, we have a couple of localisms: *Ballybackanowhere* and *Ballygobackwards*, the latter popularised by the Irish comedian Jimmy O'Dea, who created a series of sketches in which he played its stationmaster; other Irish *nowherevilles* include *Backo'beyond* and, proving that arseholes of the universe are not confined to a single map, *Backarseanowhere*.

Cities: Smoke & Mirrors

No CITIES, NO slang.

Look in a dictionary. How does it define slang? Which words do the lexicographers choose to explain this much argued-over form of language? What we find are these: 'casual', 'playful', 'ephemeral', 'racy', 'humorous', 'irreverent'. The overriding images: speed, fluidity, movement. No time, nor need for lengthy, measured consideration. The keywords are abbreviation, terse, in your face: slang's words are twisted, turned, snapped off short, relaunched at a skewed angle. Some with their multiple and often contrasting definitions seem infinitely malleable, shape-shifting: who knows what hides round their syllabic corners. Look at *hot*: thirty-four columns of close-knit print. *Red*, twenty-one. *Dog*, thirty-four again. Or, why not, *fuck*: thirty-six more. These are among slang's heavyweights, but the rule pertains across the board. It is not, I suggest, a language that works out of town; it requires the hustle and bustle, the rush, the lights, the excitement and even the muted (sometimes far from muted) sense of impending threat. To use slang confidently one needs that urban cockiness. It doesn't work behind a yoke of oxen, even athwart a tractor.

Then there are the value judgements: 'sub-standard', 'low', 'vulgar', 'unauthorised'. The word we are seeking is *street*. Street as noun, more recently street as adjective. The vulgar tongue. The gutter language.

Let's eavesdrop on a predecessor. John Camden Hotten: publisher, plagiarist, pornographer. Exemplary slang lexicographer too, whose dictionary – the first to use the word 'slang' in its title (although its author preferred to term himself a 'London Antiquary') – appeared in 1859 (six revisions would follow) and told readers that:

> 'slang represents that evanescent, vulgar language, ever changing with fashion and taste, . . . spoken by persons in every grade of life, rich and poor, honest and dishonest . . . Slang is indulged in from a desire to appear familiar with life, gaiety, town-humour and with the transient nick names and street jokes of the day . . . slang is the language of street humour, of fast, high and low life . . . Slang is as old as speech and the congregating together of people in cities. It is the result of crowding, and excitement, and artificial life.'

The congregating together of people in cities. The congregating of people together elsewhere too, for instance in the crowded, terrifying, hellish trenches of World War I, that great generator of slang on all sides, but above all, the city street.

No cities, no slang. It is unsurprising that the word itself, plus lesser conurbations such as *towns* and *villes* plus thoroughfares such as *streets*, *lanes* and *alleys*, and local areas such as *hills*, *hollows* and *bottoms* have all imposed their contours on slang's larger map.

The city is where the law lives (the outlaw – Robin Hood, Billy the Kid – stays clear). In a world yet to welcome a full-scale police force the *city bulldog* was a constable, who took his canine identification from his predecessor, the *bandog*, a bailiff in slang and properly a large guard-dog; the term re-entered use in the 1980s to describe a cross-breed of Neapolitan mastiffs and US pit bull terriers. There may also be a link in both to *dog*, to pursue. The *city college* was a prison, London was full of them, and prisoners were *collegians*, underpinning the 'school for crime' stereotype but perhaps offering no more than an ironic take on their far from academic situation. The term applied specifically to the most important, Newgate (which boasted thirteen recorded nicknames); the term worked for New York's Tombs too. While public capital punishment was the mode, the *city scales*, on which the malefactor was *weighed off*, and the *city stage*, on which he or she *danced* before a thronging audience, both stood for the gallows. Less threatening uses offered *city sherry*, bitter beer, and *city wire*, a fashionable lady, from the seventeenth century's use of wiring in clothing and hair.

Such concrete uses are historical; modernity prefers its city figurative, an all-purpose suffix *-city*, that suggests a state of being, a concrete or abstract concentration, defined as a supposed place and delineated by a qualifying noun. The term seems to have emerged from jazz, and has been attributed to the saxophonist Lester Young, who supposedly coined it around 1938.

The *-city* suffix is open to suggestion: among the best-known compounds are such abstracts as *edge city*, the extremes of experience, whether spiritual, physical, drug-induced etc; usually blended with overtones of fear and challenge; *nowhere city* (also *nowheresville*), a situation, place or person who or which is seen as irrelevant, pointless, of no use at all; *fat city*, a utopia in which all is well and prosperous (the opposite being *thin city*, though far less common) and the less well-known *biscuit city*, in which an extreme situation 'takes the biscuit'. Taken literally, *fat city* also stands for gaining weight or being fat. *Jump city* is the beginning, when events 'jump off' and equally well known as *jump street*. *Tap city* or *tapsville* comes from the tradition of tapping the table to signify that one passes the bet, plus the use of *tapped out* to mean moneyless, indicates both the literal state of being unable to raise a stake for further betting and beyond that a metaphorical place devoted to borrowing or begging money, in other words, poverty. *Wig city*, from *wig out*, to lose one's mind (one's *wig*), is a state of eccentricity, even madness; it can also mean a psychiatric institution.

Using a range of more concrete terms, both slang and standard, one finds *fist city* (with its synonyms *fist hollow* and *duke* city, from *dukes*, the fists), a fist fight; *barf city*, from *barf*, to vomit, anything particularly unpleasant, *weep city*, tearfulness, *beef city*, from beef, to complain, wherein one makes a fuss, *box city*, dead, where a *box* is a coffin and *cement* or *silent city*, both graveyards. *Doll city* is full of *dolls*, pretty girls, and may apply to a single example, *dope city* (or *scag town*, from *scag*, heroin) is any area of a town known for its high level of drug sales or consumption and *slice city* an assault with a razor or a knife (next door was *slice town*, a red-light area). Finally *sue city* (punning though not especially pointedly on the town of Sioux City, Iowa) involvement in a court case or similar legal situation.

Cities are proud, demanding a known place in the wider world, and urban boosters are keen on the instant identification that comes with nicknames. The most recent, popularised via rap where conventional city pride is not invariably on the agenda, is *Chi-raq*, a mixture of Chicago and Iraq, pointing up the alleged similarity of the respective levels of violence, but this sidesteps 'city' as such; Chicago is far better known as the *Windy City*, not to mention the *Big Windy*, the *City of Winds*, *Madame*

Windy, Windtown, Windville and *the Windy*. According to etymologist Barry Popik the original windy city was Homeric Troy, followed by Siena, Italy, known as the *Citta dei Venti*, i.e. 'city of winds'. Then, in the early 1880s, the *Chicago Tribune* newspaper, keen to promote Chicago as a summer resort, focused on the cool breeze off the adjacent Lake Michigan. The name stuck, though one also meets *Chi-Town* and the windy city can also apply to Port Elizabeth, South Africa.

Noir fiction, almost always set on the mean streets, celebrates a variety of pseudonyms, best known among them surely *Bay City*, created by Raymond Chandler, as the epitome of all-embracing urban corruption. The city in question has always been seen as Oakland, California, otherwise known, though in fact not fiction, as *Bump City*. One might have expected real cities to avoid the name, but it is that adopted by San Francisco, regularly abbreviated as *'Frisco*, though not by its natives, and also known, from the earthquakes which if not that frequent are regularly expected, as *Shaky City*, which stands on San Francisco Bay.

Nicknames suggest a primary characteristic, in the city's context of that which the metropolis produces, or at least wishes to be known for. That these may hark back to a more prosperous era, long before the concept of a rust belt, is not for these pages. Thus we have *Motor City* or *Motown*, Detroit, Michigan, *Music City*, Nashville, Tennessee, also known as *Guitar Town*. With its links to country music as the epitome of middle-American values, the adjective *Nashville* can also refer to any unsophisticated, suburban, middle-American town or person. *Beer City* or *Beer Town*, Milwaukee, Wisconsin (and the celebrated ad for Schlitz, 'the beer that made Milwaukee famous') and *Rubber City*, Akron, Ohio (its primary industry, tyre-making). After those, *Burrito City*, El Paso, Texas and named for an imported Mexican dish, seems a little forced and *Sin City*, which stands for any centre of vice and corruption but particularly Las Vegas, Nevada, like wishful thinking.

It's not just an American thing. For the use of *banana* as an urban nickname, see page 199, **Funny Foreign Food**. The *Holy City*, from the city's many churches, is Adelaide, South Australia. *Sun City*, however is not the luxury hotel and entertainment complex near South Africa's Rustenberg, but an ironic nickname for Diepkloof Prison.

Finally *Jersey City*, twinned with *Bristol City*. But these have no urban link: usually as plurals they are rhyming slang for the female breasts, or as slang has it, *titties*.

After the city, the *town*, a word that finds its origins in a variety of Germanic languages where terms indicated an enclosure, fence or fortification, and thus the buildings and ultimately people within. The idea of town as meaning somewhere culturally unique, i.e. 'not country', begins with Chaucer around 1400 as does that of town as meaning those who live there, i.e. 'not peasants and farmers' and with that the default, if unspoken identification with London. It is this last that underpins slang's uses, and slang's take on London is not so much that of the great centre of government and wealth, but the home of louche urban pursuits and individuals, and those who fall into their clutches.

Thus we find a selection of whores; the *town-crack*, from *crack*, the vagina, the *town miss* or *lady* (and the *lady* or *woman about* or *of the town*). The more recent *town pump* (otherwise *town punch* or *punch board*) is probably not professional, but her amateurism is unrestrained (nor is she limited to London). The whore requires a pimp, she finds him in the *town trap*, which plays on *trap*, to ensnare, and the *town bull*, though he, named for the bull housed in turn by the cow-keepers of a village, is as much a lecher and womaniser as actual flesh-merchant; his galli-vanting gives the phrase *lawless as a town bull*. So too is the *town stallion*. Satisfied with her own, or perhaps her husband's money, the *town tabby* is simply a smart, rich old woman; *tabby*, one of so many terms that equates a woman with a cat, is in fact far from feline (that develops later and from the same roots) and comes from *tabby*, striped or watered silk (originally produced in the Baghdad suburb of *Attabiy*). It occasionally means the female genitals and pubic hair too. More recently prostitution has given *go all over town*, otherwise known as *go around the world*. This sexual service, where the tongue does the 'travelling', denotes licking and sucking the client's body, including the genitals and sometimes the anus.

Preyed on by such as the *town shift*, a confidence trickster, constantly changing his address to keep ahead of the authorities and outraged victims, is the *town toddler*. This is not a baby (though the two coinages are pretty much simultaneous, around 1790) but one who, perhaps equally innocent, wanders around town, gawping and gullible. Two centuries on he might be helped by the presence of a *town clown*, a policeman, but this zany is American, and his town is the small one from whence the toddler came.

The standard English use of *on* or *upon the town* suggests one who is enjoying the swing of fashionable life; slang's use strips away the fashion, leaving only the dedication to urban pleasures, smart or otherwise. It has meant working as a prostitute and thus to *take to the town*, either taking up a life 'on the game' or living as a professional criminal. To be *in town* was to be well off. Thus the logical definitions of *out of town*: in prison, originally for debt, penniless, bereft of stimulation or excitement, mentally wanting and socially unfashionable.

The far-seeing Captain Grose, never one to overlook a sneer at the impoverished Irish, gives us the *town lands* and *stream's town*, which are in turn part of the *Tipperary fortune*: 'Two *town lands* [the breasts], *stream's town* [the genital area] and *ballinocack* [the anus].' He could have looked closer to home, at London's similarly impoverished East End, and found much the same: the *Whitechapel portion*, a woman's inheritance and defined in 1698 as 'two torn smocks and what Nature gives' i.e. the female breasts and genitals.

Despite an underwhelming and noticeably unappreciated effort to rechristen certain areas of London 'mid-town', presumably a misguided homage to New York, the triumvirate of *up-*, *mid*-and *downtown* remain an American concept. Specifics differ as to cities but slang has naturally adopted at least the first and last. *Up* means residential and rich, while *down* can be both the business area and the poor one. Thus uptown has meant sophisticated, worldly, rich and to *go uptown* (*on*) is to act in a snobbish manner (towards). In drug terms, at least initially, uptown meant cocaine, seen for a while as the drug of the wealthy and aspirational. Downtown, generic for the city government, the police department and similar authorities also means the police headquarters – 'take him downtown' – and, on a rough geography of the body, the female genital area, especially in the context of cunnilingus, for which one *goes downtown*. It can also refer to an area mainly lived in by the black community. In drug terms to *go downtown* is to use the depressant heroin. Paradoxically, though, moving downtown can also refer to social advance: newly prosperous Harlemites signified their new status by leaving the ghetto and moving downtown, i.e. to more prosperous parts of New York, by going 'down' one went 'up in the world'.

Like city, *town* can provide a range of nicknames. Too many to list every one; let us stick to initialdom: *C-town*, Cleveland, Ohio, *D-town*, Dallas, Texas, *G-town*, Georgetown, Washington D.C., *H-town*, Houston, Texas, *K-town*, Koreatown, i.e. the Korean area of a city, *O-Town*, Orlando, Florida, *P-town*, both Provincetown, Massachusetts and Portland, Oregon and *V-town*, Vallejo, California.

A few more notable towns include *Itchyamtown*, Edinburgh, which is underpinned by slang's inevitable characterisation of Scotland – *Itchland, Louseland, Scratchland* – as overrun by insect life, and *Snoek-town* from Dutch *snoek*, the snake mackerel (*Thyrsitesatun*), which thus represents Cape Town, once the home of the snoek fishing and processing industry. The treacle refiners of Bristol gave it the nickname *Treacle Town*, which also refers to Macclesfield (which apparently prefers *Silk Town*), of which legend recalls a day when a wagon full of treacle barrels overturned in the streets and the poor fought to scrape up the liquid as it oozed along the gutters. *Tinsel Town* usually refers to Hollywood, capital of *La-La-Land*, but the name also works for Sydney, Australia, especially in contrast with its slow-paced rival Adelaide, known as *Tortoise Town*.

There are more variations on the urban theme, notably *ville*, but before looking at them, let us consider the many subsets of town and city life which note areas by ethnicity or economics and as well as -*town* incorporate a variety of allied suffixes. They also have names all of their own.

Racism has its own finely calculated degrees of what makes 'white' and what 'black' – Jews, for instance, fail to qualify as the former for the diehard supporters of the neo-Nazi fan-club – but slang is happy to go with the usual divisions. That said, in terms of dwellings, white, being the default setting, doesn't get much of a look in. There is *hunkie-* or *honkytown*, a black term that is based on *honkie*, a modified form of *bohunk*, the original name of the middle-European immigrants (*Bohemians* and *Hung*arians) who worked in Chicago stockyards, and *Peckerwood Town*, from the red *woodpecker*, symbol of whites, rather than the black *crow*, symbol of blacks. Synonymous *Broomtown* is more recent; perhaps it refers to a predilection for cleanliness? For the rich, who chose more salubrious dwellings, there was *Swell Street*, the West End of London and thus wealth in general, or *Nob Hill*, from *nob*, an aristocrat. Both New York (near Bowling Green) and San Francisco boast a Nob Hill, the latter first colonised by wealthy veterans of the California Gold Rush. Wealthy New York Jews had *Allrightnik's Row*, Riverside Drive, based on English (doing) *all right* plus the Yiddish suffix *-nik*, a person, although Yiddish had its own *olraytnik*, an upstart, a parvenu.

Black town, that part of a larger urban area in which the black community lives, is far more productive. The rule is simple; take a piece of racist vilification and compound it with, usually, -town. There you are. In alphabetical order we find *boogie town*, *browntown*, *coontown* (or *coonsville* and *coonville*), *darktown* and *darkytown*, *dinktown*, possibly from *dinge*, a *dingy* or black person, and *jig-town*, from *jigaboo*, itself either from *jig*, a dance and ultimately French *giguer*, to leap, to gambol, to frolic (the classic nineteenth-century black stereotypes); or modelled on *bugaboo*, which, in the thirteenth century, was the name of a demon, and since the eighteenth century, the fear of demons in general; or Bantu *tshikabo*, a meek and servile person, used derogatively by slaves.

Little Africa fits the model of *Little Italy*, *Little Korea* and others. *Catfish Row* refers to a supposed staple of a black person's diet. The N-word gives *nigger row* and *nigger town*, *nigger hill* and *niggerville*. *Nigger yard* is any rough slum area; the original use was Caribbean, for that area on a plantation where the slaves were quartered. *Shine*, from the tone of a dark black skin, brings *shine-town* and *spade*, as in 'black as the ace of . . .', *spadesville*.

In addition there is the *black belt*, which can either refer to a specific black community or a whole geographical area. *Black bottom* and *coon bottom* come from *bottom*, the low-lying river-side area in which such settlements were often established. *Buttermilk bottom*, first used of the black section of Atlanta, Georgia, depended on the stereotyped link between buttermilk and black appetites. Finally the *jungle*, a term as stereotyped as any right-winger might wish, but with meanings that far transcend basic black. It can mean a city's black zone, but its use began as nothing more than the suburbs or backwoods. It has also meant any unpleasant place, a very cheap London lodging house for tramps and in South Africa a knife. Perhaps best known is the hobo use: that area of a town or city, often outside the city limits, where criminals, tramps and vagrants *jungle up*, that is congregate together.

All these are essentially negative. The one black coinage is not. This is *chocolate city*, coined by George Clinton, founder of the funk band Parliament-Funkadelic and playing on the colour and 'sweetness' of dark chocolate. Originally Washington D.C., it can be applied to any centre of African-American life. Of these one remains best known: Harlem, *H Town*, *Soul City*, the *land of darkness*, focused on 125th Street and on what 1940s Harlemites termed the *Big Red with the Long Green Stem*, Seventh Avenue, between 130th Street and 150th Street, the centre of Harlem nightlife. In that same elaborate language, listed in full in jazz journalist Dan Burley's *Handbook of Harlem Jive* (1944), any 7th Avenue corner was categorised as a *three-pointer of the ace trill in the twirling top. Big Red* was New York, *long green* referred to money, while *main stem, drag* or *stroll* meant a main street, and modified as the *main drag of many tears* it reflects the bars and theatres where otherwise depressed and frustrated people can attempt to drown their sorrows. Harlem also hosted *Sugar Hill,* that area of Harlem otherwise known as Coogan's Bluff, between Amsterdam and Edgecombe Avenues, between 138th and 155th Streets. As well as the rich, many black intellectuals and artists chose to live in the area, known for its grand apartment houses, once the original white population had moved out during the 1920s. The name had its own punning alternative: the *heavy lump.* The *sugar* was money. Sugar Hill, with *sugar* redefined as sex, was used in the South for the brothel and 'red-light' area of the black part of any southern town. New York City also had *San Juan Hill,* from the Battle of San Juan Hill (1898) in which many black troops were involved, covering those blocks between 10th and 11th Avenues, between 59th Street and the low 60s. Rap would term Harlem *New Jack City,* along with any other city with a thriving ghetto lifestyle.

It was jazz too that seems to have originated New York's most enduring nickname: the *Big Apple,* on which Harlem's Big Red was a play. The ultimate etymology remains debatable but the consensus traces it back to the jazz phrase, playing 'the Big Stem in the Big Apple', the Big Stem being Broadway. (Broadway was also known as *mazda lane,* a reference to the ultra-bright lights that also made it the *Great White Way*). The first recorded use so far is from the gossip columnist Walter Winchell, in 1927: 'Broadway is the Big Apple, the Main Stem, the goal of all ambition, the pot of gold at the end of a drab and somewhat colorless rainbow.' However he equates the phrase with Broadway only, and the direct link to the whole metropolis would have to wait a further year.

Other terms for New York include the *big town* and *big burg*, the *real puddle* (a play on 'a big fish in a small pond' and its antithesis), *up top* (as seen from the perspective of the South), *York*, and *the Start*. This was usually linked to London and was a tramping term; the city being the *start* from where one set off on one's wanderings around the country. It first appears in America in a slang dictionary of 1859, and it may be that the author, police chief George Washington Matsell, simply 'Americanised' the earlier use.

Compared with black America, no community has gained the same density of terminology. Even the Jews, usually hard on black heels when it comes to slang's vilifications, rate only *kike-town*, *Jew town* and *little Jewrusalem*, with New York City regularly punned as *Jew York* and *Hymietown* (from *Hyman*, a 'typical' Jewish name). Anti-semitism is on the up in post-Brexit UK but we have yet to see a resurgence of an old favourite: *Jerusalem the Golden* (plus *Jerusalem-by-the-Sea*, *Jerusalem-on-Sea*), a name for Brighton, from the large number of Jewish people who retire to Brighton and other towns along Britain's south coast. Nor have *Asia Minor*, named for the wealthy Jews who bought themselves luxury houses in London's Belgravia, nor the *holy land*, used of any Jewish area, yet come back to life; the north London suburbs of *Abrahamstead*, *Cricklewitch* and *Yidsbury* remain purely historical, though one still encounters *Goldberg's Green* for Golder's Green, perhaps the most visible of Jewish concentrations.

For the rest it is as one might expect; the Poles in *Polack-town*, the Italians in *Wop-town*, the Germans in *Dutch*, i.e. *Deutsch town* or *cabbage town*, tipping the hat to a supposed love for sauerkraut. Irish *bucktown* is seen as the home of *bucks*, youthful tearaways, though the name has also been used for Brooklyn and

Dublin, the capital of the Republic of Ireland, and worked for Irish ex-pat centres too. Fiction offered *Pig Alley* (there was a real street, in what is now Tribeca) in what was the first organised crime movie: *The Musketeers of Pig Alley* (1912). With a gangster 'hero' named Jack Doogan, the milieu was definitely Irish. The name *Hogan's Alley*, backdrop to the late nineteenth century 'Yellow Kid' newspaper cartoons, suggests much the same.

Pigtail alley was all-purpose poor, and the reference was presumably to the presence of at least some Chinese, though the reference may have alluded to porcine standards of living; the name was certainly given, though far from exclusively, to New York's Chinatown, based around Mott Street. Lastly Hispanics, who live variously in *dago town, dago center* or *dago hill, Mex town, Spicktown, Taco Town* or *Tamaleville*. Still using food stereotypes, Mexicans can also live in *Beantown*, which brings one round to another centre of bean-eating, Boston, Massachusetts, 'the home of the bean and the cod'.

Baltimore, Maryland, was known in the nineteenth century as *mob town*, although the mob in question was the unchained masses rather than the US Mafia. Still, there are plenty of names for criminal zones, effectively no-go areas for the law-abiding and upright. The first, from London, was the *rookery*, a general term for any such and based on the standard *rookery*, a gathering-place and breeding centre (usually high in a tree), for rooks; on the other hand there is the cant term *rook*, to defraud, to over-charge and that, while not the origin, may well underpin the term's urban recycling. London boasted a number of rookeries, the two best known being *Alsatia* and *St Giles*, otherwise known as the Holy Land.

For Alsatia one may consult page 86, **Mystery Tour: Far Away Places**, where it features among the fictional or semi-fictional places that feature in the slang lexicon. St Giles was (and is) situated at the bottom of Oxford Street, covering the area around the eponymous church – Giles was the patron saint of beggars – and now covered by New Oxford Street and Centre Point. It took its nicknames from standard English *holy ground* or *land*, an area within church jurisdiction in which villains or persecuted people could gain sanctuary. One of its main buildings – suitably verminous and over-populated – was known as Rat's Castle, and like the Alsatians locals were big on criminal slang, known to outsiders as *St Giles Greek*, in which *Greek*, as in 'it's all Greek to me' was generic for wholly incomprehensible. The occupations and cynical devil-may-care philosophies of the inhabitants are summed up in the chorus of an old ballad, allegedly very popular in the area: 'For we are the boys of the holy ground / And we'll dance upon nothing and turn us around.' Dancing upon nothing required a gallows and a rope and feet that moved but failed to find purchase on supportive earth: such was the fate of many holy-landers.

Down the road lay Holborn Hill, an extension of Oxford Street, leading to the City proper and on its way passing Newgate prison. Thus the phrases *walk* or *ride (backwards) up Holborn Hill*, *push* or *ride the cart up Holborn Hill*, and *sail up Holborn Hill*. Prior to 1783 London's main site of public execution was the great Triple Tree (a three-cornered edifice that could 'turn off' twenty-one villains at a time), positioned at Tyburn, now Marble Arch at the far western end of Oxford Street. Thus a condemned Newgate prisoner had to make their way west (one of the mooted origins of *gone west*, failed or broken), a journey – complete with three traditional stops for a pint of ale – which he or she made either standing in a cart, or sitting on the coffin that had been loaded with them. They sat backwards, either because it was believed to increase their ignominy, but more likely to avoid seeing the approaching gallows until the last possible moment. An alternative execution site was at Tower Hill (site of the Tower of London). This gave its own phrase: to *preach on Tower Hill*, an ironic use of *preach* and referring, perhaps, to the criminal's last words on the scaffold: but no talking was implied, it was simply to be hanged.

In modern America such rookeries, using the topsy-turvy world of criminal coinages, would have been known as *right towns*: any town or small city where the authorities – police, local politicians – have been bribed into allowing criminal activity to flourish. The opposite was a *sucker town*, a town or city in which any criminal activity is unwise – the authorities have proved impervious to corruption – the inference is that the populace, suckers, are too innocent to accept bribes.

Otherwise we have a variety of terms. With the accent still on poverty, though the line between that and outright criminality is as fluid as ever, we have *billy-goat hill* (also *billy-goat alley*, *goat's gulch*, *goat town*). Either the original inhabitants actually kept goats or their taste for various social excesses exhibits a certain 'goatishness'. Usually such people were poor, but improvements were possible: one such *goat's gulch* in Kansas was gentrified and re-nicknamed 'Angora Heights'. *Tobacco Road*, the title of Erskine Caldwell's once notorious novel about Georgia sharecroppers, published in 1932, was used for any primitive rural area and its inhabitants.

Hell, less equivocal (though modernity has brought gentrification here as elsewhere) provided *hell's kitchen*, *hell's half acre* and *hell's bottom*, the first specific, the others more general. Hell's Kitchen was the Irish-black slum area that covered part of the West Side of New York City from c.1850 to 1910; bounded by the Hudson River and 8th Avenue, it ran from 39th Street to 59th Street. The name may have applied initially only to a single tenement or it may have been picked up from the name of a saloon in the red-light area of Corlear's Hook (itself one of the possible origins of the slang term *hooker*, a prostitute, given the number of girls who used the area as their base). The toughest part of Hell's Kitchen was known, at least to the writer O. Henry, famed for his short stories of New York life, as the *stovepipe*, a narrow enclave running along 11th and 12th Avenues. Hell's half acre could be applied to any disreputable area or place, for instance the slum area of a town or a specific low-class dancehall or bar. Writing in his gold-rush memoir *Land of Gold* (1855) the British visitor H.R. Helper noted that 'Among the more fanciful names that designate localities in various parts of the mines are the following: [. . .] Mad Ox Ravine, Mad Mule Canyon, Skunk Flat, Woodpecker Hill, Jesus Maria, Yankee Jim's Diggings, Death Pass, Ignis Fatuus Placer, Devil's Retreat, Bloody Bend, Jackass Gulch, Hell's Half Acre.' *Hell's bottom, hell's point* or *hell's hollow* were other ways of labelling a disreputable or out-of-the-way area.

Like bottom, *hollow*, similarly invoking the 'lower depths', is another useful brand, appearing in a variety of compounds which describe an area of a town or an out-of-the-way place, usually combined with a reference to poor or foreign groups. Examples include *dead man's hollow, frog hollow, Irish hollow, piggy hollow, punkin hollow, skunk hollow, sleepy hollow* (celebrated as the title of Washington Irving's 1820 story 'The Legend of Sleepy Hollow'), *smoky hollow* and *snuff hollow*.

Among the remaining terms for downmarket areas were the *back slums*, favouring criminal over poverty-stricken locals, *pig town, crap-town, lousetown* and *bunkum-town*. *Codfish flats* suggested the poverty of fishing communities though it should not be confused with New England's *codfish aristocracy*, a mocking description of those nineteenth-century nouveaux riches whose fortunes sprang from the Massachusetts cod industry. There was *hunger street* or *lane*, *bedbug alley*, *rag-cat alley* and *cancer alley*, the last noting that poverty was made even grimmer by the pollution pouring from nearby factories. *Death alley* wasn't necessarily homicidal, but you could never be sure, while *pepper alley*, from *pepper*, to beat up (and sometimes shoot) suggested at least a degree of violence; a real Pepper Alley, on the south bank of the Thames, was equated with crime, violence and debauchery though its origins were most likely in the spice trade. *Jim town* (perhaps from *gimcrack*, shoddy) meant a shanty town, though sometimes a Hispanic area. A *cigar box* suggested flimsiness, in this case of the buildings constructed for the poor: *cigar-box row* was a whole street of them. The houses were close, probably terraced, and there was much neighbourly conversation. This *gab*, or chat, gave *gabby row*. A *dead-end street*, however, was nothing to do with the city; like another landmark, *mutton hill* (from *mutton*, the female flesh), it meant a vagina.

On a global scale we have the *arsehole* or *asshole of the universe* (see page 79, **Mystery Tour: Far Away Places**); downsized to a locality we have the *armpit*, though *arsehole* / *asshole* works too. A place can also be *rough as a docker's armpit*. One such place (though it stood in for many) was the *bloody bucket*, otherwise the *bucket of blood* or *blood-tub*. There actually had been such a tavern, the nineteenth-century *Bucket of Blood*, in Havre, Montana; its reputation spread and the term became generic for similar establishments. But it was not really the first. London historian Peter Ackroyd reports on London's Water Lane, one of the main streets of the Alsatia sanctuary, which boasted 'a dwelling . . . known as "Blood Bowl house"'. This notorious pub, properly known as the Red Lion, is pictured in plate IX of Hogarth's *Industry & Idleness*. Here we see the 'idle 'prentice' Tom Rakewell at the moment of his betrayal by his mistress Moll. He sits, debating the merits of a hatful of stolen trinkets with a villainous, patch-eyed accomplice; around them a soldier pisses against the wall, a dead, or certainly unconscious body is tossed through a trapdoor, a gang of fellow villains enjoy a tussle, brandishing chairs at each others' heads, a serving woman, her nose covered by a mask (has she lost it, we wonder, to the pox?) carries in a pot of ale while at the head of the stairs, for we are in a basement, a constable slips a coin into faithless Moll's outstretched palm.

Blood Bowl House had a history. One version cited a countryman who was taken there and had his pocket picked; when he complained, he was told that if he did not shut up, the 'blood bowl' would catch the flow from his slit throat. Alternatively, according to the engraver's biographer, it derived 'from the various scenes of blood that were almost daily exhibited, and where there seldom passed a month without the commission of some act of murder'. In either case it was a long-established centre of *fencing*, or selling off stolen goods.

Beyond the city, the small town. No love was lost in urban eyes. There was *hog island* or *hog-town*, which suggested a pig-sty and meant any small, impoverished, out-of-the-way settlement; thus the description *hog-wallowing*, which referred to an inhabitant of such a place. *Dog town* (a town whose inhabitants numbered 'one man and his dog') was both a small town and a rundown, possibly criminal area of a town. It began life as theatrical jargon, an out-of-town (i.e. out of New York City) theatre used to try out a new show before 'bringing it in'. Prior to that one 'tried it on the dog'. *Dogpatch*, perhaps influenced by dogtown, was created as the name of the hillbilly settlement in which the syndicated cartoon strip by Al Capp, *L'il Abner* (1934–77) took place. The *hick town*, or *Hicksville*, took its name from *hick*, a generic name for Richard and used of peasants, it lay beneath the celebrated *Variety* magazine headline noting a small-town distaste for films about their own world: 'Hix Nix Stix Pix', a concoction that included another word for the back of beyond: *the sticks*. *Frogtown* suggested the village pond while a *jay town* or *jayville* used *jay*, a sucker, to underline the rubbernecking vulnerability of visitors to the big city. There was the *one-horse* or *one-pub town*: neither ran to anything more plentiful for either transport or entertainment, the *slab* and the *two stemmer*: based on the big city's Main Stem, such a town had only two streets.

The railroad lay behind two more synonyms for insignificance: the *jerkwater town* and the *tank town*. These small, rural locations, through which trains passed but stopped only to pick up water rather than passengers, had a trackside water tower and a trough from which a train could scoop or 'jerk' water from between the tracks without actually stopping. An alternative etymology, based on earlier railroad practice, suggests that the crew had actually to leave the train and jerk the water in buckets from local wells, then run with it to the waiting locomotive. A further suggestion, perhaps least likely, cites buckets that were attached to the locomotive by a leather strap and that were used to jerk the water from streams running alongside the track. The tank town played the same role, and one can note the late nineteenth-century theatrical use of *water tank show*, a small touring company.

Last is cruellest: the *bad* or *narrow place* or *spot in the road*. Could anywhere have been less important? The phrase probably boasted more variations than the towns did populace: aside from these were *crack in the track, stop in the road, broad place in the road*, and, returning to the railroads, *whistle stop*.

Still rural, but far back in time, is the mysterious and quite lost *deuseaville*, the countryside, the age of which is indicated by the variety of its speculative spellings – *deasyville, deausaville, deuce-aville, dewsavell, dewse-a-vile, dewse-a-vyle, deyseaville, duceavil, deusavil* – and the problem of finding out just where it came from. The *-vile /-ville* suffix is easy enough, it came from Latin and meant town, but after that all is up for grabs. Eric Partridge suggests a corruption of *daisy-ville* but dewse = *deuce* = the devil and thus a generic negative; given that London, the big city, is *Rum ville*, literally 'good town' (though the connection here might be a proposed equivalence to mighty *Rome* itself), might not the country, its opposite, be 'bad town'? What we do have is *deuseaville stampers,* who were members of a criminal gang who wandered the country roads and frequented country inns in the hope of picking up information about possible robberies.

There are obviously many proper names ending in -ville, but recent slang use, as it does for certain aspects of -city, opts for something more abstract. Most suggest the world of beatniks, i.e. the 1950s and, like -city, what the -ville denotes is set up by the noun or adjective that goes with it. Thus there are *dragsville*, very boring; *sticksville*, very rural or suburban, and *endsville*, variously the best, the ultimate; the limit, the end, as far as one can go, and thus death; absolute, irretrievable failure; and of a place, out-of-the-way, without quality, thus extended as *east of Endsville*. Endsville can also be *gonesville*: knocked out, whether literally or figuratively; vanished, escaped, gone or dead; eccentric, insane; emotionally carried away and like endsville, used to decry a distant or unimportant location. One also finds *weirdsville*, anywhere considered strange or out of the ordinary; a bizarre situation, *creepsville*, any unappealing place or situation and *skidsville*, from *on the skids*, a state of poverty.

Rum- or *Romeville* aside, and passing by its role as the ultimate *town* (the country bourgeoisie, consciously teasing, also used *the village*), London, fount of all English-language slang, has generated a number of nicknames. The best-known is probably *the Smoke* or *Great Smoke* (and thus the rhyming slang version, the *Old Oak*, with its sense of something both old and solid). The source was the pall of pollution that, before the clean air legislation of the 1950s, hung over the industrialised city, generating smogs that in turn gave it such names as the *Big Fog*, *Fogtown*, *Fogville-on-Thames* and the *Gilded Fogpot*. Its natives, the Cockneys, have given *Cockneyland* and *Cockneyshire* and it is those Londoners, proud and parochial, who term the world beyond *the stones*, i.e the London streets, as *over the border*, or even *China*. And as borrowed by New York, there was *the Start*, which had been used a century earlier to refer to Newgate prison. This may modify the etymology: in that context it may have signified the start of a condemned person's ride from Newgate to the gallows at Tyburn, several miles to the west, but it might also have borrowed start as meaning a shock or surprise, in other words that experienced on entering prison. A link to one's starting a new life, for better or worse, on leaving Newgate for freedom seems a little optimistic for slang.

For a vocabulary which prefers to tell it like it is, little or no philosophising on offer, slang's take on the city's thoroughfares is surprisingly abstract. After -city and -ville, we reach *street*. There are, of course, a variety of concrete expressions, though these often reach beyond the named street in question. For instance *Dream Street*, a term coined by the short-story writer and chronicler of Broadway, Damon Runyon (1880–1946) as a nick-name for 47th Street, New York City, between 6th and 7th Avenues; the block, recognised as the headquarters of American vaudeville, was the site of the stage door to B.F. Keith's Palace Theater. *Wall Street* and Sydney's *Bourke Street* stand for the world of finance, *Threadneedle Street* for the Bank of England, while *Queer Street* stands for a variety of difficulties, economic ones included. Problems are also found at the *Chequer Inn* or *King's Head Inn in Newgate Street*, otherwise known as Newgate prison, *up King Street*, from King Street, Sydney, the site of the Supreme Court, which hears bankruptcy cases (the equivalent of London's *Carey Street*), and via London's China Street which gave a *China Street pig*, properly known as a Bow Street officer. Then there is plain *shit street*, a land-locked version of that unfortunate location *shit creek*.

Yet slang's *street* is less solid. It deals with a concept rather than a map. Like *road*, (used without an article) which has succeeded it, it represents the mythologised world of 'real life', which exists on the streets, rather than in the protected environments of home, office, family and the rest. The university of life, as it were, and the school of hard knocks. Before that it meant freedom, the unrestricted street that follows one's release from prison, a concept known equally as 'the world' and thus popularised by soldiers awaiting their discharge from foreign duties. Unchained one could *run the streets*, spending one's time in self-indulgence, partying, drinking and enjoying the freedoms of a non-domestic life.

Thus one is *streetified*, well versed in the ways of the urban lifestyle as seen on the inner-city streets, and has *street cred*, which was coined in the rock business and is popular in any of the industries that target the young consumer. One can have *street smarts*, the ability to survive on the streets; one is *streetwise*. There is *street legal*, which may be technically illegal, but wholly acceptable in the 'real life' context of the street. In all senses this use of *street* reflects a core belief, that the 'artist' must relate genuinely to the 'people', i.e. the working-class youth of the streets and housing estates and thus, opting sincerely or otherwise for mass culture over a privileged elite, he or she must at least assume an air of rebellion and informality.

It is the mindset that gives *hold court in the street*, ostensibly launching a gun battle (and implying that even death is preferable to prison), but underpinned by the sense that the traditional court, with its wigs and formalities, is not to be trusted and that the public arena is all that counts. Alongside is *front street*. An actual Front Street, once a mercantile centre, can be found in New York, but it is irrelevant here. Front Street is to do with *fronting up*, with *front* otherwise known as *attitude*, individual honesty or its pretence, exposing oneself, being on public display and thus open to attack, whether verbal or physical; a situation in which one must be responsible for one's words and deeds. The concept gives *play on front stree*t, to abandon pretence, to act openly, *put one's business on front street*, *take it to the street* or more bluntly *put one's shit on the street*: the phrases can mean to make indiscreet disclosures about oneself or another person, to trick or deceive or to confront and defy.

Next junction: the *alley* and the *lane*. It would appear that the narrower the street the coarser grows slang use of the image and both terms seem to adapt naturally to bodily parts, notably the vagina, the throat and the anus.

Slang can be restrained but it prefers otherwise. Thus the plain and simple *cunny alley* denotes the vagina, with its geographical variations *coney court, cunny court, cunny gate* or *gateway, cony-hall* and *cunny hall*. It may be assumed that *Gropecuntlane*, a name found in several British cities, and currently offering the earliest (c. 1230) use of cunt, belongs in this group. (Although *cunt* was the only 'obscenity' not to cross unremarked from Middle to Early Modern English – around 1450 – the word was once considered as unremarkable as *cock* or *piss*, which would not go 'off-limits' until the eighteenth century.) Fans of romance fiction might prefer *Cupid's alley*, and its extension *take a turn in Cupid's alley and Hair Court*, to have sex, but harsh modernity plunges headlong down *spam alley*. (Cupid is predictably keen on cunt; synonyms include *Cupid's anvil, arbour, arms, cloister, feast, furrow, grotto, warehouse, nest* and *pit; Cupid's kettledrums* are the breasts and Cupid's *spear* and *battering ram*, the penis.)

The smock, now associated with artists, was a female under-garment, thus an early pornographic work *The Nun in her Smock*, otherwise known as *Venus in the Cloister*. There was an actual *Smock Alley*, running off Petticoat Lane in London's East End: it was well known for its brothels and as well as signifying the vagina (also known as *smock castle*), the term also stands for any brothel area. Smock was a useful term, standing in for sex and in particular prostitute in a variety of compounds: among them the *smock shop* was a brothel, *smock servants* and *smock vermin* were whores, the *smock hunter, hero* and *soldier* were womanisers and the *smock merchant, agent, attorney, pensioner, tearer, tenant, smocker* and *smockster* were pimps.

A *smock fair*, otherwise a *marketplace*, was the red-light area; synonyms included the punning *easy street* (the girls rather than the life) and the unlikely *maiden lane*, while in Australia Sydney's Palmer Street was known as *douche can alley*, noting the use of douches by the street's prostitutes and punning on music's Tin Pan Alley.

Other terms for vagina included *long lane* (a real Long Lane still runs next to the Smithfield meat market though the pun is probably coincidental) and *leather lane* (again there is a real Leather Lane, a street market and in this case, the wordplay, on *leather*, human flesh, was certainly intentional: Clerkenwell, where the market is situated, was notorious for commercial sex). *Spew alley* is hardly congratulatory, but is a little early for the campus use of *spew* as semen. The *thatched house* (*under the hill*) is another pun, between the pubic hair and the actual Thatched House Lodge, Surrey, built for the keepers of Richmond Park in 1673 and subsequently owned by prime minister Sir Robert Walpole (1676–1745). There was *love lane*, which gave the laboured *take a turn in Love Lane on Mount Pleasant*, to have sexual intercourse and *shooters hill* (another real place and yet another pun, this time on *shoot*, to ejaculate). Again one could *take a turn . . .* along the narrow by-way, as one could *down* or *in cock alley*.

The real-life *Cock Lane* (again just by Smithfield), was in the fourteenth century the only street on which London's prostitutes were licensed to ply their trade in public. In 1666 the Great Fire was supposed to have stopped at its junction with Giltspur Street, while in February 1762 thousands of the curious flocked to number 33 Cock Lane to hear the scratchings and knockings of the alleged 'Cock Lane Ghost'. A committee of investigation, among them Samuel Johnson, duly pontificated. Disappointingly, it was all a trick.

After the vagina, the throat. *Spew alley* appears again, this time more logically. Among other terms are *gutter alley* and *peck alley* (from *peck*, food), and both *beer street* and *gin lane* (a century on in use but presumably acknowledging William Hogarth's celebrated engravings of 1751). *Gutter lane* may have echoed an actual street, but Eric Partridge preferred a link to Latin's *guttur*, the throat and to the Devonian dialect *gutter*, to eat greedily, as well as to *guttle*, to eat heartily and to *guzzle*. Those who wished to *go down gutter lane* were drunkards or gluttons. *Lane* meant throat by itself but was better known as the *red lane*, plus the *narrow lane*, *red lane alley* and *red lion lane*.

As for the anus, it is pretty much all puns and proprietary names and an unwavering focus on the infantile link between excrement and *chocolate* and slang's infatuated sniggering at sodomy. The exception is the *dirt road* or *dirt run*, usually in the phrases *go up the* (*old*) *dirt road* or the *dirt route*. Otherwise we have the *Cadbury alley* and *Cadbury canal*, the *Bourneville Boulevard* and the *Hershey Highway*. *Rocky road* evokes the popular chocolate-flavoured ice cream. Those who lack the sweet tooth have the *Vegemite valley* (Vegemite being Australia's home-produced alternative to Marmite). The use of Vaseline to ease anal sex, and a possible play on California's Silicon Valley gives the *Vaseline valley*, which is defined as the gay cruising area of Central Park in New York or a stretch of Oxford Street in Sydney which is acknowledged as the city's gay centre.

Whether in its uses of *city*, *ville* or *town*, or the images such conurbations and their thoroughfares provide for human bodies and functions, slang and the city are intimate friends. No city no slang to be sure, but slang amply repays the debt.

On the Road: Tramps & Hobos

In the main, for a term to qualify as slang – if we leave out such alternative registers as dialect or colloquialism – the assumption is that it should not be linked to a specific user group. If you want a term for the parts of the body, or for drunkenness or eccentricity, then the speaker's job is irrelevant. But some terms do spring from specific jobs. These are defined as jargons, a word that may have begun as meaning, in French, the twittering of birds, but has long since meant the specialist slang of specific occupations. And job-generated slang, say that of programmers, coal-miners, printers or lawyers, all of which are rich in such coinages, stands outside the mainstream. Such is the theory. The reality is otherwise.

We can sidestep the occupational slangs of the butcher and the baker and a wide variety of other job descriptions, but the language of some 'jobs' ensures that their terminology will gain a place within the slang dictionaries. It is not a matter of numbers, although that can matter, but of an innate outlaw status that renders their speech beyond the linguistic norm in just the same way as does that of out-and-out criminals. In such cases a language that might otherwise have been corralled as a jargon and limited to those who performed a given job, spills over into the realm of slang in general. Two such sources stand out: the *hobo* or *bum* (tramp in Britain) and the drug user. The former group offers around 550 terms; the latter well over 2,500 (and these exclude the 'trade names' of the various substances of recreational choice). For our puposes, let's look at those who wander in fact, rather than in their own heads.

On one level – the simple fact of moving around – the hobo/tramp is the descendant of the 'sturdy beggars' of the sixteenth century. It was this group, the 'canting crew', that is those who spoke *cant*, the criminal jargon of the time, whose world inspired what might be termed the first ever 'slang dictionaries'. These were a cross-European phenomenon. For a variety of reasons – among them the end of the Hundred Years War and the Dissolution of the Monasteries in England – there were many more wanderers than previously. Nor were they simply passive beggars: armed with a range of trickery they were also con-men (and women) and thieves. They lived off the land and off those gullible enough to fall for their deceptions. They spoke an incomprehensible language. All over Europe authorities and scholars set out to explain them, and their special language, believing that if one knew what they meant, one might be able to avoid the consequences of what they did. What the authorities came up with were known as 'beggar books'. They were not completely new; there had been an Arabic equivalent, complete with a list of the main beggars and their tricks, in the tenth century, but these were a European first.

The earliest appeared in Germany, albeit with a Latin title: the *Liber Vagatorum* (1509). This 'Book of the Beggars' also enjoyed a number of editions, perhaps the best known of which was that of 1528, which boasted a preface by none other than Martin Luther. It may perhaps seem odd that Luther, the father of Protestantism and more usually engaged in fighting the mighty Roman Catholic church, would bother with so minor a book, but for him begging, as carried out by what he saw as the innately corrupt mendicant orders of that church, was a source of evil and as such worthy of stamping out. As he stated in 1520:

'Probably one of our greatest needs is to abolish all mendicancy everywhere in Christendom. No one living among Christians ought to go begging . . . In my view, nowhere else is there so much wickedness and deception as in mendicancy . . . I have calculated that each of the five or six mendicant orders makes a visitation of one and the same place more than six or seven times every year. Besides this, there are the common beggars and those who beg alms in the name of a patron saint, and then the professional pilgrims.' And he admitted in the Introduction to the *Liber Vagatorum*, 'I have myself of late years been cheated and slandered by such tramps and liars more than I care to confess.' But his main aim in backing the book was moral: 'the book . . . should become known everywhere, in order that men can see and understand how mightily the devil rules in this world; and [. . .] how such a book can help mankind to be wise and on the look out for him, viz, the devil.'

The book offers some 295 words, of the roots of which just over half are German, followed by 22.1 per cent Hebrew, 6.8 per cent Dutch, 6.4 per cent Latin, and small specimens (all under 2 per cent) drawn from Romani, French and Spanish. Nearly 30 per cent have no ascertainable etymology. Among the words are *hanfstaud*, a shirt (literally 'hemp-rub'), *kabas*, the head (from Latin *caput*), *betzam*, an egg (from Hebrew), *diftel*, a church (from German *stiftel*, literally a small cathedral), *dotch*, the vulva (possibly a corruption of German *tasche*, a pocket), *crackling*, a nut (German *krachen*, to crack), *mess*, money (German *messing*, brass), *rolvetzer*, a miller and *schöchervetzer*, an innkeeper (German *schenken*, to retail liquor).

In addition to these general terms are those that denote the beggars' tricks. *Wilner*, those who like the English *ring-dropper* pretended to 'discover' a piece of silver, which they then sell to a victim; *Joners* (perhaps linked to French *jouer*, to play), card-sharps; *Sönzen-goers*, prototype begging-letter writers, and armed with false documents; *Schwanfelders*, who stripped naked in the hope of exciting pity and thus alms. There are the *Lossenders*, literally the 'let-loose', who claim to have been imprisoned in far-off countries and there persecuted for their Christian faith, the *Klenkner*, those who pretend to wounds the gruesomeness of which is balanced only by the ingenuity that conjures them up from perfectly healthy flesh; the *Dobissers* or fake priests also known as *Schleppers*; the *Grantners*, who pretend to the 'falling sickness', again a form of epilepsy; the *Gickisses*, or beggars who pretend to blindness, and claim to be on a pilgrimage to Rome or Compostella; the *Voppers* who beg on behalf of a relation possessed of the devil; *Dallingers*, posing as ex-hangmen and now repentant; the *Seffers*, who cover themselves with salve so as to appear very ill and the *Schweigers* who concoct a case of jaundice, using a mix of horses' dung and water.

There are also those that use children – never their own – for begging, those who pretend to epileptic fits, the necessary foaming counterfeited by a piece of soap in the mouth, travelling quacks, and tinkers who rather than mend a kettle, knock a hole in it, thus providing work for an accomplice.

The *Liber Vagatorum*, then, set the pattern, and it was widely emulated. In France there was *La Vie généreuse des mercelots, gueux, et Boesmiens, contenans leurs facons de vivre, Subtilitez et Gergon*, published in 1596. The title means 'The Heroic Life of

Beggars and Bohemians, their way of life, their tricks and their language.'

Its pseudonymous author called himself Péchon de Ruby (roughly equivalent to 'The Smart' or perhaps 'Naughty Kid'). Conforming to pattern, he offers a glossary of criminal argot and lays out a hierarchy of villainy. At the top of which stands *le Grand Coesre*, the king of the beggars and presumably cognate with such rulers as a *Caesar* or *Tsar*. 'A very good-looking man, with the majesty of a great monarch [. . .] and a great beard.' His coat, if we are to believe the author, consisted of six thousand coins sewn together.

The King of the Beggars story was popular. In England one found *Cock Lorel*. The name, used in slang to mean the leader of a gang of rogues, combines the adjective *cock*, first-rate, and *losel*, a worthless rogue, a profligate. The equivalent, perhaps of today's 'Guv'nor' or 'The Man'. It is usually found as a proper name and features largely in the literature of Elizabethan villainy. 'A great rascal, but evidently a man of talents', his first appearance is as the eponymous anti-hero of *Cock Lorel's Bote* (*c*.1500). According to the anonymously written verses, he is a 'ship-master', whose 'crew' is a group of rogues drawn from the workshops and gutters of London. Together they 'sail' the country, engaging in a variety of villainies. He appears in a number of works, as well as in the glossaries compiled by John Awdeley (whose *Fraternity of Vagabonds* was 'confirmed by Cock Lorel') and Samuel Rowlands (in *Martin-Mark-all: Beadle of Bridewell*), who suggests that while he was 'the most notorious knaue that ever lived' his 'captain's' role was purely allegorical and that he was, in fact that by-word for villainy and sexual deceit, a tinker. Whatever his trade he remains at the head of his marauding beggars, sometimes plotting against the state, on one occasion even entertaining the Devil to dinner at the gang's hideout in Derbyshire's Devil's Arse (now Peak Cavern) so named from the farting noises that accompanied waters flooding through the cave. According to Rowlands' generally fictitious 'history' of the canting crew, Cock Lorel's reign supposedly lasted c.1511–33. As well as supposedly establishing a number of rules whereby his villains should conduct themselves, he was the first to lay out the 'quartern of knaues called the five and twentie orders of knaues,' a hierarchy of beggary much imitated in a succession of canting dictionaries (at its eighteenth-century peak there were sixty-four job descriptions).

Italy would also contribute to the genre, albeit later still. The primary work was *Il vagabondo, ovvero sferza de' bianti e vagabondi* ('or the scourge of bandits and vagabonds') by the Roman Dominican friar Giacinto de' Nobili alias Rafaele Frianoro; it appeared in 1621 and enjoyed at least seventeen editions. Spain's equivalent was Juan Hidalgo's *Vocabulario de germanía* (1609, 'brotherhood' in Catalan and thence *hermanos*, brothers), published in Barcelona by Sebastián Cormellas.

It would have been surprising had England not joined the party. The first homegrown beggar book *The Hye Waye to the Spytel Hous* – or, roughly, Road to the Charity Ward – appeared around 1534, the creation of the London printer Robert Copland. The *Hye Waye* is a lengthy verse dialogue, supposedly conducted between Copland and the Spytell House Porter. The clinic in question, while unnamed by Copland, is generally accepted to have been St Bartholemew's Hospital, London's oldest, founded in 1123 near the open space known as Smithfield, then best known for its regular burnings of malefactors and heretics, now London's central meat market. Trapped in the hospital porch by a snow storm, Copland strikes up a conversation with the Porter, taking as their subject the crowd of beggars who besiege the Spytell House: 'Scabby and scurvy, pock-eaten flesh and rind / Lousy and scald, and peeléd like an apes / With scantly a rag for to cover their shapes, / Breechless, barefooted, all stinking with dirt.' The pair then discuss why some are allowed in and others rejected. Within this framework Copland notes and the Porter describes the various categories of beggars and thieves, as well as the tricks and frauds that are their stock in trade. They further note the way folly and vice lead inevitably to poverty and thence disease and finally, willy-nilly, to the Spytell House.

Copland's guide is not a true 'beggar book', the *Hye Way* does not offer a 'canting vocabulary', but it does provide vivid descriptions of a wide range of what would be known as 'the canting crew', 'diddering and doddering, leaning on their staves, / Saying "Good master, for your mother's blessing, / Give us a halfpenny".' Some, explains the Porter, are justified in their beggary. Others are not, and the porter explains how, after a hard day's conning the kindly public, the counterfeit 'cripples', like their succesors in John Gay's hit play *The Beggar's Opera* (1728), stripped off weeping sores, crusty bandages and suppurating wounds, tossed aside their crutches and were miraculously restored to health:

> By day on stilts or Stooping on crutches
> And so dissimule as false loitering flowches,
> With bloody clouts all about their leg,
> And placers on their skin when they go beg.
> Some counterfeit lepry, and other some
> Put soap in their mouth to make it scum,
> And fall down as Saint Cornelys' evil.

These deceits they use worse than any devil;
And when they be in their own company,
They be as whole as either you or I.

After Copland, John Awdeley, sometimes known as John Sampson: his most important work was *The Fraternity of Vagabonds* (1561). 'As wel of ruflyng Vacabondes, as of beggerly, of women as of men, of Gyrles as of Boyes with their proper names and qualityes'. But the star of the sixteenth-century show appeared in 1566: Thomas Harman's *Caveat or Warening for Commen Cursetours Vulgarely Called Vagabones*. The most influential of any beggar book, it reproduces the now regular pattern, even if in its glossary it lists but 114 terms other than those of the begging specialities themselves. But Harman, a magistrate who allegedly swapped alms for a few samples of language, was a pioneer sociologist and in its socio-linguistic rigour it would play a greater role in the canting collections that followed than any predecessor.

Cant moved on from vagabonds, the focus moving to out-and-out criminals, but they did not go away. The last and best-known example being yet another self-styled 'beggar king', one Bampfylde Moore Carew, whose original 'autobiography' appeared in 1745 and was still going strong in an edition of 1880. Its title is a book in itself: *The life and adventures of Bampfylde-Moore Carew, commonly called the king of the beggars: being an impartial account of his life, from his leaving Tiverton School, at the age of fifteen, and entering into a society of Gipsies, wherein the motives of his conduct are related and explained: the great number of characters and shapes he has appeared in through Great-Britain, Ireland, and several other places of Europe, with his travels twice through great part of America: containing a particular account of the origin, government, laws, and customs of the Gipsies, with the method of electing their king, and a dictionary of the cant language used by the mendicants.*

The modern tramp or hobo, while utterly different in so many ways, is still at heart the descendant of Carew and his predecessors. Writing in his *Tramping with Tramps* (1899) the researcher Josiah Flynt notes the fact, and references Martin Luther's foreword to the *Liber vagatorum*. And like them, as well as possessing a substantial non-standard vocabulary, he is nomadic rather than urban. For the purposes of recording that language we too must be nomads, and journey from Europe to America.

The hobo was a traveller rather than a career criminal or con-man, and had a far larger territory to cover. The beggar walked, the hobo rode, on trains, travelling via systems he called the *Q* (the Chicago, Burlington and Quincy Railroad used at harvest time), the *Mop* (Missouri Pacific), the *Dope* (the Baltimore and Ohio), the *Original Ham and Egg Route* (Oberlin, Hampton and Eastern) and the *Katy* (the 'bible belt' lines of the Missouri, Kansas and Texas Railroad, also known as the 'Moral, Klannish and Theological'). The practice, it seems, began when veterans of the US Civil War hopped freight trains to get themselves home. (The UK seems to have predated this, with the publication in 1845 of *Tales of the Trains* by Charles Lever, known as the 'Tilbury Tramp', but the relatively tiny UK network could never develop the same mythology: British tramps walked.) The first piece of hobo writing was Bret Harte's 'My Friend the Tramp' (1877): after that and until World War II hobo-related material became a publishing mainstay, whether as sociological investigation or memoir. The language, offering the best proof of authenticity, was put on prominent display. By 1931, and published in London by Eric Partridge's Scolartis Press, the lexis justified Godfrey Irwin's full-scale dictionary: *American Tramp and Underworld Slang.*

If one believes Jack London, one of the first to set down his experiences in *The Road* (1907) the language was as alluring as the lifestyle, with its fantasies of freedom, adventure and travel. The young London was fascinated by what he heard and attempted to set it down verbatim, capturing the fragmented conversation of a dozens bums in noisy chorus: '"When I was down in Alabama," one kid would begin; or, another, "Coming up on the C. & A. from K.C." [. . .] and yet another, "Nope, but I've been on the White Mail out of Chicago." "Talk about rail-roadin' – wait till you hit the Pennsylvania, four tracks, no water tanks, take water on the fly, that's goin' some." "The Northern Pacific's a bad road now." "Salinas is on the 'hog,' the 'bulls' is 'horstile.'" "I got 'pinched' at El Paso, along with Moke Kid." "Talkin' of 'poke-outs,' wait till you hit the French country out of Montreal – not a word of English – you say, 'Mongee, Madame, mongee, no spika da French,' an' rub your stomach an' look hungry, an' she gives you a slice of sow-belly an' a chunk of dry 'punk.'" And I continued to lie in the sand and listen. [. . .] A new world was calling to me in every word that was spoken – a world of rods and gunnels, blind baggages and "side-door Pullmans" . . . " bulls" and "shacks," "floppings" and "chewin's," "pinches" and "get-aways," "strong arms" and "bindle-stiffs," "punks" and "profesh." And it all spelled Adventure.'

London's tramping stories reflect his fascination. He began writing them in 1895, publishing them in small magazines, then collected them in *The Road* in 1907. That was the end of his tramping, although he featured the more sedentary poor in his investigation of London's impoverished East End, written up as *People of the Abyss* (1903).

Among the hobo-specific terms he gathered were these: *carry the banner* (to walk the streets as a tramp), *blind* (an order to leave a town (presumably on the railroad). It also meant a baggage car that has no door at the end leading to the inside; thus it cannot be accessed while the train is in motion; thus *ride the blinds*, to travel in such a wagon, *blind baggage tourist*, one who travels on such cars; *jump the blind baggage*, to ride in such a car. In addition were *blowed-* or *blown-in-the-glass stiff* (an elite hobo, a veteran), *bo* (a hobo), *bull* (a railroad policeman), *cannonball* (an express), *comet* (the aristocrat of tramps, travelling only on express trains and only for lengthy journeys), *deck* (to ride the roof of a freight car), *dewdrop* (for guards and security men to pelt tramps with stones), *ditch* (to throw a hobo from a moving train), *flopping* (anything under or in which one sleeps), *on the fly* (of a train, while moving), *throw one's feet* (to go around a town begging), *ghost-story* (a far-fetched anecdote), *hit the grit* (to jump from a moving train), *hog-train* (the world of hoboing), *on the hog* (unsatisfactory, unwelcoming), *hold down* (to ride a car roof), *hold-me-down* (a regular job), *horstile* (the invariable spelling of hostile, and referring to unfriendly local authorities), *main stem* (the main street), *monica* (or *moniker* and several other spellings, one's 'road' nickname), *mulligan* (a stew made of whatever meats and vegetables are available), *light piece* (a coin, obtained through begging), *perfesh* (a professional, i.e. a full-time hobo), *punch in the wind* (to ride on the roof), *ride the rods* (to ride on the steel bars beneath a freight car; as a generic, to be a tramp), *road kid* (a juvenile tramp who was possibly in a homosexual relationship with an older partner), *shack* (a brakeman), *side-door Pullman* (a freight car), *slam the gate* (to beg from private houses), *slough* (to imprison), *stew bum* (a down-and-out alcoholic), *stiff* (a hobo or a drunk), and *strong-arm* (the act of throttling a victim so as to immobilise them for theft).

With its emphasis on trains, the individuals good and bad one might encounter on them, and begging, this offered much of the core vocabulary. Though *jungle*, an area usually outside of town where vagrants gathered to *jungle up*, swap information and stories, sleep and eat, is not found until 1914.

One term London uses is *bo*, usually found as hobo's abbreviation, but for him *hobo* described not the man but the small-town jail cell in which he was imprisoned. London's definition was anomalous: hobo almost invariably meant tramp and the first recorded use to date comes in the *Morning Oregonian* of 14 September 1888: 'I see by your puzzled look you do not understand what a hobo is. I will tell you what we mean by the term. It is a word used to classify all tramps and vags. The word first originated with the Independent Order of tramps, and was used by them as a sort of password. One tramp walking along the street seeing another whom by his general appearance he thinks belongs to the order says "hobo". If the party thus addressed recognises the word, he stops and an acquaintance is struck up. Again, this tramp walking alongside a lot of freight cars stops at one in which he thinks there is a brother and repeats the magic word. It is a sesame and if this surmise is correct, the car door is drawn back and the man outside is received within.' The greeting of 'ho bo!' (i.e. boy) implied here is undoubtedly one of the proposed etymologies, but there is as yet no concrete solution. What mattered to the hobos themselves was the precise status that 'hobo' gave them – he was not a bum, nor even a tramp. Mencken, in *The American Language* (3rd edn, 1936) understood the nuances: 'Tramps and hoboes are commonly lumped together, but in their own sight they are sharply differentiated. A *hobo* or *bo* is simply a migratory laborer; he may take some long-ish holidays, but soon or late he returns to work. A *tramp* never works if it can be avoided; he simply travels. Lower than either is the *bum*, who neither works nor travels, save when impelled to motion by the police.'

London was not the first to write of hobos. Josiah Flynt (1869–1907), a university-educated sociologist who, a little earlier than London, had spent several years on the road in the 1890s, had published *Tramping with Tramps* in 1899. It offered a glossary of 'Tramps' Jargon'. In a brief introduction he noted that the language was quite indigenous. There was no Hebrew, Romani or other European input. Hobos were as self-sufficient in vocabulary as in life: 'They think that a good word is as much the result of inspiration as is a successful begging trick; and they believe, furthermore, that America is entitled to a cant language of its own.' Even if as ever, the underlying requirement was the same: the need to talk in public 'without being understood by others than those intimately connected with the life.' He added that it was a mutable language, but always a simple one. 'The main rule of the grammar is that the sentence must be as short as possible, and the verb omitted whenever convenient. [. . .] Hoboes say in two words as much as ordinary people do in four', a pattern that he suggests reflects their continual onward move-ment, but seems a characteristic of much general slang and cant. He claimed some three thousand terms for the hobo vocabulary (though he offers barely 125 in his glossary) but many of them, as seen in his writing and that of his successors, are not especially hobo-centred but are drawn unchanged from general slang or cant.

Flynt's hobo glossary predictably overlapped with London, but offered various extras, which focused more on begging than on transportation: *ball* (a silver dollar), *beef* (an act of betrayal, also used verbally) and thus *beefer* (an informer), *blanket stiff* (a hobo), *break out* (to take up tramping), *dead* (either professing ignorance or having abandoned the road), *dump* (a lodging house or restaurant), *flicker* (to fake a collapse), *Galway* (a catholic priest), *hoosier* (used generically for a farmer), *jigger* (a fake sore or wound), *mark* (a good place to beg; a generous donor), *moon* (a night), *Pennsylvania salve* (apple butter), *peter* (knock-out drops), *repeater* or *revolver* (a veteran), *shove* (a gang of hobos), *sinker* ($1), *slop up* (to drink heavily), *snipe* (a cigarette or cigar butt), *square it* (to rejoin the respectable 'square' world), *tomato-can vag* (the lowest order of hobo 'who drains the dregs of a beer barrel into an empty tomato-can and drinks them'), and *toot the ringer* (ring a doorbell).

In 1917 hobo life gained a best-seller and a star: *From Coast to Coast with Jack London* recounted, or claimed to do so, stories of the author's adventures crossing America with the celebrated London during his tramping days. He signed himself 'A-No 1, The Famous Tramp.' It was not A-No 1's first book: between *The Life and Adventures of A-No. 1* (1910) and *Here and There with A-No. 1* (1921) he wrote thirteen, and died a rich man on his royalties. Leon Ray Livingston (1872–1944) had been born in San Francisco and took to the road and rails from the age of eleven. He supposedly gained his monica (slang for a tramp's nickname and subject to a good dozen spellings when it was written down) from a veteran vagabond who informed him 'You're OK, you're A-No 1, kid.' The books were published for a few cents each and on the cheapest of paper (today's researcher has the invidious choice of leaving them untouched, or very likely snapping off every page that is turned); they were very successful. Thirty years after his death Lee Marvin played an approximate (and much more violent) version of the 'famous tramp' in Robert Aldrich's *Emperor of the North*.

Livingston, who carved his monica everywhere he went (plus an arrow indicating his next direction) claimed that his intention was not making money but pursuing a lifelong campaign to keep young people, generally adventurous boys, from the perils of the road. As he put it in *The Curse of Tramp Life* (1912), a book 'absolutely suited to be read by the most delicate child as well as the most dainty lady,' his primary object was 'to prove to boys and men of restless dispositions, that by their heeding the "Lure of the Wanderlust," they not only wreck their own futures, but very often the lives and happiness of their parents, and sometimes those of their families as well.' Secondarily: It shows to intending runaways 'what terrible punishment they must expect, should they be caught beating their way upon railroad trains'. And added 'DO NOT Jump on Moving Trains or Street Cars, even if only to ride to the next street crossing, because this might arouse the "Wanderlust," besides endangering needlessly your life and limbs. Wandering, once it becomes a habit, is almost incurable, so NEVER RUN AWAY, but STAY AT HOME, as a roving lad usually ends in becoming a confirmed tramp.'

For those who listened, many did not; and setting aside the spirit of adventure, the hobo ranks were inevitably swelled by circumstance; soldiers returning jobless from World War I, and the thousands of those who lost their jobs in the Depression.

One term common to Flynt, London and every hobo writer was *gay-cat*. In 1921 Patrick and Terence Casey made it the title of their hobo novel. The term has a number of meanings pertinent to hobo life: a young or inexperienced tramp, a hobo who accepts occasional or seasonal work and a tramp's younger, homosexual companion. While a concrete etymology is unknown it is possible that this use of gay may suggest a transitional role between hetero-sexual *gay*, meaning immoral, and gay in its homosexual use. That said 'The Kid' who appears in *The Gay-cat* is not openly homosex-ual, although this too may be contemporary self-censorship by the author. Certainly the implication in much of the literature suggests that these younger companions may have had a sexual relation-ship with their older peers. There are a number of synonyms: *lamb, punk, gazooney* and *road kid*. Defining the widely used *prushun*, also found in Flynt, A-No 1, the Caseys and others, Irwin (1931) states: 'A boy enslaved by an older tramp or "jocker." The boy is forced to beg and at times to steal for the jocker, and is often forced into unnatural practices. Those "prushuns" who stay with their "jockers" for any length of time find themselves absolutely at a loss when the older tramp dies, unable to think or act for them-selves. On the other hand, if the "jocker" fears that the "prushun" may betray him to the law, or if the boy grows so large that he is a danger to the older man, the "jocker" has little compunction about "losing" [i.e. murdering] the luckless "prushun."' The etymology of prushun is unknown too. It is sometimes found spelled as Prussian, but the relevant national stereotype is one of *kadavergehorsam* (discipline that would make a corpse stand to attention) rather than playing the catamite.

The Caseys added an Appendix to their novel, laying out the core vocabulary over a few pages. Calling up a century-old name they describe it as 'the flash language, that peculiar argot or slang of the thief and hobo. It is as old as history and has been used as a means of safe communication in public for years.' They suggest that 'in this country today' some three thousand 'flash' terms may currently be in use.

The hobo, whether fiction or as an object of research, plays a major role in the books of the 1900s–30s. Among the prominent titles are by *The Hobo* (1923) by Nels Anderson (which includes a glossary) and Anderson's pseudonymous *Milk and Honey Route* (1930) by 'Dean Stiff' (a given name that perhaps contributed to Kerouac's adoption of 'Dean Moriarty', his fictional recreation of the endlessly peripatetic Neal Cassady), *The Hobo's Hornbook* (1930) by George Milburn, *Adventures of a Supertramp* (1908) by W.H. Davies, *Hobohemia* (1956) by F.O. Beck, *Boxcar Bertha* (1937) by Ben Reitman, *Adventures of a Woman Hobo* (1917) by Ethel Lynn and *Boy and Girl Tramps of America* (1934) by Thomas Minehan. The Chicago novelist Nelson Algren, who put in his time on the rails, often touched on the hobo world, notably in such Depression-era pieces as 'Thundermug', 'So Help Me', 'If You Must Use Profanity' and 'A Place to Lie Down' written in the Thirties and issued posthumously in the collection *Texas Stories* (1995).

Across the Atlantic the London section of George Orwell's *Down and Out in Paris and London* (1933) laid out his experiences among the tramps. The book has a variety of slang, but it is not especially that of tramping; as he explains his topic is London slang (or as he describes it, 'cant') and swearing. Lying in the *spike*, the down-and-outs' hostel, he notes such terms as he hears, but the list is short and nothing like that special language of the hobo. Other British tramp studies include and *Travels of a Tramp-Royal* (1932) and *Tramp-Royal on the Toby* (1933) by Matt Marshall, but again here there is relatively little compared with the wide-ranging US vocabulary. As the British beats would find twenty years later, one might yearn for the romance of travel but even Lands End to John O'Groats bears no comparison to New York to San Francisco or Chicago to New Orleans. And the language that they and their successors the hippies would use was pure-d American-made.

Nonetheless, the British tramp did have some lingo. Examples on offer include these: *atch* (to arrest, i.e. catch), *b.d.v* (i.e. bend down Virginia, a cigarette stub), *bimp* (a five-shilling piece), *black and white* (tea and sugar), *boat* (penal servitude, which presumably harks back to transportation), *bottom road* (that which leads south from London to the coast), *brass knocker* (left-over food), *camphor and moth* (rhyming slang for broth). *Carriage drag* (a one-month sentence) expands on drag, which had meant a three-month sentence since 1833, *chant* (to sing for alms), *chice* or *chis* (nothing, and linked to the synonymous *shice*, a version of *shit*), *chuck-bread* (waste bread), *click* (money acquired through begging or trickery), and *clods* (copper coins). *Cock-broth* (strong, nourishing soup) was coined in 1661. There was *crow* (a lookout), *semi-doss* (a penny bed, extending the simple *doss*, first found in 1839), *dolly* (a candle) and *dolly up* (to heat water with a candle), *on the downright* (wandering as a beggar), *feather* (a bed), *fiddling* (selling matches), *finish* (methylated spirits) and *flappers* (the boards carried by a 'sandwich-man').

Hallelujah was a Salvation Army hostel for the homeless; and slang added *hallelujah garment*, a swallow-tailed coat, as worn by preachers, also known as *hallelujah peddlers*, *hallelujah-hawking*, working as a door-to-door evangelist, thus *hallelejah-hawker*, the *hallelujah lass*, a young female Salvationist, and the *hallelujah stew*, which was served in hostels. The odd one out is *hallelujah masher*, defined as a second-rate dandy; the example suggests that the heaven he was proclaiming was strictly mercenary.

Other tramping terms include *galtee* (to spend), *gorm* (chewing tobacco), *hole* (one shilling), *huey* (a town or village), *jack off* (to leave), *jib* (the tongue, from Romani *chib*, the tongue and earlier Hindi *tschib*, language), *kill-me-dead* (rhymes with bread), *kite* (a cigarette paper), *knocker* (an arrest), *lettary* (a lodging, from Italian letto, a bed and doubtless linked to Polari's synonymous *letty*), *lunan* (a female), *mashing* (a portion of tea leaves and sugar, enough for one cup of tea), *mickey* (the casual ward, which was rhyming slang and ran mickey = mike = spike), *monkery* (countryside, from the Irish tinker slang Shelta: *munk'ri*, the country), *reesbin* (a prison and also Shelta), and *mooch it* (to live as a tramp; one of a number of terms found in pan-European slangs meaning concealment and/or cheating; these in turn suggest an old Germanic word meaning darkness or mist).

Nark (a beggar who works part-time and lives permanently in a common lodging house), seems to be part of a group that, based on Romani *nak*, the nose, includes an informer, a miser and a generally irritating person. W.H. Davies in *The Adventures of Johnny Walker* (1926) explains 'These three men were "narks". In other words they were town beggars: men that had lost their homes and had to take refuge in a common lodging-house' and adds 'All true wanderers hate him.' The implication is that he doesn't move often enough to be trusted.

The *two penny rope* was generic for a casual ward, a development of a primitive (and cheap) sleeping arrangement in which two ropes were strung across a room, with rough bedding (usually sacking) strung between them, on which bedless tramps could lean and fitfully sleep for a 2d. payment. Dickens gave it a walk-on in *The Pickwick Papers* (1836–7): ''Ven the lady and gen'lm'n as keeps the Hot-el, first begun business, they used to make the beds on the floor; but this wouldn't do at no price, 'cos instead o' taking a moderate twopenn'orth o' sleep, the lodgers used to lie there half the day. So now they has two ropes, 'bout six foot apart, and three from the floor, which goes right down the room; and the beds are made of slips of coarse sacking, stretched across em.' Come the morning the ropes would be untied; it was a rough awakening.

A final group include the Romani *motto* (drunk), *mousey* (cheese), *Mrs Greenfields* (the open air, thus *sleep at Mrs Greenfields*, to camp out), *props* (trousers), *raclan* (a married woman, from Romani *rakli*, a girl), *ruffer* (a bed outdoors, possibly tied into old cant *ruffmans*, the bushes, though one should note simple 'rough sleeping'), *saddle* (an overcoat), *shackle-up* (a midday meal cooked on the road). *Shamrock tea* is weak (it has only three leaves in it), a *sinker* (one shilling), *skimmish* (alcohol), *slush* (lodging-house tea or coffee), *squealer* (a pork sausage), *tea and sugar man* (a casual labourer), *toby* (to tramp the roads, from Shelta *tobar* or Romani *tober*, the road), *two-ender* (two shillings), *whale and whitewash* (fish in white sauce), and *work the noble* (to beg from an upper-class person).

The hobo persists, as does the tramp, but in common with so many once independent areas of slang, the unique language seems to have faded.

The Body: Only Man is Vile

I F WE LOOK at what makes slang tick, the image we get is something like one of those pictures which draw a man on the basis of those physical bits and bobs that matter most. The picture we get starts off with disproportionately outsized genitals, pretty big arms and hands, maybe a substantial mouth, all balanced by an insignificant head and brain. Though the face, given human vanity, may be reasonably large as is the mouth within it. Science terms this image a *cortical humunculous*, a neurological 'map' of the body; the counter-language is less sophisticated. If you work from slang's priorities, it's all about sex and the physical appendages that make it happen. And although those pictures have also been conjured up to show off female priorities, slang remains overtly male. Or, if gender-neutral the default tends to assume a man (it rarely says 'a male arm', though it might, men's point of view being ever-paramount, note a 'female leg').

For our purposes here, let's do a bit of gelding. Let's resist *it*, as both varieties of *down there* stuff are so conveniently called. *Tits* and *arse*? Maybe, but frankly they're pretty well represented elsewhere and it's time to bring in the less celebrated parts. Slang isn't an especial devotee of equal opportunity, other than in its no-holds-barred nastiness, but let's go for a little affirmative action. Let's look beyond those toys for boys and those dark, forbidding passageways. Let's look instead at the head, face and mouth, at the arms and legs and the hands and feet. This not all-inclusive – I have had to resist the 101 terms for nose (*foghorn, leading article, sensitive plant, trumpet* . . .) and those for ears (*listener, hearing-cheat, lug, ginger-beer* . . .). Space is not helpful and slang remarkably encyclopaedic. So let us start at the top, and make our way down. Well, as I have explained, down-ish.

The Head

The head is well supplied by rhyming slang and those terms may as well be disposed of now. In some ways they're an uninspiring lot, not much wit on the lines of such classics as *saucepan lids* and *trouble and strife* which had some kind of relevance to the word you were looking at. Just rhymes.

So there's *ball o 'lead, cherry red, crust of bread* (which is 'on the top'), *penn'orth of bread* and *gingerbread* plus the slightly arcane *twopenny* which expands to *twopenny loaf,* and thus *loaf of bread,* which rhymes itself but actually comes a little later. There is *lemon spread,* which at least suits all that bread, *lump* or *pound of lead,* which given rhyming slang's urge for self-abbreviation comes as *lump 'er.* There are *rosy red* and *ruby red* and the inevitable human beings, notably *Uncle Ned,* the fictional *Judge Dread,* and *Kelly Ned,* i.e Ned Kelly, the Australian bushranger. *Rocky Ned* was, however, a horse, albeit another Australian: a buckjumper, known as the 'four-legged fury'. *Tile* usually stands for a hat, but it can mean the head beneath and rhymes with *battle of the Nile,* commemorating Nelson's victory over Napoleon on 1 August 1798. *Penny-a-mile* is less impressive: it refers to

Victorian cab-fares. Finally *toffee wrapper*, which rhymes with *napper*, and *bundle of socks*, which links to *thinkbox*.

There are a range of boxes or at least some sort of container. The *box* itself (which gives *out of one's box*, crazy), the *bonebox*, *cheesebox*, *dreambox*, *facebox*, *fusebox* (for a *bright spark?*), *pepper box* and *pepper-caster*, and, as noticed, the *thinkbox*, which can be *thinking box* or *thinkpad*. There is the prosaic *tin can*, and a number of containers, usually for liquid: the *pan* and *pannikin*, the *canister* and the *pipkin* (an earthenware cooking pot). *Crock* is also a pot, and another that, as *off one's crock*, means out of one's mind. The *conk*, also meaning the nose and in that guise usually a recipient of violence, most likely comes from Latin *concha*, a shell, and Greek *kogcha*, anything hollow. *Mazard* comes from standard English *mazer*, a hard wood (usually but not invariably maple) used as a material for drinking cups, otherwise known as *noggins*, another word for 'head'.

What it contains is the brain, and that makes the head a *brain bucket*, *brain barrel* and, for boxing fans, *brain canister*. It can be a *brain pot*, an *idea-pot* and a *knowledge-box*; the mysterious *geranium* presumably mispronounces cranium. A *nous box* uses the Greek *nous*, long-since adopted in English and defined as instinct or common sense, as opposed to actual learning. As *machinery* it drives the rest of the human system, among other things the *guessing gear*.

It sits at the top of the body and takes a number of slang names from the heights, human and otherwise. Such terms include *attic* (with its extension *queer in the attic*, meaning both mad and drunk; craziness is also implicit in the modern *rats in the attic*), *garret*, *coop* (the image is of pigeons), *cockloft* (literally the room over the garret) and simple *loft*, *gable* and *belfry* (in which of course one may be *bats*). Architecture underpins *dome*, *turret, cupola* (a rounded vault or dome forming the roof of any building or part of a building). Altitude adds *topknot, top piece, topflat, top deck, top end, top-loft, top storey* and *upper storey, upper extremity, upper apartment, loft, works* and *crust*. The *weathercock* is the highest head of all, though that may be the *sky-piece*. After *chimney* and *lid* nature offers *kopje*, a small hill, and *crag*, a high one. There is *tree*, usually found as *out of one's tree*, another hint at instability, and finally the punning *crown office*, which leads to the phrase *the Scotch greys are in full march by the crown office*, the lice are crawling on one's head (Scotland being invariably linked to such infestations) and *get into the crown office*, to get drunk.

The head is a *lump* or *chump*, otherwise a short thick lump of wood chopped or sawn from timber, a *block* (thus *off one's block*) or, still woody, a *knot*. There is also *doorknob* and *bonce*, originally a large marble. It is also equated with a range of edibles. These include *biscuit, crumpet, scone, bean, beanie* or *beano, coconut* and its variations *coko-box* and *coco, squash* (though *squash-headed* is foolish), *turnip* (a popular bet was 'all one's head to a turnip') and *swede* (US rutabaga and thus *crash the swede* or *set the swede down*, to go to sleep), *onion* (an eccentric is *off his* or *her onion*), *costard* (meaning a large apple and as such the root of that prime user of Cockney slang, the *costard* or *coster-monger*), and *pumpkin*. Other foods include the *cauliflower*, which elsewhere denotes a large white wig 'such as is commonly worn by the dignified clergy, and was formerly by physicians' (Grose, 1785) as well as the foaming head of the glass of beer. Elsewhere still the vegetable can mean the vagina, and we are again grateful to Captain Grose for telling us why: 'The reason for this appellation is given in the following story. A woman, who was giving evidence in a case wherein it was necessary to express those parts, made use of the term cauliflower, for which the judge on the bench, a peevish old fellow, reproved her, saying she might as well call it an artichoke. Not so, my lord, replied she, for an artichoke has a bottom, but a **** and a cauliflower have none.'

Along other food-based synonyms are *gourd*, which also means pumpkin, as does *calabash*, with roots in the Persian *kharbuz*, meaning 'melon', and occasionally 'water-melon'; *packy*, another term, is used in dialect for the calabash. Last comes *casaba*, which in standard English is *cassava*, defined by the *OED* as 'a plant, called also by its Brazilian name Manioc [. . .] two varieties (or species) of which are extensively cultivated . . . for their fleshy tuberous roots'.

From fruit, as ever, to nuts. *Acorn* and *filbert* are both en-slanged but neither, however, come near approaching *nut* itself, which is especially productive of combinations that show the head in a variety of roles, often violent or deranged.

Nut is especially fond of psychiatric institutions: These include the *nut bin, box, college, factory, farm, foundry, hatch* (underpinned by the well-known asylum at Colney Hatch near London, opened in 1851), *hut* and *place*. The *nut alley* (in a prison), *nut ward* and *nut wing* (in a hospital) are all specialist departments. The inmates include the *nutbag, nut-boy* and *nutball*, the seemingly edible *nutbar, nutburger* and *nut cake*, plus the *nuthead, nut-job* and *nut-nut*. Even their supervisor, the *nut doctor*, sounds dubious. The *nut wagon* and the *nut train*, both of which one 'rides' are insanity itself. To *go off one's nut* is to go mad, or at least lose emotional control, which can also be *blow, do* or *go off one's nut*.

Is it all madness? No. Among other compounds – *nut job*, a head-butt, *put* or *stick the nut in* or *on*, to give that blow – there's a trio of Australianisms: the *nut ducke*r, one who deliberately ignores a friend in the street, the *nut worker*, who works out ways of avoiding hard work and who the horny-handed equate with the white-collar worker, and the act of *nodding* or *ducking the nut* (as well as *the scone, the head* and *the skull*) all of which mean to plead guilty.

The images keep on coming. The presence (or lack) of hair gives *wool-grower, mop* and *moppery, barber's block*, the wooden 'head' on which a barber placed a wig as well as *wig* (or *wig-block, wig-box* and *wig-stand*) itself. Hats offer *headpiece, hatpeg, -rack* or *-stand, kadoova*, which may be linked to *kadi*, a hat, and its variation *kaboona*, and *derby*, which as well as the head is a hat in itself. *Kabeeza* may be associated to these. There are *egg, pimple* and *poundrel*, though why? It means a pair of scales. *Bazooka* recalls the anti-tank rocket launcher, first used in World War II; it may come from Dutch *bazu(in)*, a trumpet, though that seems to indicate the mouth rather than the entire head.

Thomas Harman's sixteenth-century glossary included *nab* (*nab-cheat*, i.e. 'head-thing' was a hat) and *nob* follows a century later (its use as a synonym for toff emerges c.1800.) Plus *noll*, which was once standard but turned slang these lead to *noddle*, another former standard use, but only for the back of the head, *noodle* (also a fool), and *nuddikin* which comes from *noodle-ken*, where *ken* means a house or home and could suggest another institution. *Napper*, plus *knapper, napper box* or *case, nopper* and *nappertandy*, which played on the real name of an Irish revolutionary, seem part of this group.

There are more, but let us conclude with just a couple of others. *Boko* is either a play on *beak* and/or *coconut* and is better known as a nose. The origin may lie in the trademark gesture of the great clown Joseph Grimaldi (Dickens adored him and wrote a biography) which was to tap his nose and utter the comment,

C'est beaucoup, that's plenty. Finally *sconce* or *sconce piece*, with roots either in sconce, a lantern or sconce, a fort or earthwork.

The Legs

The first recorded slang term for legs is *stamps* (1567), taken directly from their function; it was followed by *pins* (from the primary meaning of *pin* as a peg, and gave such phrases as *on one's pins*: to be feeling well, or in good form and the underworld's *fake a pin*, to injure one's own leg in order to obtain some kind of medical discharge or support. After that came *gams* (1780, from French *jambes*, thus *flutter a gam*: to dance), and *hams* (from the standard use of *ham*: the bend in the back of knee, which progresses to mean the buttock and upper thigh taken together and thence to the whole leg). Hams thus creates *ham-cases*: trousers, perhaps using Romani *hamyas*: knee breeches, *ham-bags*: girls' drawers (c.1900, and presumably a pun on *handbags*) and *ham frills* (c.1925 girls' running shorts). *Ham hocks* and *hammers* are modern developments. The *pestle of pork* borrows from standard English *pestle*, the leg of certain animals used for food, especially the haunch of the pig.

Rhyming slang for legs, with a possibly coincidental pun, offers *ham and eggs* along with *bacon and eggs*, *scrambled eggs* and *scotch eggs* or *pegs* both of which are found as *scotches*, plus *clothes-pegs*, *cribbage-pegs*, *Dutch pegs*, *Easter eggs*, *fried eggs*, *mumbly* or *mumblety-pegs* (a game based on one's feet and the throwing of pocket-knives just near them), *Gregory Pegs* (from movie star Gregory Peck) and *Mystic Megs* (the clairvoyant), and *wooden pegs*.

A group indicates the leg's role in moving or holding up the body: *wheels*, *locomotives* and *propellors*, *pillars*, *bracers*, *stand-ons, supporters, underpinners, underpinnings* or *under-standings* and *uprights*. Other terms include *drivers, stumps* (nineteenth century, and found mainly in the rather archaic phrase *stir one's stumps*), *cabbage stumps* (nineteenth century), *timbers* (originally only wooden but soon any leg), *trams* (twentieth century), *trespassers* and *pods* (which usually referred to children's legs; thus *podding*: toddling). *Shanks'* or *Mother Shanks' pony, mare, nag* or naggy are all usually found in *ride shanks' pony*, to walk and punning on standard English *shanks*: legs. There is also the US regional use: to *ride one's mother's colt, granny's colt, mother's pony* and so on. *Sticks* leads another subset, which includes *drumsticks, bunting sticks, poles, props, spindles, stems* (a noir-ish term for a woman's legs), *stilts, twigs* and *back-er-sticks* (from days when tobacco was sold in short twists a few inches long. *Chalks*, which come in sticks and are best known in the phrase *walk your chalks*, to move or leave, seems to be part of the group.

Slang can be very specific, especially when it comes to mockery. Who would have thought it would notice so many varieties of 'non-standard' leg? To have knock-knees was to be *cross-legged* or *baker-legged*: the condition was seen as a side-effect of the job, while in folk myth knock-knees are one of the 'proofs' of effeminacy; knees themselves were *marrowbones* or the rhyming *biscuits and cheese*. To be *box-ankled* was to have legs so made that the ankle-bones knock together. Bandy legs were *queer gams* (*queer* as in odd, not gay) and *cheese cutters* and those that had them were said to *buy their boots in Crooked Lane and their stockings in Bandy-legged Walk*. Those with crooked legs were *buckle-hammed*, from *buckle*, to warp or bend and to *walk dandy-dude* was to kick out one's leg when walking, perhaps a one-time affection of some lost species of exquisite. One who was splay-footed was a *skew-the-dew* or *marley stopper*, from the image of stopping a *marley*, i.e. marble with one's foot.

Those with *catsticks* or *trapsticks* (both from popular games) had thin legs, they were *spider-shanked* (thus *spider-shanks*, a man with very thin legs, although *spider's legs*, in Scotland refers to very thin hand-rolled cigarettes). There was the nickname *spindleshanks* and the phrase *calves gone to grass*, which produced the once-jocular remark 'veal will be cheap, calves fall' on noticing a man whose calves fall away. Australia adds *lolly-legged* (from *lollipop*, or at least its stick) used for thin, spindly legs, and by extension one who is physically uncoordinated.

Thick legs are *piano legs*, *tamp braces* (unattractive female legs) and *spiddock pot legs*, which pot was large, made of earthenware and had a hole through which one pushed a spigot. Otherwise it was all Irish: *Irish arms*, *Irish legs*, *Irish stamps* and the phrase *beef to the heel like a Mullingar heifer* (Mullingar being an Irish town). Men who wished to comment on a passing woman retreated to backslang to remark appreciatively: *doog gels*, good legs.

In a world before prostheses, the solution of a *peggy*, a one-legged individual, was the wooden leg which was an *ammunition leg*, *queer timber* or a *timber-toe*, which made the wearer *half-timbered* or *half-a-foot*. Depending on which leg was missing (and this extended to arms), the sufferer was either a *rightie* or *leftie*. The wooden appendage was also a *jury leg* which seems to follow the pattern of the nautical *jury-rig* or *jury-mast*, temporary rigging or mast, a short-term arrangement that replaces equipment swept away in a gale or during a battle. Finally there was the nickname *dot and carry one* or *dot and go one*: in an era before properly moulded 'feet' were available, the dot is the impression made by the bottom of the wooden leg, while the good leg is 'carried'.

A lame leg was a *swinger* or *gammy leg*. The term seems to come from gam, but in dialect gammy is left-handed – always seen as a defect – and the Irish lexicographer Bernard Share suggests *geamhchaoch*, bad from the tinker's language Shelta. *Stumps* are legs and *stumpy* hints at single-leggedness but means only short, which brings in *duck-legged* (*duck legs* being short legs) and the *duck's disease*: like a duck, one waddles around with one's buttocks close to the ground. Scotland offers *gipe*, otherwise an awkward person or a fool, for one who has long legs.

Finally, since the foregoing has been relatively free of sexism, there are of course a couple of terms that equate the woman, and her sexuality, with her legs. *Margarine legs* and *peanut butter legs*: both are 'easy to spread' with the difference that the latter are also 'smooth and brown'.

The Feet

Slang has its exotica, but in these bodily parts it is equally practical. As with the legs, many terms for the feet look at their primary role: walking. This gives *walkers, pads, paddles* and *padders, creeps* and *creepers, shufflers, stampers* and *stomps, steppers, toddlers, scrapers, trods* and *trotters* (and rhyming slang *Gillie Potters*, named for a music hall star and later radio comedian, real name Hugh Peel). A foot could be an *everlasting shoe*, and the crossover with footwear, generally heavy boots, gives *mud-faker* and *mudhook*, plus *mud-hopper, -masher, -splasher, -splitter* and *-squasher*, all of which meant both the human appendage and a heavy shoe or boot. The same multi-tasking goes for various terms for large feet: *barges, boxcars, canal boats, steamboats* and *battleships, clod-hoppers* and *-mashers, ant-killers, beetle-crushers* and *-squashers*. The use of *trilby* for a foot, and a briefly fashionable woman's shoe (men wear the trilby hat, from the same source) takes the name of the heroine of the eponymous 1894 novel by George du Maurier: her feet cited as being particularly attractive. Big feet were also *airy-fairies*, a jocular reverse on the term's usual meaning, on the same lines as calling giants *tiny* and shrimps *lofty*. Properly small feet have been *tootsies*, a playful or affectionate name for a foot, and expanded into *tootie*, *tootsey*, *tootsie pootsie*, *tootsie-wootsie* and *tootsum-wootsums*. There are probably other variations: baby talk is inexhaustible.

Shanks' pony aside, most terms for walking relate, with complete logic, to the feet. Terms include the *ankle express* and *ankle excursion*, the *hobnail express* and the *shin stage*. One can *hoof it* or *beat it on the hoof, travel by Mr Foot's horse* or in Australia *per Harry Pannell*, which firm manufactured stout walking boots. Walking as performance gives black America's *slidewalk*, a specific style of walking: one foot takes normal paces, the other drags; one hand is tucked into the side, the other is positioned with the wrist pressed to the waist and the elbow sticking out. This is a variation on the better known *pimp walk*, or *pimp strut*, less a walk than an elaborately choreographed stroll. As explained by the slang collector J.L. Dillard: 'The gait is slow, casual and rhythmic . . . almost like a walking dance, with all parts of the body moving in rhythmic harmony.'

Like those of the leg, the foot's imperfections naturally appeal to slang. Clumsy feet are *curby hocks*, which in a horse are the hock or other part of a horse's leg which is afflicted by a hard swelling. To have a club-foot is to be *bumble-footed*, thus to *bumble-foot*, to stumble, while the afflicted foot itself is a *double-breaster* or an *Irish hurley*, which puns on the Irish game of *hurley* or hurling, in which the ball is hit with a stick or *club*. A flat-footed person is either a *gut-foot* or *kidney-foot*, and one who walks flat-footed has been to *Palmer House*, a nod to the walking done by the hard-working waiters of Chicago's Palmer House Hotel; the flat feet themselves are *Palmer Houses*. A *council-of-ten*, from the Council of Ten, a secret tribunal of the Venetian Republic (1310–1797), are the toes of a man whose feet turn inwards when he walks.

Deformations aside, a number of phrases depend on the foot. *California socks* or *overshoes* (as used by tramps and/or unsuccessful gold prospectors) were and perhaps remain makeshift 'socks' created by wrapping the feet in sacks, often flour sacks, over which boots can then be put on. To *have a foot up one's ass* is to be treated unfairly or, to be victimised and one escapes by *taking the foot out of one's ass* and ridding oneself of ill treatment, victimisation and exploitation. To *make feet for children's shoes* was to have sexual intercourse, the assumption being a pregnancy. The Caribbean's *cock up one's foot* or *feet* (semi-synonymous with standard English's *put one's feet up*) is to sit around looking important while others work. It can also be used of a woman who sits with her legs sprawled in what is considered an indecent manner.

To *play footsie* (or *footie-footie*, *footie* or *foots*) is to nudge someone's foot with one's own – out of sight of companions – as a possible prelude to further intimacy. It can be found in South Africa as *voetjie-voetjie* and *footchy footchy*. A *shrimper* is a foot fetishist – the toes are supposed to resemble pink shrimps – thus *shrimping* is sucking toes for sexual satisfaction. The *hot foot*, however, is far from sexy, but a malicious trick played on an unsuspecting sleeper. Matches are thrust end-first into the gap between the upper and sole of the shoe (or between naked toes if vulnerable); the matches are lit, and the shoe 'catches fire' or the flesh is painfully singed.

The Arm

Perhaps slang's most widely known use of arm comes in the *short arm* (which can also be the *middle* or *third leg*), and specifically the *short-arm inspection*. This, of course, refers not to the arm but to the penis, and the health check to which military, prison and other authorities submit it.

In truth the arm mainly shows up in slang as an adjunct to other terminology, typically that of injectable drugs. Thus we have *go on the boot*, to leave the needle in one's arm after injecting a drug, then jerk the needle so as to draw blood, and *Grand Central Station*, a pun on the numerous tracks to be found at the New York terminus, and the *tracks* to be seen on the scarred arm of a long-term heroin user.

The arm as arm is relatively under-described. There are *pipes* and a *brace of hookers*, the *props*, the *flapper*, the *flipper*, the *meat-hook* and the *pumphandle*. There is the *rammer*, the *smiter*, and less aggressively, the *wing* (thus the nickname *wingy*, for a one-armed man). Lost but once a staple of baseball writing was the *soupbone* or *souper*. Rhyming slang provides a few more: *burglar alarm* and *fire alarm*, *chalk farm* (from the north London district), *Indian charm* and *lucky charm*, *five-acre farm*, *Emmerdale Farm* (from the UK soap opera *Emmerdale Farm*, now renamed *Emmerdale*) and *Warwick Farm* (from Warwick Farm, a Sydney racecourse).

To walk arm in arm is to *link it*, to *latch on*, to *crooky* (the bending of the couple's arms) and if a man has a woman on each arm, he is *carrying milk-pails* (the image is of a milkmaid with her yoke and two pails). The US campus adds *escargot*, a man walking arm in arm with his date, which either looks to the French *escargot*, a snail, suggesting that such couples appear as tightly curled up as a snail in its shell, but the word may simply elide 'his cargo', implying that the woman is something the man carries along. The *Armstrong heater* refers to one's arms when embracing a loved one and puns on *strong-arm* and the brand-name of a stove; *Johnny* or *Captain Armstrong* is a corrupt jockey who holds back his mount to (lucrative) order.

To *have long pockets and short arms* is to be miserly, mean, and to *make a pot with two ears* is to set one's arms akimbo. To *cross-fam* was an underworld term that described a method of picking a pocket by crossing one's arms in a particular position. Still with crime, a *mason's maund* (from *maund*, a wound, probably coun-terfeited to gain sympathy) was a fake sore, placed above the elbow and counterfeiting a broken arm caused by a fall from a scaffold. To *chuck a scrammy* is similar, an Australian term for pretending to have a withered arm (from dialect's *scram*, with-ered) so as to get off work (a *scrammy* is someone who actually has such an arm). *Batwings* or *bingo wings* are a cruel hit at the excess flesh that accumulates on the upper arm of an older woman (an *old bat*, but that may be coincidental), and, in the case of the second term, is seen as she stretches her arm upwards to claim 'House!' at the game of bingo or lotto.

A *fit in the arm* was a blow and to *have a fit in the arm* was to aim a punch or blow. The lexicographer James Redding Ware explained it in his dictionary of 1909: 'In June 1897 one Tom Kelly was given into custody by a woman for striking her. His defence was that "a fit had seized him in the arm", and for months afterwards backstreet frequenters called a blow a fit.' Finally *Saturday night palsy*, *Saturday night-itis* or *paralysis*: this is the temporary paralysis of the arm, especially a weakness in the wrist, after it has rested on a hard edge for a long time, as during sleep following a bout of drinking.

The Hand & Fingers

Offer slang a point of view and one can be pretty sure that it will take the negative. Thus the words it has found to describe the hand and its fingers (bracketed together since it is often only context that makes it clear which is meant in a given use) are not those of stroking, caressing, soothing and similar aspects of human kindness rendered physical. Instead we have a range of terms that can be summed up as promoting self-gratification. Self-gratification, as will be seen, in every sense.

Eats first, morals after, said the playwright Bertolt Brecht, and the first thing at which slang's hands grab is food. There are *biscuit hooks* and *snatchers*, and the same duo are attached to *bread*; *crumb-snatchers, clam-diggers, flesh-hooks* (which may be sexual but more likely edible), *jelly snatchers, lunch-hooks* or *grabbers, meathooks, potato grabbers, -grablers* and *-stealers* and *grubbing utensils*. The fingers are *Adams' knife and fork*, *greasers* or *fangs* and the index finger the *lickpot*.

There are, however, no morals, only immorality. We find *pickers and stealers* (from the mid-sixteenth-century catechism: 'To keep my hands from picking and stealing') and plain *stealers, thieving hooks, cornstealers* and *cotton-pickers, grabs, grab-hooks, grabbers, grapples, grapplers, grappling irons* and *gripes* (from *gripe*, the act of grasping). There are *claws* and *clampers, nabblers, divers* and the *fork*, the last couple in the context of pickpocketing where to *dive* is to thrust one's hand into a strange pocket and the *diver* is also the pickpocket in person. To *fork* was a technical term, meaning to pick pockets using the fore and middle fingers, extended like the tines of a fork, which are thrust into the pocket, then closed tight on any object within; this is then withdrawn between the 'fork'. *Glom* can be a hand, but *glom* or *glaum* have meant to grab or steal since the late nineteenth century and all uses come from Scots *glaum*, to snatch, to grab, to seize with the jaws, to eat greedily. A possible link to Irish *gabhlach*, a forked instrument used in fishing, used in modern Irish slang as golly-fishing, may lie behind the seventeenth century's *goll*.

Among other veterans are the *bunch of fives* (also *box of fives* and *set of fives*), the *daddles* or *daddlers* and thus *tip someone a daddle*, to shake hands, and the dukes, usually found in the context of fist-fighting, and properly part of rhyming slang where *duke of York* equals fork. Prize-fighting also likes *mauley*, *mawley* and later *maulers*, which comes either from standard English *maul*, the Gaelic *lamh*, the Shelta *malya* or the Romani *mylier*, each of which means hand. *Mitt*, yet another boxing term, cuts down *mitten*, which was borrowed from winter's hand-warmer to mean boxing glove a century before it became a fist. Although *forefoot* was popularised by Shakespeare, the earliest of all hand/finger terms was *fumble* which appears in the mid-sixteenth century as hands, and gives *fambling cheat* ('hand thing') a ring.

Grabbing, stealing and . . . groping. The hand was a *pussy glommer* (again from *glom* or *glaum*) long before the 45th President, as were fingers slanged as *cunt scratchers* and *cunt-hooks*, *gropers*, *feelers*, *ticklers* and *wigglers*. Yet slang prefers staying nearer home and the masturbatory hand is well catered-for. There are the *dick-beater* and *dick-skinner*, the *wanking spanner*, *wanker's spanner* and *wanking paddle*. Grasping at least a fantasy of female involvement there is the *dry-mouthed widow*, *Miss Fist* and *Mother Fist* (each with *her five daughters*), *Mother Five Fingers* and *Mrs Hand*, *lady five fingers*, *five-finger(ed) Mary* or *Annie*, *Mary Fist* and *Mary* or *Minnie Five-Fingers*. To masturbate is to *audition the finger puppets* or *the hand puppet*, or *to lay a little five-on-one* (that's five fingers, one penis or vagina). For girls only, is *the button finger*, used to stimulate the clitoris or *button*. But the palm (there is no avoiding it) goes to the family of that name. There are to be found *Mrs Palm and her five daughters*, *Madam Palm and her five sisters*, and the alluring *Rosy Palm* (who has her own *five sisters* or *five daughters*) which also give the phrases *have a (big) date with Rosy Palm*, *date Rosy Palm and her five sisters*, *entertain*, *get off with* or *visit Rosy Palm and her five daughters*. Sometimes the Palms are Palmers: *Rosy Palmer*, *Patsy Palmer* and both *Mrs* and *Mr Palmer*, who has *his five sons*.

Both hands and fingers find a role in rhyming slang. The former has *brass band*, *frying pan*, *German bands* (a staple of British entertainment that vanished abruptly with the declaration of World War I, and the departure of the once popular German bands from British streets), *Margate* and *Ramsgate Sands* (popular day-trip destinations for the East End), *Ray Milland*, *Mary Ann*, and *Martin-le-Grand* (one of the last vestiges of St Martin's le Grand, a monastery and college founded c.1050; its bells rang the nightly curfew, and prisoners on their way from Newgate to Tyburn regularly passed it; those who managed to escape were able to claim sanctuary within its walls – thieves and coiners were accepted, Jews and traitors were barred. It was suppressed in 1540, and its only memory is a street name). Since a hand can also be a *fin*, there are *Lincoln's Inn* and *strong and thin*.

The latter includes *bees wingers*, *bell ringers*, *comic singers*, *lean and lingers* and *longer and lingers*, *melody lingers* and *wait and lingers*. Australia gives *manly-warringahs* (from the Australian Rules football club Manley Warringah; warringah, a term from the Guringai language means 'sign of rain', 'across the waves' or 'sea') and *onkaparinga* (from the brand name of a make of woollen blanket).

The fingers also find a place in gesture, the best-known of which is to *give the finger*, which simply involves raising the middle digit in a gesture of contempt. Synonyms are to *give, flip* or *hand someone the (big) bird*, and to *flag, flip, give* or *shoot a bone* (the reference being to the *bones* that are inside the finger). New Zealand prefers to *give someone the ta-tas* (*ta-ta* meaning 'goodbye'). South Africa's *zop* is a gesture of derision created by poking the thumb between the middle and index fingers and the equivalent of the Italian *fico*, which means both fig and cunt. There is the gross *smell your mother!* insult, usually accompanied by waving the middle finger under the insultee's nose; the implication is of recent sexual foreplay. Still sexual is *play at pot-finger*, to stimulate a woman by sticking one's finger in her 'pot'. This in turn leads to *stink-finger* (also *stinky-finger, stinky-pinky*) which is manual stimulation of the female genitals by the middle finger, an experience the Beatles famously (in 'Penny Lane') apostrophised as *finger pie*.

The Face

Since the face has no direct functions, but plays host to such organs that do such as the mouth and nose, it largely lacks the images that other parts of the body have borrowed from standard English. The exceptions are *index, title-page, chart* and *map*, noting the way in which facial expressions can indicate emotion. The *phiz* (variously found as *fiz, fizhog, fizz, fizzog, phis, phisimiog, phisog, phizzog, physiog,* and *phyz*) adds to this list. Its source, the standard term *physiognomy*, originally meant the art of judging character from a study of facial features (for some this also allowed prediction of the future). So too, perhaps, is *frontispiece*, though that favourite of prize-fighting reporters and fans suggests hiding rather than revelation. Boxing also gives *furniture*. One can also argue a case for *clock* and *dial*, as well, since these are actions with which we associate the face, as for *kisser*, *smiler* and *feed-bag*.

Other early terms go their own way. *Muns* simply borrows German *mund*, the mouth; nineteenth-century sellers of hot-cross buns used in their sales pitch: 'One a penny, two a penny, hot cross buns, / Butter them and sugar them and put them in your muns.' The first half has survived, the second has not. *Mush* was once thought to come from the softness of the flesh; it is more likely to have come from regional French *muse*, the mouth or muzzle. *Muzzle* is used on its own merits. *Jib* (and its developments *chiv*, *chib* and *chivvy*), like much early slang, is a Romani term, chib or jib, the tongue, which in turn like many Romani words comes from Hindi, in this case *tschib*, meaning language. Mug, which remains popular, apparently comes from a variety of eighteenth-century drinking *mugs*, bearing a grotesque human face, although Anatoly Liberman has noted Scots *mudgeon*, a grimace.

It is hard to discover many links between the rest. *Esaff* is backslang, *beezer* a possible development from *bowspirit*, the nose, and can mean nose itself, *balloon* and *chump* (a lump of wood) are based on the shape, *mattress* seems to take the original slang meaning, a beard, and apply it wholesale, *mag*, originally chatter, seems to do the same. It is hard to see how *mulligan* fits, unless it was used exclusively for Irish faces. There is no need to look at the remaining few terms *grill*, *dot*, *grip*, *kite*, *coupon chopper* – the same disconnections emerge.

The face does attract a good deal of rhyming slang. Such terms include *boat-race*, *airs and graces*, *roach and dace* and *kipper and plaice, cherry ace* and *deuce and ace, chips and chase* and *handicap chase, Jem Mace* (the UK prize-fighter Jem Mace (1831–1910) and *chevy chase* (plus *chibby chase* and *chivvy chase*) which borrows the proper name Chevy Chase, the site of a celebrated seventeenth-century border skirmish and thus the subject and title of a popular ballad. The jaw gives *jackdaw* and *rabbit's paw* but *rabbit*, as *rabbit and pork*, more usually means talk or speech.

The chin is variously the *button* (originally prize-fighting jargon), and the rhyming *Errol Flynn* or *Gunga Din*. The nineteenth-century *nutcracker* denoted a Mr Punch-like profile with a curving nose and protruding chin. Cosmetics, with which the face is adorned include *lippy* (i.e. lipstick), *slap* (originally theatrical) and *war paint*.

The face underpins a few phrases. One can have a face *like a blind cobbler's thumb* (covered in pockmarks, resembling needlepricks), a *hatful of bronzas* (i.e anuses, from the colour), *a stripper's clit*, like *a bum* ('dirty and daggie', from *dags*, bits of excrement hanging off a sheep's posterior), a *douchebag*, a *toilet seat*, a *wet week*, a *busted* or *twisted sandshoe*, a *bucket of smashed crabs*, a *smacked arse*, a *bull's bum*, a *festering pickle*, an *abandoned quarry*, a *painter's radio* (streaked with dirt), a *stopped clock*, a *yard of tripe*, *half-past-six* (the ends of the mouth point down) and *yesterday*. Many are Australian; none are desirable.

There is the derogatory *Croydon facelift*, a British female hairstyle which pulls the hair back tightly from the face, supposedly giving the effect of a facelift; it is stereotyped as that of working-class young women. The older *Whitechapel shave* again stigmatising the working class, whitening applied to the face to lighten the 'five o'clock shadow' since the poor cannot afford a barber to shave them. The face also suffers at the hands of a *chalker*, an Irish thug, the equivalent of a London Mohock, who specialised in roaming the streets and slashing the face of any unfortunate victim; thus *chalking*, carrying out this species of urban terrorism or 'amusement' as Grose grimly notes it in 1785.

The Mouth

The mouth is practical. It holds the teeth and tongue, it leads to the throat, it permits eating and speech. On occasion it can kiss. Such are its functions, such are the bases of its descriptions in slang.

Teeth first: the *bonebox*, *domino-box*, the *ivory box* or *case* and *box of ivories*, the prosaic but factual *toothbox*. The teeth themselves often rhyme – *Bexley*, *Hampstead* and *Hounslow Heath* – but also offer *chatterers*, *choppers*, *crunchers*, *gnashers*, *grinders*, *mompyns* (fifteenth century, literally 'mouth-pins') and the *pearly gates* among several others. For speech the mouth can be the *spoke-box*, the *oration trap* or *box*, *clack-box* and *rag box* or *shop*, both *rag*, which 'waves' and *clack* being terms for tongue. It is the *chaffing-box* or *closet* (there is also the *chaffer*, but that tends to be the throat as in *moisten one's chaffer*, to take a drink). The *sauce-box*, which might suggest food, but is surely *sauce* as in cheekiness or teasing. The *feedbox* is unarguable, as is the *gob box*, which uses one of the veteran terms for mouth, *gob*, which reaches back to 1550, though the gob might refer to another meaning: clots of sliminess and thus the mucus that one spits. The *sausage box* is specific, while the *lung-box* and *bacca-box* recall a less prohibitive attitude to smoking.

Speech has also brought the *flapper*, *screech*, *yawp*, *gab*, *blabber* or *bullshitter*, *chatterer*, *clacker*, *giggling* or *laughing gear* and *laughing* or *talking-tackle*. *Jib* has been noted for face, it also works for mouth, as do *map*, *muns*, *muzzle* and *napper*. The *mummer* was once one who mutters and murmurs and thus an actor in a dumb-show; slang has given them a voice.

If gob is a veteran, so too is *trap*, though a couple of centuries the junior. *Shut your trap*, be quiet, remains a slang regular. What it traps is food, though there is room for *clapper-trap*, where *clapper* is the tongue, and *flap-trap*, its action, plus *talk-trap*, *flatter-trap* and *kissing-trap*, coined ironically in the violent world of prize-fighting. *Smacker*, usually a kiss, also means a mouth, as does *busser* from *buss*, to kiss. *Claptrap* seems another but it is not. The *clap* here is applause and the term suggests some piece of theatrical, and later social business that will milk that applause from an audience; the image of nonsense is contemporary, both existing since the early nineteenth century. *Flytrap* is a joke and presumes a gawping mouth, while *clam-trap* or *clamshell* suggest the bivalve, opening and shutting. The rest is consumables. The *grub-trap*, which could be a *shop*, a *street*, a *mill* and a *grubber*. Both *beer* and *gin traps* (though a *gin-trap* also referred to a snare for rabbits and such) and *rabbit-trap* qualifies here too; a *meat-trap*, *-mincer* or *-safe*, a *bread-trap* and a *bun-trap*, a *hash-trap* (*hash* as stew, not dope), a *pudding trap* and *duff trap* (*duff* being stodgy and based on suet, much relished in the navy), a *turnip-trap* and, less conventionally tasty, an *opossum-trap* and a *rat-trap*. Potatoes are the big one: *potato-trap*, *-box*, *-jaw*, *pratie-trap* and *tater-trap*.

The final container is the hole into which we shove our food and which gives *bacon-hole*, *porridge hole*, *pie-hole* and *piechopper*, *doughhole* and the most popular: *cakehole* (another one to 'shut'). *Faghole* and *smokehole* deal with cigarettes, and *wordhole* and *blowhole* (for *blowing off* or boasting) with speech. The *gap* and *gapper* go here too, as must the *pan*.

The mouth qualifies as a place and as such becomes a *cavern* or *tunnel*, a *gate* or *wicket* which can be locked up by a *dub*, a key, which in turn gives *dubber*. Given the link of wicket-gates to churches the use of *graveyard*, where the teeth are the tombstones, is logical. The *garret* seems out of place, it's usually the head, and the *gazabo* requires a stretch: does the mouth really resemble a form of garden hut, or a turret on the roof of a house? That, however, is properly spelt gazebo, while *gazabo* can be slang for fool. The link is still tenuous.

Beak, *nib* or *neb* all link the mouth to a bird's equivalent and *maw* is usually used of non-human animals. Otherwise the concept of eating gives *feeder* and *biter*, *cafeteria* and *dining room*, *grog-shop* and *gin lane*, *coffee-mill* and the *feedbag*, usually a horse thing, which one 'puts on'. *Beefeater* is another prize-fighting creation: 'Tom sent his sinister mawley upon Bill's beef-eater' reported the *Sporting Times* in 1860. Beefeater, Yeoman of the Guard aside, could also mean a true Briton, man or woman, and the first recorded use, in 1623, notes it as a translation of the French *rosbif*, still found, though the country's image has changed from what goes into the mouth to what comes out of it and *les rosbifs* are now *les fuckoffs*. The sexual sense of *eat*, to administer oral sex, gives *cocksucker* and *cunt*.

There are few rhymes: *east and south*, *north and south*, *queen of the south*, *sunny south* and *salmon and trout*. *Moey* is from Romani *mooï*, the mouth, Australia's *chook's bum* describes pursed lips as more appealingly does the *rosebud*, and Ireland's *puss* is a sulky look. *Transporter* was a criminal thing: the image was of the sentence of transportation that comes from a judge's mouth. The *alligator mouth* is to be avoided, it went with boastfulness: *he's got an alligator mouth and a hummingbird* (or *canary*) *ass* is another version of *all mouth and trousers*, while the wise advise, *don't let your alligator mouth overload your ass.*

Finally the productive *chops*, which begins as a standard English term for 'jaw' but has been borrowed by slang for the mouth. One can *beat* or *bust one's chops* (or *gums*) and thus talk incessantly, work very hard or make a great fuss about something. To *bust someone else's chops* is to nag, to criticise. One can be *down in the chops* which is depressed. To *flap one's chops* is to talk too much or to gossip, while to *flog one's chops* returns to hard work or unchecked talk. To *run one's chops* about is to complain and *slice one's chops* to chatter. *Lick the chops* should mean food but it is a musician's term: to tune up before a performance, and the chops are musicianship, a reference to the use of one's mouth and lips in playing a wind instrument.

The Eye

Windows to the soul, says the popular cliché and who is slang to argue? The eyes can be the *front windows*. But the soul plays little part in slang's world-view and as with the rest of the body, much is down to functionality. The eye sees, it is a *lookout* or a *seer* which may suggest something prophetic, but probably does not.

As such a number of slang's synonyms simply borrow from standard English: *blinkers, winkers, leerers, oglers, peekers, peepers* and *peeps* (thus *peel one's peeps*, to keep a lookout) and *squinters*. *Clockers* clock, or take notice of what's happening, *gagers* gauge the situation, *gogglers* goggle and *spotters* spot. There are *glimpses* and *slanters*, which *take a slant*. There is the simple *optic* and prize-fighting's *ogle*. The *gig* reverse-engineers *gig-lamps*, spectacles, while *gim* is either a misspelling of *glim*, a light, or a pair with *gim*, to stare.

In through those windows comes light and the eyes, which can be simply *lights*, conjure up a number of compounds that reflect the fact: *deadlights, domelights, glasiers, headlamps* and *headlights, skylights, toplights*, the modern, artificial duo of *neons* and *dimmers*, and the long-established *shutters*. The flowery *day-opener* comes from boxing. Light illuminates them, they shine and become *glisteners, sparklers, twinklers, beads, pearls* and *oysters. Immies* reflect *immy*, a highly rated marble, made to resemble a semi-precious stone, and *killem-shots* suggest the killing glance of a pair of sparkling, and traditionally female eyes. *Saucers* is less romantic, though *eyes as big as saucers* was coined in the fourteenth century. *Baby-blues*, sometimes *icy blues* are generic, they can be brown, green, whatever. *Banjo eyes* suggest the round, white drumskin on the instrument and denoted large, wide-open eyes.

To squint was to have a *boss-eye, queer ogles* or *peepers, squeench-eye* or *squinny-eyes*. Bright, clear eyes were *rum ogles*. One who was *cunt-eyed*, the image being of a slit, squinted. Francis Grose, who includes a number of such conundrums in his dictionary, defined the *seven-sided animal* as 'A one-eyed man or woman, each having a right side and a left side, a fore side and a backside, an outside, an inside and a blind side'. Grose is also responsible for the threat, 'I'll knock out your eight eyes' and explains it as 'a common Billingsgate threat from one fish nymph (the far from traditionally nymph-like fish-seller, or, in slang, *fish-fag*, itself incorporating *faggot*, a woman) to another: every woman, i.e. according to the naturalists of that society, having eight eyes, viz. two seeing eyes, two bub-eyes, a bell-eye, two popes-eyes, and a ***-eye.' Bub-eyes are *bubbies*, the breasts, bell-eye the belly and a pope's eye the lymphatic gland in a leg of mutton, regarded as a delicacy; here presumably the urinal and anal orifices. The final, censored term remains mysterious, it is presumably and despite its three letters, since Grose was always squeamish in this area, a reference to the vagina.

There is rhyming slang: *baby's cries* and a range of *puddings and pies* both sweet and savoury: *apple pies, jam pies, lamb's fries, meat pies, mince pies, mutton pies, pork pies* (*porky pie* too, but that's usually a lie) and *mud pies*. There is *Nelly Blighs*, from Nellie Bly, the pseudonym of Elizabeth Cochran Seaman (1864–1922), a famous pioneering feminist newspaper reporter, who took her pen name from the title of a Stephen Foster 'minstrel' song, featuring a black maid.

Of all the face, the eye seems most prone to injury. Blows to the eye include the *poultice over the peeper* as well as the *blinder*, *blinker* and *bung*. To *star* or *mill the glaze* originally meant to break a window for the purpose of stealing whatever lay behind it; borrowed by prize-fighting it meant to knock out someone's eye. The result of all this violence: the black eye. No other injury (as much as slang even notices them) has received so exhaustive a coverage.

The simple black eye can be a *beefsteak eye* (the traditional palliative being a raw steak laid across the painful optic), a *bruiser* and a *bunger*. It is a *casualty*, a *goog* (the bruised eye resembles a *goog*, Australian for egg) or a *graper* (another supposed resemblance, to a plump black grape), a *shiner* (generating the rhyming slang: *morris minor*, the term is currently favoured as meaning fellatio) and a *stinker*. A *mouse* suggested the greyish tones of a burgeoning bruise and a *Monday mouse* was the tangible aftermath of Saturday or Sunday night's (drunken) fight. The witty *half a surprise* plays on the musical hall star Charles Coborn's song lyric (c.1886), 'Two lovely black eyes/Oh what a surprise' (adapted from the slushy 'My Nellie's Blue Eyes'). On stage

Coborn dressed as a somewhat leery toff: fair enough, he also wrote 'The Man Who Broke the Bank at Monte Carlo'.

To give a black eye was to *darken someone's daylights* or *skylights* and to *get someone to go to bible class*, which pun referred to the well-known rowdiness and horseplay of a printer's 'chapel' or workshop. *Raspberry-jam* indicated an unfortunate double: black eyes and a bleeding nose (a *cranberry eye* was merely blood-shot, while *gooseberry eyes* are blank and lifeless), while a *pair of spectacles* resisted the blood. Blackness indicated a person *in mourning*. Thus the *full suit of mourning*, a pair of black eyes, *half-mourning*, a singleton (the bruise might have turned purple which fitted the hierarchy of Victorian costumes: half-mourning being that colour) and the *peeper in mourning*.

The late eighteenth century ascribed such wounds to a stereo-type: the drunken, fighting Irish. Thus the *Irish beauty*, a woman with a pair of black eyes and *Irish wedding*, a brawl, where, to quote Grose once again, 'black eyes are given instead of favours' and the *Irishman's coat of arms*, a black eye and a bloody nose. There were other coats of arms, given the make-up of the first Australian convict vessels, possibly Irish too: the *Botany Bay coat-of-arms*, a broken nose and black eyes, reflected the violence that was prevalent at the convict settlement; it was also known as a *colonial livery*. The painful eye and nose was also *Lord Northumberland's arms*, in this case the joke was on the red and black spectacle-like badge that is the basis of the Percy family, i.e. Lord Northumberland's arms.

The eye generates a number of slang phrases. Probably the best-known is the military coinage *eyes like pissholes in the snow* (variations include . . . *in a snowbank* and *two burnt holes in a blanket*). Such eyes, deeply sunken and often bloodshot, are taken to reflect a night of excess. This also left one with eyes *set at eight in the morning*, i.e. staring in different directions. To *have big eyes (for)* is to experience a great desire (for); *bedroom eyes*, *come-to-bed eyes* and *sweet eyes* indicate an unrestrained sexual come-on and another militarism, *a little bit of eyes right* (playing on the similar *bit of all right*) is an attractive girl.

Sore eyes can be *pabble-blinkers* (perhaps from *pebble*, one feels as if there is a small rock beneath the eyelid), *bung-eye* is an eye infection caused by flies, and *duck's meat* is mucus. To be *gravy-eyed* is to be bleary-eyed, and gives the nautical *gravy-eye*, the notoriously tedious 0400–0600 watch. *Bung eyes* protrude as do *bug eyes* and *glarum goggles*. To *eye-shoot* is to stare aggressively, possibly with a *coke stare*, the rigid, highly aggressive gaze that may overtake the more paranoid cocaine user. The *eye-limpet* (it sticks to the socket) was an artificial eye and the punning *guccis*, in gay South Africa, are bags under the eyes.

One eye and a winkle was a blind person or a person with one eye, and the *winkle* is presumably the penis. There is the *Nelson*: a score of 111 in cricket, the digits represent the much reduced admiral's 'one eye, one arm and one arsehole'. The link of a single eye to the penis is productive. It gives such images as *one-eyed bob*, the *one-eyed guardsman*, *one-eyed pants python*, *one-eyed rocket*, *one-eyed brother*, *one-eyed* or *hairy Cyclops* which is of course tautological, since all Cyclops are one-eyed, *one-eyed monster*, *one-eyed stag*, *one-eyed (wonder) worm* (or *one-armed trouser worm*) and the *one-eyed zipper fish*. The supreme example of the form, as fans of Barry Humphries' Aussie ex-pat Barry McKenzie will know, is the *one-eyed trouser-snake*, though Bazza is not responsible for its synonyms: the *one-eyed bed snake*, *one-eyed trouser mouse*, *tan trouser snake* and *trouser serpent*. That the hapless Bazza, one of life's great virgins, fails ever to make it *spit*, is quite another story.

Pox: Knocked by a French Faggot-Stick

Playing, rather than being doctors and nurses (see **Doctors & Nurses**) has a downside. At least for grown-ups. Not, thanks to developments in modern medicine, as far down as once it might have been, but pleasure still brings some possibility of pain. Those who revel in such outcomes proclaim the triumph of morality; the rest of us prefer to eschew superstition and reach for the penicillin. Either way what we have is STDs: sexually transmitted diseases.

Slang doesn't do morality. It does God and his boy Jesus, but only in terms of turning them upside down in its usual manner and furnishing the angry world with a range of words and phrases that, if you believed, would be listed under blasphemy, but on the whole come across as something of a joke: *'slight!* (God's light!), *'snails* (God's nails!), *gadswogs* (God's wounds!), plus *where the five 'n' arf?* based on the old measurement of 5.5 yards, a *rod*, and thus a rhyme with God.

The words 'morals' and 'morality', like the fugitive 'love', are conspicuous only by their absence. There are less than twenty-five instances of 'immoral' or 'immorality', and these, predictably, are men's judgement of women's choices. *Breechy*, for instance, usually used of cattle that are liable to break through the pasture fence; in this case it's the woman who 'jumps the pasture fence'.

164

As far as ethics are concerned it certainly doesn't lay down the law. (Those supposedly immoral women are if anything, in this male-orientated language, objects of approval and to be taken advantage of.) If it deals with a topic then it lays out a stall, nothing more. It is up to the speaker to buy, or walk on. Thus the vocabulary of venereal disease, the misery that devolves upon pleasure.

So alongside health and its administrators (see **Doctors & Nurses**), let us look from another angle at the physically ailing. Nor just any ailment, for that is not slang's choice. It deals, as we have noted, with mental problems, but slang does not really bother with such problems as the common cold. There's the rhyming slang *silver and gold* or *warrior bold*, and one can be *bunged up* while *to sit in the garden with the gate unlocked* means to catch a cold, but that's about it. There are a few terms for influenza (*dog fever*, *dog's disease*, the rhymes *inky blue* and *lousy lou*) and the Antipodean *wog* which has nothing to do with race but uses an earlier meaning: a germ or parasite, an insect, in other words a 'bug'. The two *wogs* are wholly different but, frustratingly, neither offers a concrete etymology. The illness may be linked to dialect's *wog*, to twitch, while the long-approved, but far from proven back-drop to the human, usually from the near East or Indian sub-continent, is '*w*esternized (or *w*ily) *o*riental *g*entleman'. That is if it isn't a clipping of *golliwog*, that distinctly non-PC blackface doll.

Of the great childhood diseases – chickenpox, mumps or measles – nothing. Only AIDS/HIV gets anything like attention, and that probably because slang sees it as sexually linked. Terms include *A-word*, *big A*, *cowie* (in Scotland), *gangster*, *the monster*, *the germ*, *the gift that keeps on giving*, *the package*, *the plague* (thus *plaguer*, a victim), *the virus*, *high five* (a *hiver* is living with the illness), and the inevitable rhyme: *shovels and spades*.

No. Our topic is *pox*. Once *pocks*, which was what indicated a variety of illnesses that revealed themselves via a rash of spots such as smallpox, cowpox or chickenpox. This is none of those. What it refers to was and remains syphilis, sometimes known as the 'great' or 'grand pox' and nicknamed for the first recorded time in 1503. As Francis Grose once branded the word *cunt*, 'a nasty name for a nasty thing'.

A moment's pause. There is the *clap clinic* and *clap shack* and *pox hospital*, and the late seventeenth century's *nimgimmer* who seems to be a *pox doctor*. But what of that mysterious figure, the *pox-doctor's clerk*? That flashy, over-dressed peacock of a man, against whom any male, irrespective of occupation, may be compared: males who are considered *done up*, *dressed up*, *got up* or *mockered-up like a pox-doctor's clerk*. Not only that but one might be *drunker than a pox-doctor's clerk*, *have a face like a pox-doctor's clerk*, *lucky as a pox-doctor's clerk* (which despite what we might assume meant very lucky) and, less so, *smell like a pox-doctor's clerk*, doused in cheap perfume and not so distant from the equally odiferous *tart's boudoir*. Did he exist? Did such specialists in venereal diseases even have clerks? Was he no more than a figurative evocation of some social horror? Regretfully, no illustrations appear online (a search offers a strange selection, the best being a plague doctor c. 1348: he seems to be dressed in a bird mask). We must accept that there is no answer. *Pox on't*!

When it comes to pox, we're talking France. The *French disease*, a neat piece of nationalist stereotyping that emerged with the publication in 1530 of a poem *Syphilis, sive Morbvs Gallicvs* ('Syphilis or the French disease'), by Girolamo Fracastoro (otherwise known as Hieronymus Fracastorius and living from 1483 to

1553), a physician, astronomer and poet from Verona. The poem tells the story of the shepherd Syphilus, supposedly the first sufferer from the disease. Fracastoro then used the term again – now as a definite piece of medical jargon – in his treatise *De Contagione* ('On Contagion', 1546). The poem arrived in English in 1686 when it was translated by the future poet laureate Nahum Tate with the title *Syphilis: or, a Poetical History of the French Disease*. The pox itself was long established.

There are possibly more Francophobe terms wherein modern slang's nudge-nudgery equates 'French' to fellatio, but the link to syphilis, found mainly around the late sixteenth and seventeenth centuries, offers a substantial list. There is *the Frenchman*, the *French gout, French disease, malady of France, French goods* (which can also be brandy, given the source of the liquor) and the *French pox*; the *French chillblains, French marbles, French measles, French cannibal, French morbus* and *French razor*. To *learn French* or *take French lessons* is to contract the disease, and *frenched* or *frenchified* means infected. The *French pig* refers to the disease in general, but specifically to the syphilitic pustule or bubo (thus *bube*, a generic for the illness and from *pintle*, the penis, which in turn goes back to Dutch *punt*, a point; a *pintle-blossom* was a pustule and *pintle-fever* VD in general) that indicates its existence. The *French crown*, otherwise *curse* or *gout*, and properly known as the *Corona Veneris*, focuses on the *crown*, a ring of spots that appears around the forehead. A *blow with a French faggot-stick* refers to the loss of one's nose through the advancing ravages of the illness, and one whose nose has already rotted away has been *knocked with a French faggot* (despite the modern slang use of *faggot* as homosexual, this means nothing more than stick and may thus be the origin of *stick*, VD, though not *up the stick*, where the stick is the penis and the phrase means pregnant). The only odd one out is *French fits*, which means delirium tremens, but even this may hint at the insanity attendant on syphilis; on the other hand it may suggest an excess of that quintessential French drink, brandy.

Why so French? Spain was the current national enemy and given that Europe's first cases of syphilis are linked to Naples (where it was contracted and then spread by French troops) such alternative slurs as the *Naples canker*, *scab* or *pox* are marginally more accurate. A *Neapolitan* designated one who carried the disease. Still, syphilis was not what slang-users primarily associated with the 'bum-firking Italian', a figure more generally linked to 'Italian tricks', i.e. sodomy. Nor had the cliché that made *French* a synonym for dirty/sexy yet arrived. The disease, first carried northwards by those French soldiers, has to be the primal 'dirt' and all else followed. One might have added oral sex, also 'dirty' for some, but that link came even later.

Straying briefly from English, the France / syphilis association was a cross-Europe phenomenon. Danes and Norwegians refer to *Franzoser*: the Frenchman, and *den franskesyge*: the French disease. In Poland it is *franca*, once more 'the Frenchman', while in Russia *frantzukaya boiezn* means the French disease, as does *francuzljiv* in Croatia, *o gallico* in Portuguese, *französische Krankheit* in Germany and *fransos* in Iceland. Spain, Italy, Slovakia, and speakers of Yiddish all use something similar. With so relentless an identification, it is hardly surprising that St Denis (in his more respectable guise the patron saint of France and of its capital city Paris) is also patron saint of syphilitics.

Nonetheless France hit back. Faced by the German *Franzosen* she retaliated with *prussiens*: 'Prussians', to characterise the disease, while *aller en Baviere*: 'to go to Bavaria' is to be treated for syphilis; an extra punch was given to the phrase by the pun on French *baver*, to drivel, a fate that tended to overtake advanced sufferers as the brain gradually imploded. Similarly *aller en Suede*: 'to go to Sweden', which meant to take the once popular sweating cure for syphilis, embodied an inbuilt pun, in this case between the proper name *Suede* and the French *suer*, to sweat. The French have also termed the illness the *Italian disease* and a pair of Italian cities provide the backdrop for Portugal's *mal de Napoles*, and France's *mal florentin*, respectively the maladies of Naples and of Florence. The *onguent napolitain*: 'Neapolitan ointment' was a salve, the active ingredient of which is mercury, which was used in the treatment of syphilis. Probably quite unconnected is the US term for Scandinavian immigrants: *salve eaters*.

It's a truly international pursuit. It just depends on those a given nation hates and like sport, an accusation of genital decay is a useful, if temporary substitute for war. Japan has *mankabassam*: 'the Portuguese sickness', and Portugal opts for *mal de Castilla*: 'the Castillian sickness', ancient Greece referred to the *korinthion chanon*: 'Corinthian ill', a knock at a people who were generally pilloried for their alleged decadence. England, as ever, targets Ireland, with *Irish mutton* and the *Irish button* (presumably a reference to the syphilitic bubo that develops in the groin; a *Welshman's button*, however, is an artificial fly, used by anglers). There was also the *Scottish fleas*, which underlined England's traditional disdain for Scotland as a land of infestations, known otherwise as *Louseland* and *Itchland*. Spain played its role as national enemy, which produced the *Spanish disease, needle, gout* or *pip*. This last is usually a disease of chickens, and the *bots*, with no national link, is also found, though this is properly a disease of horses caused by an infestation of botfly larvae in the digestive tract. In the county of Somerset any form of venereal disease was known as the *Welshman's hug*. The Dutch, who fought many bitter battles against Spanish rule, used *gezienhebben Spanje*: 'to have seen Spain', to mean that one was suffering, although the phrase could also mean to have suffered punishments other than venereal ones. The Netherlands also uses *Spaansche pokken*, Spanish pox. Germany backs up its excoriation of France with that of Spain, offering *spanische Krankheit*: the Spanish disease, and the polysyllabic *Spanischfliegenpflaster*: literally 'Spanish-fly plaster', but here a syphilitic blister, and possibly linked to *cantharides*, the alleged aphrodisiac known as *Spanish fly*, with its roots in Greek *cantharis*, the blister-fly.

Not every name has been nationalistic. To return, and stay with English, the aching symptoms gave the *bone-ache*, often extended by 'Neapolitan', the loss of the nose led to the nautical *break one's boltsprit*, and to lose one's hair was to *moult one's feathers*. A diseased whore who transmitted her own syphilis was thus a *barber*, which also played on the imagery of the barber's shaving water and the whore's vagina being 'hot'. To *piss out of a dozen holes* evokes the rotting penis (thus the contemporary *take* or *spring a leak*, to be infected), to *play a game at loll-tongue* was to have one's saliva checked for traces of syphilis (the treatment, salivation, was known as *sal*). We have the familiar *old joe* and the *old rale* or *rail* (possibly from dialect *rail*, to stagger) which notes the way in which the developing disease gradually impairs mobility. The *old dog* 'bites' the sufferer, while to be *one of the knights* projects the disease as weakening one's 'sword'. The belief that those who went on long sea voyages suffered from fevers, possibly intensified by the image of the genitals being in the 'southern' part of the body, gave to *go under the South Pole*, to suffer from syphilis or venereal disease. A last example was the deeply unpleasant *full hand, full house* or *nap hand*: card imagery that was defined as a simultaneous dose of both syphilis and gonorrhoea; sometimes body lice and/or pyorrhea joined the fun.

Where would we be without a *dose* of rhyming slang. It is not always clear which of these refer to syphilis or to gonorrhoea, given their relatively modern coinage, but no matter. Rhyming with pox are *band in the box*, *boots* or *shoes and socks*, *cardboard box*, *coachman on the box*, *goldilocks* and *jack* (*in the box*), which in turn gives *the jack*, and the state of being *jacked up*. Proper names include a pair of clergymen: *John Knox* (Scottish and Presbyterian) and *Ronald Knox* (English and Catholic), the music hall duo of *Nervo and Knox* (Jimmy Nervo and Teddy Knox, once members of the much-celebrated Crazy Gang, a staple of 1940s variety shows) and the journalist *Collie Knox*. Finally *Surrey*, *Tilbury* or *Whitehaven docks*. *Bang and biff* and *Will's whiff* (a long defunct miniature cigar) come from syph, *bumblee* from VD, and *handicap* and *horse and trap* from *clap*, which is usually gonorrhoea.

The *gentleman's complaint*, as some termed gonorrhoea, was and remains first and foremost the *clap*, occasionally *clapper*. The word comes from Old French *clapoir*, a venereal bubo, which also gives *clapoire* or *clapier*, a place of debauchery and the illness one can contract there. Standard English until the late sixteenth century, it starts appearing in cant/slang lists by 1800; in 1611 the *Dictionary of the French and English Tongues* defined clapier as a 'rabbits' nest' (as well as a name for 'old time Baudie houses') which thus punned on standard *coney*, a rabbit and slang's *cony*, both vagina and whore and both possible sources of disease. Clap gives *clappy*, suffering from venereal disease, *clapster*, a regular sufferer, and *clap-trap*, both vagina and brothel. The meaning of nonsense has nothing in common: it began life in the theatre where it was defined as any bit of business that milked the applause: it 'trapped the claps'. Coincidentally, slang's *applause,* gonorrhea, is a heavy-handed pun on clap. A *bullhead clap* was an extremely severe dose.

As well as the clap there was geography. Just as prostitution gave slang a succession of terms that depended on its current 'headquarters', e.g. *Fleet Street houri, Bankside lady, City Road African, Drury Lane vestal* and *Haymarket hector* (a pimp), venereal disease had its personalised London. Covent Garden yielded up *Covent Garden ague* or *gout. Drury Lane*, nearby, had *ague* too. (The *Covent Garden abbess* was a procuress or brothel-keeper and a *Covent Garden nun* or *lady* a whore.) Nor was it only London. There was the *Barnwell ague*, which came from Barnwell near Cambridge. Defined as 'a place of resort for characters of bad report' it gave rise to the University decree of 1675: 'Hereafter no scholar whatsoever [. . .] upon any pretence whatsoever, shall go into any house of bad report in Barnewell, on pain [. . .] of being expelled from the university.' The town of Tetbury, Gloucestershire, was similarly unsavoury: according to Captain Grose, a *Tetbury portion*, i.e. an inheritance,was 'A **** [cunt] and a clap.'

Gonorrohoea hurts. You *piss broken glass* or failing that *razor blades* or *pins and needles*; you could also have *picked up a nail*. It manifests itself by *tokens*, whether a discharge or gangrenous spots, and which one can *tip* to an unfortunate partner. What you see is a whitish discharge. For women this is either *the yellows* or *the whites*. Neither bode well. Thus the seventeenth-century news sheet *Mercurius Fumigosus*, telling in 1654 how 'Mistris Squirtington, so miserably troubled with the yellows, that she lives in perpetual fear lest her husband should act the Town-Bull of Smithfield, and ride every jade he comes near.' For men it was *gleet* or *gleat*, borrowed from old French *glette*, slime, filth, purulent matter and known to medicine as urethritis. Gleet may be linked to *gluts*, defined by the *Swell's Night Guide* of 1846 as 'to be sick of a mot', i.e. rendered ill by a woman.

The discharge has also been known as *glue, creamies, drip, drips* or *dripsy* and the disease is thus *the dripper*. The pus can also be a *running horse* or *nag*. Running meant oozing, while the horse referred to *horse-pox*, an especially severe strain of the disease. The *Mercurius Fumigosus* of May 1655 launched itself on an orgy of double entendres, mixing horse images and the slang sense of *ride*: to copulate. '[They will supply] Oysters ... to strengthen the backs of the Horse-coursers, that are Ranke Riders, In requitall whereof, they have promised to finde them a Teame of Running Naggs, to help them home with their Ware, which Running Naggs shall be so fleet, that they shall run faster than a Winchester Goose can flie.'

An *oyster* was a prostitute (or her vagina), *ware* meant the penis, and the *Winchester goose* or *Winchester pigeon* was no bird but VD and reminded people that the popular brothels of Southwark came under the jurisdiction of the Bishop of Winchester; abbreviated as *goose*, it was the basis of a reference to a well-known whore: 'No Goose bit so sore as Bess Broughton's'. (*Goose*, as in poke or tickle, is different: the image is of pecking.) If the disease produced spots, then it became a *botch*, a Biblical term meaning ulcer or plague-spot and found in Deut. 28:27 'The Lord will smite thee with the botch of Egypt, and with the emerods [i.e. haemorrhoids], and with the scab, and with the itch, whereof thou canst not be healed.'

The terminology did not always specify the problem. In many cases one simply *cops a* non-specific *dose*. Among the older synonyms are the *crinkums* or *grincomes* (among a wide range of spellings) which come from the *crinkum-crankum*, the vagina in slang and a narrow twisting passage in standard English, and which emphasises the sense of twisting pain that accompanies the disease, and the *flapdragon*, which plays on a game: *flap-dragon* or *snapdragon*, in which, explained Samuel Johnson, 'they catch raisins out of burning brandy and, extinguishing them by closing the mouth, eat them'. In this case it is the penis that is 'hot'. *Haddums* comes from the punning phrase 'been at had 'em and come home by Clapham'. There is *Venus's curse* and *Cupid's itch* plus *scrubbado*, from standard English *scrub*, 'the itch' – the Spanish suffix *-ado*, gives an underpinning of racist stereotyping, while Latin's *noli me tangere*, 'don't touch me' was popular in Scotland, although the *Scotch* or *Welsh fiddle* were English slurs. The *fiddle* or *violin* also symbolised the vagina, thus the seven-teenth-century riddle commencing: 'I've two holes in my Belly and none in my Bum / Yet me, with much pleasure, Italians do thrum . . .'

More recent terms have included the *African toothache*, *Chinese rot* and plain *cock-rot;* the nineteenth-century's Lingua Franca gave *kertever cartzo*, which comes from *cattivo cazzo*, 'bad cock'. There is *yook* (perhaps from the exclamation *yuck!*), and *the brophys*, an Irishism which used the nickname of the supposed insects, relations of body lice or crabs, which allegedly carried the disease. The days when the London street Piccadilly was thronged with prostitutes (known as *Edies*, their smarter sisters in Mayfair proper were *Toms*) gave *Piccadilly cramp*. There are more, but perhaps the most unnerving was *lobstertails* or *lobster-toes*, African-American terms from around 1960. In *Deep Down In The Jungle*, his collection of 'toasts' (narrative poems usually featuring pimps and whores and created and recited in prison), Roger D. Abrahams offered this excerpt from the adventures of the trickster-hero Shine (itself a term for a black man): 'He went to a place called 'Dew-drop Inn.'/ He asked the broads to give him cock for a lousy fin. / She took Shine upstairs and she gave him a fuck, and all this pats. / He came out with the syphs, the crabs, lobstertoes, and a hell of a case of the claps.' Quite why a lobster is unknown, perhaps its colour, perhaps its nipping claws; *cock*, in this context, meant the vagina, as it does in the Southern US, and refers to the *coquille*, a cockleshell or cowrie.

Words that meant being infected focus on heat. The burning sensation in one's *dropping member*, a penis that could no longer function due to pain. First recorded is *burn*, which would give the cynical nautical joke 'to be sent out a sacrifice and come home a burnt offering', to be sent off to fight for one's country, but to return carrying venereal disease. To *burn one's poker* or *one's tail* (both meaning penis) was to catch a venereal disease. The *flame* or the *fire* were VD itself, to give it to one's partner was to *set them on fire* and those who suffered, sometimes known as *fireplugs, passed through the fire*. Still with fire, or at least the light it casts, g*lymmar* or *glimmer* meant a lantern (and much later an electric torch); for our purposes it became a dose of clap. Thus in 1612 the playwright Thomas Dekker, in his treatise of criminal language *O Per Se O* noted that 'however cold the weather be, their female furies come hotly and smoking . . . carrying about them Glymmar in the Prat (fire in the touch-bore) by whose flashes oftentimes there is Glymmar in the Jocky.' *Prat* being buttocks and thus here the vagina, *jocky*, from *jock*, the penis; the *touch-bore*, more usually *touch-hole*, was the vagina, both terms meaning in standard English the vent of a firearm, through which the charge is ignited.

To be infected was to *knap* [i.e. catch] *the glim*. To *pepper* was to infect and those who suffered badly were *peppered*, sometimes extended to an invasion of crab-lice. One who was *pepper-proof* was (temporarily) free of problems. One could be *clawed off*, defined as 'swingingly Poxt'. Covent Garden has been mentioned, here we find *break one's shins against Covent Garden rails*, yet another synonym for venereal misadventures. Modernity, as all too often, is less inventive; to give someone the clap is simply to *fuck them up*.

Once infected one *has a cold*, is *fly-blown, hot-tailed, loaded (up)*, *piled (for French velvet), placket-stung*, where *placket* refers to the slit at the top of an apron or petticoat and thus the vagina beneath) and *in for the plate*, a laboured play on horseracing jargon: horses that qualify for the *plate* (the main race) have first won the *heat*. Heat returns in *sunburned* and *warm* (and one can *warm* someone else). The *burning pestle* is a diseased penis, and the *knight of the burning pestle* a sufferer; Beaumont and Fletcher used it for a play title in 1607. Persisting in the imagery is *scald*. This began life meaning scabbed, afflicted with the 'scall' (any scaly or scabby disease of the skin, especially of the scalp; *dry scall* was psoriasis, *humid* or *moist scall* was eczema). In what is the first attempt at a slang glossary, Robert Copland's *Hye Way to the Spyttel House* (c.1535) the porter at Bart's Hospital describes the beggars crowded round the doorway as 'Scabby and scuruy, pocke eaten flesh and rynde, / Lowsy and scalde, and pylled lyke as apes, / With scantly a rag to couer theyr shapes.' The disease itself was *scalder*.

There was also the idea of being the victim of a weapon. The seventeenth century borrowed the sea's *shot* or *hulled between wind and water*. One could equally *shoot* one's partner in the same place. The nautical phrase refers to that part of a ship's side that is sometimes above water and sometimes submerged, in which part a shot is particularly dangerous. World War I added *cop, get* or *stop a packet*, which usually meant to get killed or wounded. According to *Songs and Slang of the British Soldier* (1930) by Brophy and Partridge, the origin was the 'packet' of gauze and lint that comprised the First Field Dressing that would be applied to a wound.

Where did it come from? The assumption was a working girl. She could be a *queer mort*, where *queer* was an all-purpose negative with zero gender connotations and *mort* a woman; she could be a *frigate on fire*, which played on *frig*, to have sex, on *fire*, VD, and on the common equation of whores, 'sailing' the urban streets, with ships. If she was diseased then she was *high*, as in the stench of rotten meat (the *meat* being both the girl and her genitals), or in the modern Caribbean, having *a gun in her baggy*. Captain Grose's dictionary, ever-anecdotal, explains the practice of *docking*, meted out to such unfortunates. It was 'a punishment inflicted by sailors on the prostitutes who have infected them with the venereal disease, it consists in cutting off all their clothes, petticoat, shift and all, close to their stays, and then turning them out into the street'. *Dock* had no seafaring link but in standard English meant to cut off the *tail*. Like the apprentices who regularly pillaged and burned the brothels where they were otherwise such enthusiastic customers, the sailors had no problems with victim-blaming.

Finally, treatment. There was no penicillin. Instead there was *Mother Cornelius' tub* otherwise known as the *Cornelian tub*. Whether there was an actual Mother Cornelius is unknown; she could have been a nurse, but equally possibly, since such women were often known as *Mother* (e.g. Mother Damnable, whose house was in Kentish Town, Mother Midnight and Mother Knab-Coney, i.e. 'snatch-sucker'), a brothel-keeper.

On the other hand there is a mention of a male Cornelius in *Travels to Bohemia* by John Taylor, 'The Water Poet' (his day-job was ferrying passengers across the Thames): 'Or had Cornelius but this tub, to drench / His clients that had practis'd too much French.' Other theories suggest the physician Henry *Cornelius Agrippa* (1496–1535) a leading advocate of hot baths for medicinal purposes; the possible use of a hard dense wood, necessary to withstand the heavy salt brine used in 'pickling' patients, known as *cornel-wood* and 'celebrated for its hardness and toughness, whence it was anciently in request for javelins, arrows, etc.' (*OED*.) There were also possible puns on *cornel* and the 'cornuted' cuckold, implying either than the sufferer has been given not just *the horn* (the symbol of cuckoldry) but also the clap, or that one's current incapacity is the result of one's own *horniness*. The tub was also the *powdering tub*, borrowed from the standard English name for the tub in which the flesh of dead animals was pickled or 'powdered'. Some doctors believed that vinegar was a cure and as well as internal or external use suggested that the mercury used in the treatment of syphilis should first be boiled in vinegar: those who received such treatment were *yeomen of the vinegar bottle*. To be *laid up in Job's dock* was to be spending time in the venereal disease ward at St Bartholomew's Hospital and like the Bible's Job, suffering. As for the *House of Lords*, used in America, one can only attribute this to republicanism.

Funny Foreign Food

S LANG CAN, BUT these pages cannot, cover all the nationalist and racist vileness on offer. It would take a book and indeed in 1996 I wrote it; punning as ever, it was entitled *Words Apart*. The solitary review suggested that so unpleasant was the content it might have been best left unsaid. This was perhaps optimistic, and today's resurgent hatreds suggest a reissue, probably much expanded. Race and nation and alongside them religion are among slang's great stimulators. They cannot be ignored. Let us at least take refuge in a subset: the way in which the braggadocio of one nation's myths blend into the stereotypes of another's 'typical' foods. The way slang uses foods for insult. Call it a mixed grill (and that's *grill*, as in taking the mick).

Eat to live? Live to eat? The choice is yours and slang plays no favourites. Food, or the imagery that it offers, plays a major role in the vocabulary. Taking in compounds, phrases and allied formations, the simple word *meat*, for instance, has 202 meanings, *fish*, 144, and *fruit* 84; *vegetables*, perhaps predictably in slang's ostentatiously macho world, a mere half- dozen. Go to individual foodstuffs and the story continues: *beef* offers 150 meanings, *apple* 90, *cabbage* 66, *banana* 55, *chicken* 41 and so on.

Meanwhile, straight across the lexical street, we find another human appetite: national pride. Patriotism, the scoundrel's ultimate refuge as the great Dr Johnson put it. That nationalism notches up the terminology will offer no surprises. Each against all the rest is the rule, and there's always been time for slang to take advantage of the appearance of a new national enemy. The *French* (117 terms), the *Dutch* (104), the *Spanish* (41), the *Germans* (21), the *Italians* (16) . . . and for that matter, for the English English speakers, the *Scottish* and *Welsh*, although of England's neighbours only the *Irish* are considered worthy of concerted assault with 126 (the Scots notch up a mere sixteen).

It would be good to stop short at national borders but slang works with the broadest of brushes and nation can easily segue into race and thence religion and all are equally identifiable by what they consume. So like slang itself, we must declare the borders open. In a perfect, or at least efficiently categorised world we could eschew the Jews. Anti-semitism, never far away, is gleefully and openly flaunting itself once more and I see no reason to offer its advocates, whether left or right, a vocabulary. Let those among them who are literate grub for their own foulness. They will find more than enough in slang. We would extend our free pass to Islam, though that may come by default: such delicacies (the mythical sheep's eyes notwithstanding) as are considered 'Islamic' do not seem to have played a part in our savaging of that faith. (Such an oversight is doubtless down to ignorance. It is hard otherwise to believe that slang would have missed the possibilities of cous-cous, although, thanks to the peerless *Roger's Profanisaurus*, we do have the *badly packed kebab*: 'An untidy vagina that looks appetising only after ten pints.')

Nor would we have to consider people of colour, whose role in slang's vocabulary of vilification outweighs even that of the

Christ-killers. We would stick to nations, who, we may assume are big enough to stand up by themselves. It is in the nature of Nation A to disdain Nations B to Z. Slang has always capitalised on this. The word *barbarian*, as used by Greeks and Romans, suggested those who lacked the civilised attainments of Greece and Rome, and comes allegedly from an echoic use of the sound *ba-ba-ba*, the stammering mispronunciation of Greek or Latin. To stick to national entities also remedies an omission: slang's seeming inability to critique anyone seen as 'white'. At least on the grounds of their whiteness. The term *white*, after all, meant upright, honourable, trustworthy and much akin and it has only been relatively recently that this has been said with the necessary irony. Resisting slang's vocabulary of racial and religious abuse also sidesteps the inevitable howls of those, besotted with the masochistic self-martyrdom of identity politics, who have wilfully discarded the ability to differentiate between the messenger and their message.

It is not a perfect world. So what follows, the use by slang of foods and those who eat them to conjure a lexis of loathing, is all-embracing. Everybody's ass, as the comedian Lenny Bruce once made clear, is up for grabs. Everybody's palate too.

National slurs are based on establishing then reinforcing the concept of 'the other' and what better means than the other's food, in its 'funny' and 'foreign' incarnation. What might otherwise be wholly appealing is rendered quite unpalatable. Gastro-nationalism, as it were, gets the benefit of several antagonistic worlds: not simply racial difference, but those ever-absorbing bones of contention, manners and taste. The cartoonist James Gillray had it down: robust *John Bull* gorges on a mighty side of beef, scrawny *Lewis Frog* can only pick at something green, quite probably his namesake, and almost certainly engulfed in garlic. What you are, as the old 1960s slogan used to proclaim, is what you eat, and never more so than in this arena of squabbling particularism. In some ways, of course, it is also a reverse on the traditional snobberies of consumption, in other words it's not so much a matter of whether or not you know how to eat, say, an artichoke, but whether or not you'd want to be seen ingesting the wretched alien object in the first place.

As is usual with slang, irrespective of type, there are certain 'inevitable' stereotypes: the *chilli-chomping* Mexicans, the British *rosbifs*, French *frogs* and German *potato-eaters* – each locked into the demands of their stomachs, but no one, whatever their personal culinary preferences, has any monopoly here. With so many contending 'dishes' on offer, our best resort is to read the menu.

Soup (best known for the neutral *in the soup*) is pretty much limited to the French, and specifically French Canadians who are known variously as *Johnny-peasoup*, *Jean Potage*, *Johnny Soup*, *French-peasoup*, *peasoup*, and *peasouper*. Quite why they crop up remains a mystery, but such immigrants may (or may not) have fascinated the American gangster Dutch Schultz, whose last words – a long, rambling and ultimately disjointed tirade – requested, 'Come on, open the soak duckets; the chimney sweeps. Talk to the sword. Shut up, you got a big mouth! Please help me to get up! Henry! Max! Come over here. French Canadian bean soup. I want to pay. Let them leave me alone.' If anyone knew, all lips were zipped. On the other side of the Great Lakes America offers *metzel*, a German immigrant, from *Metzelsuppe*, a soup made with sausage. Still in America the *Borsht Belt* describes that part of the Catskill Mountains where the great Jewish resort hotels were once bursting with vacationers from New York City. The name comes from allying a staple starter, *Borscht* – chilled beetroot soup with sour cream – to their clientele. Presumably it has shifted to the menus of the Russian restaurants now pushing for space on Long Island's Brighton Beach.

After soup, pasta, and in particular macaroni.

Pasta, literally paste, i.e. flour moistened with water or milk and kneaded, comes from the Greek πασταί (*pastai*): barley porridge, via a Latin use that meant 'a small square piece of a medical preparation'. The usual story is that Marco Polo brought it back from China, where it appeared in the form of noodles, at the end of the thirteenth century but the reality is that Italy, Germany, France, Japan, China and Korea each lay claim and all cases rest. No matter: pasta, in its many and varied forms, remains a staple of Italian cooking and pasta, or at least its two best-known varieties – spaghetti and macaroni – has become synonymous with Italians too. *Spaghetti* itself, plus *spaghetti-bender, spaghetti-eater, spaghetti-head* and the abbreviation *spag* all mean Italian. With garlic-flavoured sauce it becomes an *Italian hurricane* (the garlic itself is *Italian perfume*). The *spaghetti western*, of course, is any of those movies, pioneered by Sergio Leone at Cinecittà in Rome, and initially showcasing the young, monosyllabic Clint Eastwood, which depend on maximum violence, minimum chat and the moodiest of scores. *Spaghettiland* can mean Italy while an *Italian special,* or less affectionately a *wop special,* means a dish of spaghetti in the world of short-order cooking. It is possible that *spick,* used of both Italians and Hispanics, comes from *spiggoty,* which takes us back to spaghetti, though a case has been made for the immigrant's apology: 'no spicka de English'. Yiddish *lukshen,* noodles, means Italian, as does *ice-creamer,* from ambulant *gelati* salesmen, as did the once self-evident *banana peddler* and the *baloney-bender*, which refers to Bologna sausage.

As for w*op* (and its feminine *wopalina*) there's nothing culinary, other than its furthest roots. It probably comes from Latin *uappu*, literally bad wine and by extension, and used as such by Horace, a good-for-nothing. This moved on to Spanish *guapo*, a dandy, and when Spain occupied the island, was adopted in Sicily where *guappu* meant arrogance, bluster and unpleasantness and in time would be used by immigrants to the US to characterise their Italian work bosses. The work the immigrants did was 'guappu work' and guappu metonymised to mean the workers themselves. (In black America *work like a wop* meant to work very hard.) Clipping *guappu* to *guapp'* we have wop. We also have the rhyming slang *grocer's shop*.

Of all pastas, slang has best loved *macaroni*. The *mac* in *mac and cheese*, but much, much older. Linguistically it boasts the longer pedigree. It crossed from the Italian kitchen into the English dictionary with the institution of the *Macaroni Club*, which, as Lord Hertford explained in 1764, is composed of 'all the travelled young men who wear long curls and spying-glasses'. The travelling, suggests the *OED*, probably gave the members a taste for foreign foods, hence the name. They dressed extravagantly – towering blue-powdered wigs, red high-heeled shoes – and gambled for high stakes. Their club, Almacks, became today's Brooks. The essayist Joseph Addison attempted to make a link with another Italian word, *maccherone* in its senses of 'blockhead, fool, mountebank' (and an earlier use of macaroni did mean a jolly fool, usually Italian) but it does not exist; Addison was perhaps writing facetiously. The macaroni, delighted as he was in his own image, was never popular. In 1770 the *Oxford Magazine* noted that 'a kind of animal, neither male nor

female, [has] lately started up amongst us. It is called a Macaroni.'
It talks, added the magazine, 'without meaning, it smiles without pleasantry, it eats without appetite, it rides without exercise,
it wenches without passion'; Horace Walpole, in 1774 when the
craze had passed, remarked dismissively, 'They have lost all their
money . . . and ruin nobody but their tailors.' By the end of the
nineteenth century it meant no more than 'an over-dressed, or
gaudily dressed person', an effeminate fop. More recently the
term has dropped all references to fashion and like spaghetti
means simply 'an Italian'. In Australian slang it has meant
nonsense or meaningless talk.

Fish

As with the Jews and pork, so the Catholics and meat, an item
which, for the truly pious, is off-limits on Friday. Fish, on the
other hand, is mandatory. Such fish-days, or fasting days once
included Wednesdays too, and were – religion aside – a way of
dealing with the realities of Medieval and Tudor economics.
Thus *fish-eater*, *guppy-gobbler*, *mackerel-snapper* and *mackerel-
snatcher* all mean Roman Catholic.

That said, aside from the *conch* (from the Greek *koncha*: a
cockle or mussel) which has served variously as a nickname for
the natives of the Bahamas, for West Indians in America and
for a 'poor White' native, often a fisherman, living in the
Florida Keys or North Carolina, the remaining fish terms
concentrate on the herring. In Canada a *herring-choker* is a
Newfoundlander or a native of any of the Maritime Provinces;
the same term is used in America for a Swede. Still in the US,
a *herring-snapper* is both a Swede and occasionally a Catholic,
while a *herring-punisher* is a Jew and a *herring-destroyer* or

herring-choker a Norwegian. In the West Indies a *herring-Jew* is a Jewish or Syrian immigrant, referring to those that made their fortunes peddling salt-fish. Jews themselves call a herring a *Litvack*, a Lithuanian, a reference to the Lithuanian and Ukrainian Jews who were so fond of the fish. A *Dutch red* is a smoked Dutch herring and a *pickle-herring* a Dutchman. The *herring pond*, of course, is the Atlantic (although *to cross the pond at the King's expense* referred to transportation to Australia). Nicknames for the herring, masking its common-ness with a variety of terms that reflect a rather more luxurious table, are *Alaska turkey, Billingsgate pheasant, Californian pheasant, Crail capon, Digby chicken, Dunbar wether, Glasgow magistrate, Gourock ham, Halifax mutton, North Sea rabbit, Peruvian quail, Taunton turkey* and *Yarmouth capon*, all referring to centres of the herring industry. The *Californian* links the herring's 'red', i.e. gold colour with the Californian Gold Rush, while Catholic Ireland's *Protestant herring* is not fit to eat. The cod, much-beloved by Bostonians, is an *Irish goose*.

Meat

Like *fish*, which in mainstream slang can refer both to a woman or her vagina (and indeed carries a wide variety of alternative definitions), *meat* also comes with sexual overtones, in this case extended to racist fantasies. *Dark-meat, black-meat,* a *piece of dark meat,* a *hot piece* (*of dark meat*) and a *rare piece of dark meat* can all signify a black woman, viewed invariably as a sex object. *White* or *light meat* can mean just the same of her white sister. But in terms of meat as food rather than, as the sex-related US slang term has it *PEEP* ('perfectly elegant eating pussy'), the language throws up a whole platter of possibilities.

To continue in the world of black America, *nigger steak* is liver (substituting cheap offal for the more expensive 'white' cut), while the short-order chef's *nigger and halitosis* is steak and onions. *Alligator-bait* or *'gator-bait* refers viciously to any black human being, especially a child; an *Aussie steak* (at least to the Australian army) is a piece of mutton, predictable, given the vast number of sheep 'Down Under'. A *Dutch steak*, taking Dutch for Deutsch, is a hamburger, while a *German dog* refers to the great American creation, the hot dog, and a *French pie*, presumably as a result of some heavy-handed culinary humour, is stew (France's *Strasbourg pie* was filled with foie gras). The West Indian *nyam-dog*, however, is a Chinese person, from *nyam*: food and a reference to a stereotyped appetite for canines. *Goulash* means a Hungarian. In the world of poultry, a *German duck* (in late eighteenth/early nineteenth century England) was half a sheep's head boiled with onions; the term (which in less appetising contexts referred to a bed-bug) acknowledged the popularity of the dish amongst the German sugar-refiners and confectioners of London's East End.

Sauerkraut, a form of pickled cabbage and served, as a larger dish, with a variety of boiled pig-meats, gives *kraut*, still popular as a nickname for a German, *kraut-eater, kraut stomper* and *krauthead. Krautland* is Germany. *Sausage* also meant a German in late-nineteenth-century England and *baloney* or *boloney*, meaning nonsense or rubbish and which is generally accepted as referring to a Bologna sausage (although the *OED* claims the connection is 'conjectural'), appeared in the 1920s. Against the Oxford verdict, lexicographer Ramon Adams refers in his dictionary of the American West, *Western Words* (1968) to 'bologna bulls: animals of inferior quality whose meat is used to make Bologna sausage', while Eric Partridge suggested Romani *peloné*, testicles; thus *balls* or *ballocks*, which can also mean nonsense. The baloney's shape leads to penis, and a range of sexual phrases meaning either masturbate (*beat the balogna, bop one's baloney*), have sex (*hide the baloney, ride the baloney pony*), anal sex (a *boloney colonic*) or fellatio (*smoke the baloney pony*).

Classic Mexican dishes, perhaps through their popularity as fast food, seem especially prone to negative and nationalist equations. *Chilli, chile* or *chili con carne* (a stew of Mexican origin containing minced beef flavoured with chillies) gives several terms for Mexicans, who are thus disdained as *chilis, chili chokers, chili eaters, chili-pickers, chili-beans, chilli-bellies* and *chilli-chompers*. A *chili chaser* is a US border patrolman, employed, absent the Trumpian wall, to prevent Mexicans entering the country illegally. Chilli itself does not, popular belief to the contrary, refer to the nation, Chile, but is a Mexican word, in place long before the Europeans arrived. Other Mexican favourites give more grounds for sneers. The *taco* (a Mexican snack comprising a fried, unleavened cornmeal pancake or tortilla filled with seasoned mincemeat, chicken, cheese, beans) gives *taco-eater, taco-head* and *taco-bender*. (A *taco wagon* is an automobile with the rear end 'chopped', i.e. lowered and seen as a Mexican creation.) The *enchilada* (literally 'seasoned with chilli', and in practice a tortilla served with a chilli-flavoured sauce) gives *enchilada-eater*; peppers in general lead to *pepper, pepper-gut* and (*hot*) *pepper-belly*; a *hot-tamale* (in culinary terms made of crushed Indian corn, flavoured with pieces of meat or chicken, red pepper, etc., wrapped in corn-husks and baked) is an attractive girl. Chilli is also used figuratively to mean second-rate (since Mexican) and thus gives a *chili chump, chili pimp, chili-bowl pimp, chili-mac* (no relation to pasta but from *mack*, a pimp and ultimately from the Dutch *makelaar*, a merchant), a pimp who has only one girl working for him or an inexperienced pimp. Such a pimp may be of any background, but the reference is to the supposed incompetence of small-time Mexican pimps.

For a bird of such weighty stolidity, sitting stuffed and uncomplaining on so many Christmas and Thanksgiving tables, the turkey has a surprisingly confusing background. In the first place it suffers from a fundamental misnomer: it doesn't come from Turkey. Its first appearance seems to have been as the *Guinea-cock* or *Guinea-fowl*, known to Greeks and Romans alike as *meleagris*. The reference to Guinea reflects the fact that the Portuguese began importing the bird from Guinea, in West Africa. The synonym *turkey-cock* appeared in the sixteenth century, and in turn underpinned the fact that Guinea, at that time, was under Turkish rule. The sixteenth century also saw, in 1518, the conquest of Mexico by Spain; among the booty the Spaniards enjoyed was the bird that would become known as the American turkey, and which had already been domesticated for some time. When Carl von Linné (1707–78), better known by his Latinised name Linnaeus, set about classifying flora and fauna, he took the African name, *Meleagris*, and gave it to the Mexican bird. Its African cousin, a substantially smaller, slenderer creature, remained today's *Guinea-fowl*.

None of which has much bearing on the naming of the turkey around the world, but might cast a little light on what otherwise appears a rather confused system. The English turkey itself sets the pattern, leading generations into the erroneous belief that the bird began life in the eastern Mediterranean. France's cant term *Jesuite* refers to the original importers of the bird: Jesuit missionaries. The majority of other names attach it to 'India', or perhaps (with a little more accuracy) 'the (West) Indies', which might just about stretch to Mexico. Thus the French *coq-d'Inde* or *dindon*, the German *Indischer Hahn*, the Italian *gallo d'India* and the Greek *indianos*, which can also mean 'Red' Indian. The same 'Indian' image persists in Arabic and in Turkish itself, where the bird is *dajaj Hindi*. Both Dutch and Germans underline the theory with *Kalkoen* and *Calecutischer Hahn* (the 'Calcutta hen'). Indeed, the eighteenth-century Italian traveller Padre Paolino believed that Calcutta, or Calicut as it then was, meant 'Castle of the Fowls'. Back in the States Native Americans, in the eighteenth century, referred to turkey (and venison) as a *White man's dish*.

The slang use of *turkey*, meaning a disaster or flop, emerged in American showbiz jargon in the 1920s, when it was cited in *Variety* magazine as 'a third rate production' and was known to professionals as a *turkey show*, a touring show, usually burlesque, mounted at a moment's notice and staffed by a third-rate cast, even stage-struck amateurs. This bit of theatre jargon would seem to be the origin of the slightly later *turkey*: a stupid, slow, inept, or otherwise worthless person; in both cases the image is of a large, waddling creature, of no real worth. *Turk*, meaning an Irish immigrant (*Greek* was synonymous) was sometimes expanded to *turkey*. The synonymous *saltwater-turkey* underpinned the journey from Ireland, across the 'saltwater' Atlantic. Yet here again the turkey may be indicating a false trail. If one sense of *turk*, a low-class whore (with its synonym *mahomet*) and others focused on sex, notably anal sex, do seem lodged in the eastern Mediterranean, another, an unpleasant boor, may equally come from the Irish *torc*, a boar or hog. Food, yes, but *meleagris*, not at all.

An unarguable Irish connection reappears in *Irish turkey*, meaning corned (UK: salt) beef and cabbage, a classic 'Irish' dish and one in which the image of poverty (as with various herring names) is deliberately contrasted with the presumed 'luxury' of eating turkey. Widely popularised via the US comic strip, 'Jiggs and Maggie' (properly *Bringing Up Father*, launched by George McManus in 1913) and sometimes known as a *Jiggs dinner*, the term is first recorded as one of the treats laid out in the ballad 'Rafferty's Party', in the *Donnybrook-Fair Comic Songster* of 1863. The dish is also known facetiously as *la bullie Hibernian* (*bullie* as in French *boullie*, boiled, and sharing an origin with *bully beef*), pretentious menu French for a distinctly plebeian dish that is also known as an *Irishman* or simply a *boiled dinner* (a meal traditionally eaten on St Patrick's Day). The Irish do no better out of *Irish horse*, which refers to tough, undercooked salt beef (especially as served to sailors) although that, in the gay lexicon, can also stand for an impotent penis. *Junk*, another nautical name for salt beef, means the genitals too though perhaps coincidentally. Only the *Irish wager* (or a *buttock and trimmings*), an eighteenth-century bet based on a rump of beef and a dozen bottles of claret, improves the national image. Normal service is resumed with *chaw* or *chawbacon* both of which mean variously a yokel, a peasant and an Irish immigrant. Finally *banjo*, an Australian coinage, refers both to the shovel wielded by so many of these immigrants (otherwise known as the *Irish banjo* and the *idiot stick*), and to a shoulder of mutton.

Find a weak point and exploit it: this is slang's mantra. The pig works as a problem-free food for millions. But not for all. Two of the three Peoples of the Book have chosen to avoid it. Whether this is based on the prevalence of pork-borne tape-worm in hot countries, or the anthropological theory that casts the pig as a 'marginal' animal, is still debated. Muslims, for whom the creature is also off the menu, seem to have avoided porcine labelling (if not the pigs' heads tossed at mosques), but as for the Jews . . .

'Let the goyim sink their teeth into whatever lowly creature crawls and grunts across the face of the dirty earth, we will not contaminate our humanity thus . . . Let them eat eels and frogs and pigs and crabs and lobsters; let them eat vulture, let them eat ape-meat and skunk if they like – a diet of abominable creatures well befits a breed of mankind so hopelessly shallow and empty-headed as to drink, to divorce and to fight with their fists . . . Thus saith the kosher laws, and whom am I to argue that they're wrong.' Thus also saith Philip Roth's fictional Alexander Portnoy of *Portnoy's Complaint* (1969), and along with circumcision and a big nose, nothing defines the Jew like this abstention from pork. How could slang resist? As in the 'jokes' that term blacks *snowballs*, the charm is apparently in the opposition. The pig is *the Hebrew's enemy* and pork and its other by-products *Jew food*, while the Jew himself is a *porker*, *porky* or *pork-chopper*. In the language of America's short-order cooks, a *sheeny's funeral* is roast pork. *Sheeny* being a Jew and possibly from the Yiddish *shayner Yid*. This term, meaning a pious (literally 'beautiful-faced') Jew was originally congratulatory, but as assimilation progressed, became used by the sophisticated to mock the new immigrants, still tied to their old-fashioned ways. The first half of the phrase, which the 'uncultured' Jews pronounced *sheena* rather than the more Germanic *schön*, was taken up by gentile Jew-baiters to create *sheeny* (and thus World War I soldier use: *sheeny*, a careful, extra-economical man).

Beyond Jewry, where pork presents no further difficulties, the pig and its processing give *smokey* and *smoked ham*, for a Native American; *pork-chop*, for an African American and *Pork and Beans*, a term that means Portuguese, both from the approximate assonance and from the fact that during World War I this appeared to be their troops' staple ration.

Other than Scotland, otherwise known as *haggisland*, from the haggis (sheep or calf offal minced with suet and oatmeal, seasoned, and boiled like a large sausage in the maw of the animal) which is seen as a typically Scottish dish (although prior to 1800 it was equally popular south of the border), Britain, or rather England is the country of beef. France's *rosbif* sums up the type, and the Dutch add *Engelschgaar*: the 'English way' when they mean undercooked or half-raw. The English have also been termed *beefeaters* (from as early as 1620), mixing the animal with the uniformed custodians of the Tower of London: the Yeomen of the Guard. These developed from the Beefeaters of the Guard, a name that referred, not especially kindly, to an earlier use of *beefeater* (or *loafeater*): a well-fed menial who earned his board and keep. Beefeater was even extended to describe a briefly fashionable woman's hat, modelled on those worn by the Yeomen.

Finally the East, which gives *chow*, meaning both food and a Chinese person and which comes from the Cantonese *cha'ao*: to fry. Thus *Chowmeinland* is China, referring to *chow mein*, the artificial dish concocted by America's mid-nineteenth century Chinese immigrants as a sop to those unsophisticated Western palates who nonetheless wanted some ersatz Chinese food. *Chop suey*, which slang has adopted to mean a Chinese person or restaurant, is another piece of fakery. A dish of stir-fried meat and vegetables, created by Chinese chefs for their Western customers, it plays no part in any Asian cuisine, but was seen as adequate for the Western palate. The original Chinese is *shapsui*, 'mixed bits'. Irrespective of geography *Jap hash*, literally 'Japanese food' (*hash* originally meaning a mess or jumble), is in fact Chinese food while *egg roll*, still in the Eastern context, while ostensibly another form of Chinese food, refers to one of

America's most recent groups of Far Eastern immigrants, the Koreans.

With a very few exceptions – *black bean*, a black person, *nigger bean*, a dark bean – beans primarily mean Mexican. *Bean-eater* and *beaner* have branded Mexican immigrants for a century. The same terms have been grafted onto the Cubans who have been appearing, in Florida rather than California or Texas, since the 1960s. Combinations with beaner give *beaner shoes*: huaraches, the typical Mexican sandals and *beaner wagon*: an old, dilapidated car seen as the basic form of immigrant transport. *Frijole-guzzler*, based on another Mexican dish, also means Mexican. The jargon of short-order cooking gives *Mexican strawberries*, reddish-coloured beans and the *Mexican navy*, as in the order 'a bowl of fire and Mexican navy': a plate of chilli and beans. Mexico notwithstanding, North America has its own bean-orientated enclave: Boston, Massachusetts. 'Good old Boston,' as John Bossidy's nineteenth-century doggerel put it, 'the home of the bean and the cod.' Bostonians were also termed *bean-eaters* by 1800 while Boston itself is still known as *Bean Town* to American truckers. The one anomaly, though it blends two 'poor/stupid' stereotypes, is *Irish nachos*, fried potato wedges and (refried) beans (rather than the actual nachos: tortilla chips, cheese sauce and peppers).

Cabbage-head, otherwise denoting a fool, referred to both the Dutch and the Germans in late-nineteenth-century America and like *Bean Town*, *Cabbage Town* meant the poor area; it could also mean that section inhabited mainly by German immigrants. A *cabbage-eater* refers both to a German and a Russian.

Nigger-toe means a potato in America, and *french fries* refer to the Québecois in Canada. *Freedom fries*, that jingoistic coinage that followed France's refusal in 2003 to lockstep after the US into Iraq, has no stated national slur, but the implication is unmistakeable: 'our' freedom is in being anything but 'old Europe'. The term, predictably, is still to be found amongst the core Trump demographic.

Germans love cabbage and sausages and get credit for both, but they also love potatoes and that seems to have eluded anglophone slang, although there are terms that equate German and 'potato-eater' in Poland, Italy, Russia, Slovakia and the Czech Republic, Portugal and Holland. In English, however, the *potato-eater* is strictly Irish. And while the German delight in the vegetable seems to be linked simply to their gargantuan appetite for the tubers, Ireland's link, as in so many other areas, is based on a sneer at peasant stupidity and poverty as much as at the actual food. Thus the snobbish usages *Irish lemons*, *grapes* and *apples* and *Irish fruit* in general (plus the *Irish root* and the inedible *Irish football*) all of which refer to the potato. So too does the *Irish apricot*, occasioning Francis Grose's remark in 1785 that 'It is a common joke against the Irish vessels to say that they are loaded with fruit and timber, that is potatoes and broomsticks.' The *Irish cherry*, another fraudulent 'fruit' is in fact a carrot. Similar terms include *bog-oranges* and *Munster plums* (Munster being an Irish county). *Navigators* (and the rhyming slang *navigator scot*: potatoes all hot) refer to the job undertaken by many mid-nineteenth-century Irish immigrants to Britain, that of a 'navigator' (and thus the slang *navvy*): a labourer on Victorian Britain's railways and canals. Contemporary life was further indicated in *home-rulers*, baked potatoes cooked and sold in the street, which emerged during the late nineteenth century, a period marked by Sinn Fein's agitation for Irish Home Rule. That agitation also provided a *Fenian*, threepenny-worth of whisky and water, a pun on 'three cold Irish', that's 'cold' as in dead and referred to the hanging of one of two sets of Fenians, i.e. fighters for Irish independence: either the 'Manchester Murderers' of 1867 or those who carried out their killings in Phoenix Park, Dublin in 1882.

Spud, a popular nickname for a potato, was also one for an Irishman (the *spuddy*, a seller of bad potatoes in nineteenth-century London, possibly combined both) as was *Murphy*, which started with the person and moved on to the vegetable. Finally, predictably, comes *potato-head*. A *potato-fingered Irishman* is clumsy and maladroit and may be linked to the plain *potato*, used of a severely disabled individual, though the link here is possibly based on the similarly dismissive use of *vegetable*. *Potato* itself has been used in Canada of a native of New Brunswick: the province grows many potatoes; the implication is one of rural stolidness and stupidity and in New Zealand to sneer at Polynesians, seen as being 'brown on the outside but white on the inside'.

Vegetable, as noted, can be cruel, but it is not nationalistic and veggies play a minor role in this variety of slang. *Spinach*, at least in America, refers to a Spaniard. Being the Welsh national emblem, a *leek* has meant a Welshman since 1695 and to *wear the leek* means to be Welsh. America's *Indian turnip*, also known as a *Jack-in-the-pulpit*, is a tuber which, when eaten raw, is burningly pungent; just as 'red' Indians supposedly hid their true nature from the white man so the tuber hides its sharpness from its eater. A *Jerusalem* or 'Jewish' artichoke (also known as a *Jerusalem potato*) is a *jewboy*, although the slur is totally misdirected on both counts. The 'Jerusalem' is a perversion of *Girasole Articiocco* or Sunflower Artichoke. First cultivated in the Farnese garden in Rome, it began its spread around Europe in the early seventeenth century.

The *Jew's ear* is a form of edible fungus growing on wood and the *Scotch bonnet* is better known either as the 'fairy-ring' mushroom or a particularly hot chilli pepper (it supposedly resembles a tam o' shanter; Guyana's nickname 'ball of fire' is more to the point). A *nigger killer* is a yam (at least c.1895), whether from the resemblance of some varieties of yam to a club (which slang also terms a *nigger killer*) or to its sheer stodginess which might choke an eater to death, while an *eggplant* (or *aubergine*) is another name for African-American, a reference to the vegetable's black-purple, shiny skin. A synonym *molonjohn*, often found as *Moulie*, used by Italians of blacks, presumably comes from the Italian *melanzana*: an eggplant. An eggplant can also be a *Jew's apple*. Last of these vegetable terms are the Australian *vegetable John*, a Chinese greengrocer, of whom there were many prior to World War II, and a *Dutch grocery* is an ill-kept, run-down, third-rate grocery although given the usual Dutch reputation for financial acumen and a devotion to cleanliness, this seems paradoxical (it is, perhaps, another example of Dutch actually meaning *Deutsch*: German).

Three fruits stand out as far as racial references are concerned: the pomegranate, the lime and the banana. *Pommy*, or in its most popular combination *pommy bastard*, is widely known to mean a British immigrant (or indeed visitor) to Australia. It is equally widely accepted that pommy is an abbreviation of pomegranate (itself from the Old French *pommegrenate*: the seed-filled apple). From there on the problems begin and no one seems properly to know why the term was adopted. The most popular assumption is that pomegranate 'rhymes' with immigrant, as does another once-popular nickname, *jimmygrant*, and certainly there are many citations of young people, now old, recalling shouting 'Pommygrant' after still pallid Britons, newly arrived from what, of course, was known as *Pommyland*. Certainly W.S. Ramson, editor of the *Australian National Dictionary* (1988), backs up this interpretation. Henry Lawson, one of the country's best-known writers, had his own take, offered in a short story of 1921: 'An' the Pommy he says "Pom-me-word" [i.e. 'pon my word] – and that's how I think Pommies got their name.' Or perhaps not. A further suggestion is that it began life as *pome*, an acronym for *P*risoner *O*f *M*other *E*ngland, but like so many concocted acronyms, designed to provide a neat etymology, this seems unlikely.

The *pome* theory is further undermined by chronology: transportation to Australia had officially ended in 1868 (it had effectively ceased in the 1850s) but there are no recorded citations for pommy before 1900 where it serves as the title of a play. The ever-popular compound *pommy bastard* appeared in 1915 and *whingeing pommy* or *whingeing pom*, an allusion to what other Australians see as one of the primary characteristics of the newly arrived British (the other being a seeming reluctance to shower), in 1962.

Lime juice, long recognised as a prophylactic against scurvy or vitamin C deficiency, was doled out to sailors who might otherwise have been struck down on the long voyages of the age of sail. Among them were those whose ships went from Britain to such colonies as South Africa, Australia and New Zealand, and this intake of limes gave rise to the nickname *limey*, first for the sailors and gradually for all Britons. It began in 1851 as *lime-juicer*, which meant both the sailor and his vessel, and the abbreviation followed around 1910. Lime-juicer could also mean a British immigrant to the US or Australia. Synonyms included *lime-juice*, *lemon-eater* and *lemon-sucker* and for a while *Limeyland*, in Australia, referred to the 'mother country'.

As for bananas, this fruit touches equally on the inhabitants of Queensland, Australia and Natal, South Africa. Thus *banana-men*, *banana-benders* and *bananaskins* are all Queenslanders. *Bananaland* is Queensland (and a *Bananalander* a native of the state), and *Banana City* is Brisbane, the state capital. At the same time Bananaland can mean Durban, capital of Natal, while *bananalander* or *banana-boy* refers to a resident or native of Natal as well as one of Queensland. A *banana peddler*, however, is American, and referred to an Italian immigrant.

Still in Africa, if figuratively, an *African grape* is that most clichéd of foods, the watermelon, supposedly *the* African-American favourite, also known as a *nigger special*. A *raisin* can be a black person, perhaps a reference to the 1959 play *A Raisin in the Sun* by Loraine Hansberry (1930–65) though that puns on 'raisin'', i.e. growing up, while a *Jew plum* is properly known as an otaheite apple, which, while its flesh is edible, has rind that tastes like turpentine. *Pineapple*, with little originality, refers in America to a Pacific Islander, while in New Zealand these same islanders are *coconuts*, another play on the 'brown outside, white within' trope.

Bread means an Afro-American while one of the many definitions for *negro-* or *nigger-head* (both sailors' terms) is a loaf of brown bread. A *bagel* or *bagel-bender* refers to the doughnut-shaped bread popular among Jews and logically means a Jew, as does *motza*, the unleavened Passover biscuits, which can also mean money. *Lox*, or smoked salmon, the 'automatic' accompaniment to bagels (and cream cheese) gives *lox jock*, another synonym for Jew. *Bagel* has another meaning in South Africa where it denotes a spoilt, wealthy, upper-class young man; his female equivalent is a *kugel*, the Yiddish for cake. Although such young people were originally (and mainly still are) Jewish, there are equivalents – at least among the girls – in the Black community (*ebony-kugels*) and among the Afrikaaners (*boere-kugels*). The jargon they speak is *kugelese*. (Slightly distanced from food, but definitely related to the kugel is the *JAP* or Jewish American Princess, sisters, as it were, under the sun.) An *Italian hero* is a large sandwich (whether the distinctly phallic look of such snacks, usually in a long roll, reflects on Italian masculinity is debatable), while in the pidgin of Papua New Guinea *bretskin* or 'bread skin' is used by country people to describe someone from the capital, Port Moresby, who eats more bread than is felt to be necessary and is thus seen as self-indulgent, fat and lazy by his country cousins.

Despite the wide variety of sweets there is, at least in the racial lexicon, only one major brand: the dark one. Thus America's *licorice* and *licorice-stick* (and France's *jus de rélisse*: licorice juice) which refer to a Black person. Thus too America's *brown sugar*, as memorialised in the Rolling Stones' song title, and *toffee* or *taffy*. Like brown sugar, most 'sweet' terms tend to the sexual, thus *chocolate, chokker, choco, chocolate drop, hot chocolate, sweet chocolate, chocolate-bar, chocolate-chip*, all of which refer to Black girls, who are doubtless seen as 'good enough to eat'. Specific brand-names – *Hershey-Bar* and *Tootsie-Roll* (both best-selling American chocolate-based sweets) – underpin the image.

The fact that chocolate, like rum, sugar, tobacco, coffee and cocoa, was at one time the product of Black slave labour, only points up the ironies. Advertising furthered the image: a brand named 'Assorted Chocolates' was adorned by a picture of a couple of 'cute' Black girls, while in Germany a variety of chocolate cake termed itself 'the edible negro'. In an American book of comic stories entitled *Chocolate Drops from the South* (1932) its author, Edward V. White, asserted that America's 'greatest source of laughter and good humor' was her Blacks. For 'he looks funny, he acts funny, he is funny. Moreover, he is serious about it all.' White, presumably, would have lauded the term *nigger spit*, another way of describing lumps in cane sugar. Other sweets, such as Canada's *eskimo* or South Africa's *eskimo pie* – both meaning what in Britain is termed a 'choc-ice' – refer to the Inuit, for whom the name Eskimo, it should be recalled, means those who eat their meat raw – hardly an especially 'sweet' concept.

One anomaly in this toothsome list is the *Mexican jelly bean*. No sweet this, but a vintage Chevrolet lowered in the rear and fitted with a *Mexican window shade* (a Venetian blind) in the rear window. Not strictly a sweet, the peanut is best noted here. *Peanut* itself meant a black person; the obvious link is to the growing of peanuts in the south, and to the black agronomist George Washington Carver, whose introduction of peanuts and sweet potatoes essentially saved the southern economy. However, peanut can also mean a person of small value, and relates to such cognate terms for black as *dink* and *jit*. Dink itself, which was also used by US troops to describe the Vietnamese, is an abbreviation of the slang *rinky-dink*: worthless, second-rate. Another 'peanut' image is that of *goober-grabber*, used as a catch-all term for the south. The word *goober*, widely used for peanut, probably comes from the Congolese *nguba*: a type of peanut. As for jit, it is an abbreviation of the slang term *jitney*, meaning five cents; the black person is equated with the low-value coin.

Like sweets, what one might term 'national' desserts also seem to have a bias towards the Black. Thus the American *niggers in a snow-storm*: stewed prunes and rice, and the cowboys' favourite *nigger-in-a-blanket*: a dish made of raisins in dough. *Prunes* by themselves refer to a black person or to a black head, and *nigger-toes* are brazil nuts. The French phrase *Anglais á prunes* refers less to a dish than to a characteristic: meanness. (*Prunes* translates strictly as 'plums'.) To the amusement of the French, the English – careful, penny-pinching travellers – note the highly priced fruit in restaurants and ask instead for a handful of (cheap) plums as their dessert. This image of parsimony persists elsewhere: *faire une anglaise*: to do it English style, refers to the practice of tossing coins to decide on who is to pay for a round of drinks, or to divide the bill (like impecunious students) in exactly equal portions. French cabbies talk of *Anglais de carton*: a mean (English) tipper.

There is more to dessert than prunes or plums. The Scots call their English neighbours *pock-pudding* or *poke-pudding*, which is a synonym for bag-pudding (from the Scots *poke*: a small bag or sack and thus any pudding boiled, like a Christmas pudding, in a bag), while in Canada French Canadians are mocked as *johnny-cakes*, a term that can be found in a doggerel verse, popular amongst Montreal children around 1900: 'French peasoup and johnnycake / Make your father a bellyache.' The cake, which exists in Canada, America, the West Indies and Australia and which is made of maize or wheat-meal and either toasted at a fire or baked in a pan, may be of black origin; the 'Johnny' may also be a red herring: some authorities claim that its original form was 'journey-cake' and, given its basic ingredients and the simplicity of its cooking, this may well be true. A *French pancake* is not, alas, a crêpe, but is in fact a rectangular academic hat or a beret.

Dairy products in language as well as the marketplace typify the Dutch. Thus Britain's *butter-mouth* (1547), *butter-box* (1600) and *butterbag* (1645) all meant a Dutchman, on account of the vast quantities of dairy products consumed and produced in

Holland. A *Dutch cheese* is a bald person, as is the South African *cheesehead* or, in Afrikaans, *kaaskop*. A *limburger*, the very smelly yet paradoxically bland cheese is a German (although the cheese is a Belgian speciality). Still with butter, there are a number of African-American terms, notably *butter baby* or *melted butter*, both of which mean a mulatto 'yellow' girl; *butterhead*: a Black who, for whatever reason, is considered an embarrassment to his race. Last in the butter stakes comes *Jew butter*, which is not actual butter, but goose grease, the equivalent of dripping and a popular spread on bread. The Jews' own term for such a spread is *schmaltz*, literally 'fat', and which, while devoid of racial overtones, can be found as a pejorative itself, implying excessive and mawkish sentimentality, especially in the world of show business.

With a few exceptions, words based on grease refer exclusively to the unfortunate Mexicans. British service slang adds *gippo*, *gippy* and *gypoo* which can mean variously stew, gravy, bacon fat, butter or any form of greasy sauce. Quite why the gypsies should be, as it were, smeared with the term is unexplained, but it may come from the simultaneous World War I use of *Gyppo* to mean an Egyptian, a race who, being Middle Eastern, might, in the way of such slurs, be presumed to be greasy. From there on the focus is strictly on Mexico. Aside from *frito*, meaning fried and itself emphasising the Mexican love of fried food, and *oiler*, which refers to the cooking rather than the commercial liquid, Mexicans have been *greasers* – supposedly from their 'greasy' appearance – since the 1840s. Similar terms include *greaseball*, which has also been used for a Greek, just as *greaser* can occasionally denote an Italian, *grease-gut* and *grease-boy*.

Rice, being the staple it is, means Chinese or Oriental, especially as *ricer*, *rice-belly*, *rice-eater* and *riceman*. A *rice queen*, in gay use, favours Easterners as lovers, while the recent *rice rocket* refers in America to a Japanese-made off-road or four-wheel-drive vehicle. Less common is *rice Christian*, which from the 1890s to the 1930s described those inhabitants of rice-growing countries who volunteered for conversion less through religious fervour and more through a desire to obtain food from gullible missionaries. *Sago*, a form of starch prepared from the pith of various palm trees, and much used as a food in the Pacific, is found in Australia as a slur on the natives of the Pacific Islands.

Buckwheat, a species of *Polygonum* (*P. Fagopyrum*) and a native of Central Asia, whence it was introduced into Europe by the Turks in about the thirteenth century, is used in Europe as food for horses, cattle and poultry; in North America, however, its meal is made into buckwheat cakes, regarded as a dainty for the breakfast table. In slang it also means a black person, either another play on the Black/White jokes that produce 'lilywhite' and 'snowball', but possibly an acknowledgement of 'Buckwheat' Thomas, the black actor in the 'Our Gang' Saturday morning movie series of the 1930s. *Wheatfolks*, an occasional name for White Americans, appears to link in to buckwheat, as well as punning on the common description 'white folks'.

Unlike the majority of these terms, which identify the properties of a given food or drink with the perceived deficiencies of a given nation, the bulk of terms that deal with tea and coffee seem more preoccupied with the drinks themselves. Thus, other than *pepsi*, which in Canada pokes fun at the French Canadians' alleged propensity for the fizzy drink, *cocoa*, meaning a black person and *black teapot*, which referred to the black servants who were once *the* fashion accessory in any smart European household, the rest seem to deal with intrinsic quality – or lack of it.

English winter and *cold English* are both iced tea, although the

American phrases, albeit subconsciously, underpin the British reputation for sang-froid; an *English martini* is tea spiked with gin. *Scotch coffee* is not coffee, but hot water flavoured with burnt biscuit, while *Negro coffee* is coffee senna. *Indian coffee*, a 'Wild West' coinage, is coffee made from old grounds; the derisive assumption was that such coffee was all an Indian deserved. *Cowboy coffee*, on the other hand, was properly brewed. *Brazil-water*, another term for coffee, sounds a little better (especially given Brazil's much touted reputation for the stuff), but the construction probably does no more than reflect such phrases as *scandal-water*, which to the eighteenth century meant tea. In mainstream use *Brazil water* was in fact the reddish dye extracted from the local species of the Sappan tree, native to eastern India. Indeed it is this dye that gave its name to the entire country, which was originally named *terra de brasil*: red-dye land. Why the dye itself was termed 'brasil' remains conjectural. It may come from the French *briser*, to break (since the wood tended to crumble on its voyage to Europe), from the Spanish *brasa*: a glowing coal (indicating its colour) or even from the Arabic *wars*: saffron.

Utensils do not figure highly in these lists, but there are a few noteworthy terms. A *stove-lid* is an African American, as is a *skillet* (otherwise a large stew-pan, often made of cast-iron); a *skillet blonde* is a Black woman in a blonde wig. The *Japanese knife trick* is the use of one's knife to convey food to the mouth, presumably reflecting on the obtuse 'trickiness' of any Oriental, as well as on the fact that the Japanese do not customarily use Western knives and forks. A *Spanish spoon* is either a long-handled dipper or narrow shovel, while a *Spanish toothpick* is a nickname for Bishop's-Weed or *Ammiviznaga*, a form of 'hot' herb. Straying briefly to Papua New Guinea the North Solomon

Islanders, who generally play the role of the Irish in Britain and the Poles in America, are known in Tok Pisin as *blak sospen*, a black saucepan (from the darker tone of their skin) and are further insulted by the phrase *as bilong sospen*, literally 'your arse belongs in a saucepan', which carries a dual meaning; on the one hand 'your skin is so black it looks burnt' or 'you are such an appalling person that you deserve to be tossed into a cannibal cooking pot'.

The American term *joint*, which began life in the mid-nineteenth century as a cant term, meaning a place where criminals could get together or 'joint up' and later as an opium den, before becoming more generally a room or place, gives *Chink joint* (a Chinese restaurant). In England both *Chinese* and *Indian* mean the restaurant and the meals it serves, thus the common 'Let's get an Indian'. However *chinois*, in France, means no more than a cafeteria, irrespective of the menu. The Afro-American equivalent is a *nigger joint* (a cheap, low-class café, and thus one frequented by poor blacks). Synonymous are *nigger juke* or *jook*, both of which incorporate the term *juke* (also found in jukebox) which means variously the cheap, raucous music played at similarly inclined roadhouses, cafés and brothels (and which give the term *juke it*: to play piano in a cheap bar or brothel), to dance, to have a good time and to have sex. From there it came to mean any building used for drinking, dancing and generally enjoying oneself. The origins of juke are debatable but may lie in Africa – in the Bantu *juka* or Wolof *dzug* – or possibly Scotland, where a *jouk* is a place into which one may dart for shelter. It is in such a café that the patrons eat *blackplate*, a synonym for soul food and, as such, traditionally black dishes. Blackplate puns on the mainstream *blueplate*, usually as 'blueplate special', coined during World War II, which refers either to a restaurant dinner plate divided into compartments for serving several kinds of food as a single order, or a main course (as of meat and vegetables) served as a single menu item.

Other restaurants include America's *wophouse*, which uses *wop*, Italian to pun on *flophouse*: the lowest level of transient hotel used by vagrants and tramps, and Australia's *steakdahoyst* or *steaka-da-oyst*, mocking Italian speech patterns to describe an Italian restaurant specialising in steak and oysters. In Australia, a Greek is known as a *grill*, from the number of immigrant Greeks who run cheap cafés specialising in mixed grills, while in America a *Greek hash-house* is a lunch-stand. This last gives what is called *hash-house Greek*, a reference not so much to the café's owner, but to Greek in the same sense as it has been used since the sixteenth century: an unintelligible jargon, in this case that of short-order cookery. Such jargon includes *slaughter in the pan*: beefsteak, *red mike with a bunch o' violets*: corned beef and cabbage, *two of a kind*: fishballs and *Adam and Eve on a raft and wreck 'em*: scrambled eggs on toast.

When it comes to gluttony, and for a people so heavily identified with food, the French themselves get off rather lightly. Perhaps the rest of the world has swallowed their propaganda: France remains synonymous with good food. But not invariably: there is *Frankish fare*, meaning excessive or over-generous amounts of food. The Dutch, seen as undiscriminating if enthusiastic trenchermen are credited with a *Dutch palate*: a coarse palate, with no appreciation of the finer comestibles, while their South African cousins, the Boers, talk of a *Kaffir's tightener* to mean a heavy meal, which, despite the reference implicit in kaffir, could hardly have been an exclusively black phenomenon. (The slang term *tightener* itself had been coined, with no racial overtones *c.*1850, and *do a tightener* meant to gorge oneself.)

From excess to deprivation, and starvation gives as many 'national' words as does gluttony. Typical are a variety of notional 'meals', the point of which is that there is no meal whatsoever. To show slang's affection for the joke, there are some 'occupational' breakfasts as well.

Thus America's *Mexican breakfast* or Australia's *Pommy's breakfast*, both of which entail no more than a cigarette and a glass of water. With an accent on the outback or the 'never-never', Australia also offers the *dingo's breakfast*: 'a piss and a look around', and a *drover's breakfast* in which a cough is substituted for the passing of water. Other starvation breakfasts include the *Norfolk breakfast*, the *seagull's breakfast* and the *duck's breakfast*. The *rabbiter's breakfast* involves smoking a cigarette while defecating and the *bullocky's breakfast* follows a similar ritual, but without the cigarette: after the lavatory one merely tightens the belt. The *bushman's breakfast* has, if nothing else, a variety of choices: these are 'a shave and a spit (or shit) and a good look around', a 'hitch in the belt and attention to natural requirements' and a 'drink of water and a good look around'.

The 'Pommies' have their alternatives too, a *vegetable breakfast* and a *Spitalfields breakfast*, both of which refer to judicial hanging. The Spitalfields meal is a 'tight necktie and a short (wind) pipe' while the 'vegetable' in question is an 'artichoke (hearty choke) with caper sauce'. (The *sheriff's breakfast*, again 'eaten' on the gallows, has the same definition). An *Irish* or *Irishman's dinner* is no dinner at all, a phrase that emerged in America and was reinforced by immigrant memories of the deadly famine of 1845–6, although a modern joke describes such a dinner as 'a boiled potato and a six-pack of beer'. The slightly longer *have an Irishman's dinner* is to be forced to forgo an expected meal.

Finally, there are some slang breakfasts that offer something (though not always solid) to chew on. There is the *Cockney breakfast*, no food, but a glass (or more) of gin or brandy and soda water; the *California breakfast*, a cocktail and a shoeshine, the *jockey's breakfast*, an Irish treat defined as 'a rasher and a ride', in other words sexual intercourse and a slice of bacon. Best of all must be the *Kentucky breakfast*, so named for its being the supposed favourite breakfast of the classic 'Southern gentleman'. Popularly defined as 'three cocktails and a chew of terbacker', one may substitute whiskies for the cocktails. A further variation is 'a bottle of bourbon, a three-pound steak and a setter dog or bull-dog.' Why, one may ask, the dog? It's there to eat the steak. Slightly off-topic, but surely linked, is the *Burketown mosquito net*. Based on the outback town of Burketown, Queensland it means the day's final relaxation: a bottle of rum and a cow-dung fire.

The Spanish, perhaps on the grounds of their much-celebrated pride, seem to volunteer starvation – echoing those who claim that one can never be too rich nor too thin. Thus to *take a Spanish supper* is to tighten one's belt rather than actually offset one's hunger with food (thus France's *un ventre à l'espagnol*, 'a Spanish belly', is one that is swollen, but only from starvation.) To pursue the motif of emaciation, African Americans have termed Whites *the thin people* while they in turn have been called *bones*, although this presumably refers to the 'Mr Bones' character, once a staple of 'black' cross-talk vaudeville acts between 'Mr Bones' and 'Mr Jones'. (The original 'Mr' or 'Brudder Bones' played in minstrel shows on the castanet-like 'bones' that were a feature of such entertainment.)

The appetite must be satisfied. There are *gourmands* and there are *gourmets* (supposedly different – the former gluttons, the latter culinary aesthetes – but the French, who should know, use them interchangeably). Then there are geophages. Geophagy, literally earth-eating, has been found in various parts of the globe, typically Tierra del Fuego, but as these terms indicate, it has also cropped up in the so-called 'civilised' West, specifically the poorer states of America. Thus *clay-eater* means a poor white, especially a native of North or South Carolina or Georgia; a synonym is *grit-sucker*, while *clover-eater*, substituting grass for earth, is a nickname for a Virginian. Similar are *rosin-chewer* and *hay-eater*. Equally strange is an appetite for wax, found in the American *candle-eater*, meaning a Russian. This, however, may not be quite as bizarre as it appears. The candles that the Russians 'eat' may well be a simple reference to the burning of candles in Russian Orthodox churches.

To conclude, a glass of wine and a cigar. Wine, at least when home-made which was the case among many immigrant Italians, gives *grape-stomper* for the maker and *purple death*, *red ink* and best-known, *dago red* for the wine. This latter comes from *dago*, from Spanish *Diego*, i.e James, and thus usually applied to a Spaniard but which, like *greaseball*, can also denote a *guinea* (there is also *guinea red*), who started off life as black (coming from the Guinea Coast) but was transferred to the Latins. Thus the *guinea stinker*, a cheap, malodorous cigar, the Italian district of *Guinea-town* and the *guinea football*, a bomb but more likely a large firecracker.

Mixed Drinks

S LANG'S TERMS FOR *alcohol* or *liquor* or simply for 'a drink' reveal that the counter-language offers nearly seven hundred variations. (*Drunk* finds 1,160 and even *drunkard* 156). This is not surprising. Along with sex and crime, alcohol, its consumers and consumption and its usually deleterious effects, provide the very essence of the counter-language. Humankind, as T.S. Eliot noted, cannot stand too much reality, and liquor definitely takes the edge off, even if it can take us straight back to sex and crime. Further enquiries for the specifics beer (363), whisk(e)y (221), gin (153), wine (150) and brandy (111) more than double that total. Nearly 1,700 terms, and too many for proper consideration here. Apologies to those who will thus miss their tipple of choice, but let us concentrate on a single group: mixed drinks, for which slang has always had a partiality.

But first, a *toast*, a word that the unrevised *OED* tells us first applied to the man or more likely woman toasted, and which took its name from a once popular drink which included a chunk of spiced toast: the woman in question ('often one who is the reigning belle of the season') was supposed to flavour the bumper – the brimming glassful that was raised – as did toast in liquor.

Setting aside the various reduplications – *chin-chin! pip-pip! honk-honk!* – and the variations on Humphrey Bogart's celebrated *here's looking at you! – here's looking up your kilt! here's mud in your eye!* – toasts, proclaimed with none but men at table, have often been distinctly sexual. There was the *beggar's benison*: 'may your prick and your purse never fail you!'; *inside and outside*, that's 'inside a cunt and outside a jail' and the *best in Christendom!* the missing word again being 'cunt'; *both ends of the busk!* celebrates not just the *busk*, i.e. corset, then of whalebone stiffening, but what was to be found at either end: the breasts and the vagina. There was also *Hans-in-kelder*, or 'Jack in the cellar', which usually meant an as yet unborn foetus.

Other than sex, toasts required that a glass should be drained. Thus *put it down!* and *down the hatch!* There were also the cries of *no daylights!* and *no heel-taps!* which referred to the filling and emptying of the container. A *daylight* was a gap left between the top of the poured liquor and the glass; a *heel-tap*, usually a layer of leather used in making a shoe heel, was anything still drinkable left at the bottom. Neither were acceptable to the dedicated *elbow-bender*.

Toasts drained, let us commence with some proper names. *Aristippus* referred to two drinks. The first being Canary wine (produced in the Canary islands), another name for the fortified wine that was known as *sack* (most likely from Spanish *sacar*, to draw out, i.e. from the barrel) and subsequently as Malaga or today's sherry. The second definition is less appealing: a diet drink, made of sarsparilla, cinchona bark (a.k.a. *Jesuit's bark* and the basis of quinine) and other ingredients, available at certain coffee houses. Why it was named for Aristippus (*c.*435–366BCE), a Greek philosopher who founded the rigorously hedonistic Cyrenaic school of philosophy is unknown, though his supposed portrait shows a certain jauntiness. It was presumably a hat-tip from a classically educated age to the school's basic belief: that pleasure was what counted. And by pleasure they didn't mean simply the absence of pain, but active, immediate gratification. Physical pleasure, in the here and now; emotional pleasure worked, but lacked that all-important sensuality.

Another liquorous mixture, a hot drink of small beer mixed with brandy, plus lemon juice, spices and sugar, was a *Sir Cloudesley*. Much loved in the Royal Navy it took its name from that of Sir Cloudesley Shovell (1650–1707), a notable British admiral who was knighted for his suppression of piracy.

Catherine Hayes was a drink made of claret, sugar, nutmeg and orange. The general belief is that the lady in question was an Irish songbird, vastly popular in Australia (where another singer, Nellie Melba, would come to name a foodstuff too). It was Hayes (c.1818–61) who was the first ever singer of 'Kathleen Mavourneen', that classic Irish lovesong, in its home town of Dublin. The sweet-voiced soprano was most likely the authoress of the sweet concoction, but there is a possible challenger: an earlier Catherine Hayes (1690–1725) who murdered and dismembered her lover (body parts into a nearby pond, head into the Thames) after deliberately rendering him insensibly drunk. Hayes suffered a more than usually miserable death: sentenced to be burned at the stake, so hot were the flames that the executioner was unable to perform the usual preliminary mercy of killing by strangulation. Instead she only died when a bystander threw a heavy lump of wood, crushing her skull.

The effects of *Sneaky Pete* (a generic name: there is no known Peter on record as an origin) 'sneak up' on the consumer. Best-known as cheap, rotgut wine (*rotgut* itself covers all sorts of third-rate drinks and goes back to 1597) it has also been used to describe marijuana mixed with wine and, terrifyingly but presumably effectively, a form of spirit distilled from household chemicals. His feminine companion is *red Biddy*, from Bridget, usually equated with cheap wine. The name can also apply to meths (of which more below), as included by James Joyce in his novel *Finnegans Wake* when he mentions one Treacle Tom who 'slept in a nude state, hailfellow with meth [. . .] blotto with divers tots of hell fire, red biddy, bull dog, blue ruin and creeping jenny'. (*Blue ruin* being gin, as well as applejack or the hangover that follows. None of the others, sadly, have been explained although *creeping jenny* is elsewhere the plant *lysimachia nummularia*, known for its aggressive colonisation of all available soil.)

Proper names aside, there are also geographical links. For instance *Brummagem wine*: any adulterated or mixed drink. This, with its negative stereotyping of Birmingham, is an extension of the older form, *Bromicham*: 'particularly noted a few years ago, for the counterfeit groats made here, and from hence dispersed all over the Kingdom'.

Australia offers a pair of off-brand uses of champagne, none of which much resemble the French original. For *Northern Territory* or *bush champagne*, stereotyped with racist glee as a favourite tipple among Native Australians, see below. The country also served the *Domain cocktail*, a mixture of petrol and pepper allegedly once popular among *Domain dossers* or down-and-outs, in the Sydney Domain, a city park which was popular for speech-making and frequented by the unemployed and the alcoholic.

A *King's peg* was a champagne cocktail that mixes champagne with brandy. The King is self-evident and its date suggests that the monarch in question was Edward VII. Edward also modified the usual recipe, substituting whisky for the brandy and adding Maraschino and angostura to create his own 'Prince of Wales cocktail'. As for *peg*, this either moralises on the idea that each drink was one more peg, i.e. nail, in the drinker's coffin, or takes us back to the seventeenth century's tankards, wherein the peg referred to 'one of a set of pins fixed at intervals in a drinking vessel as marks to measure the quantity which each drinker was to drink' (*OED*).

Finally, and perhaps inevitably, a pun: a *war cry*, a mixture of stout and mild ale, played on the Salvation Army newspaper *The War Cry* and the belief that while the Army spoke 'stoutly' it used only 'mild' terms.

No one pretended that this stuff didn't have a kick: wasn't that the point? Rough whisky might be *spill-skull, bust-skull, pop-skull, swell-skull* and *swell head*. Australia offered *blow-my-skull-off,* which mixed wine, opium, cayenne pepper and rum; it doubtlessdidjustthatandwasmuchprizedatthemid-nineteenth-century gold diggings; an alternative recipe mixed boiling water, sugar, lime or lemon juice, porter, rum and brandy. A *shake-up* was a form of cocktail, made from a variety of liquors, plus wine.

After which, one needed a *corpse reviver*, another non-specific mixed drink, tossed back in the hope of curing a hangover. It was usually listed among typical mid-nineteenth-century 'American drinks', all luridly innovative to the visiting Brits. There was even a comic song, 'The American Drinks', created by the music-hall star Arthur Lloyd (1840–1904): 'I suppose you've all tasted American drinks at one time or other,' he asked his audience, 'curious names they have tho'. For instance there's . . .

A stone-fence, a rattlesnake, a renovator, locomotive,
Pick-me-up, or private-smile, by Jove is worth a fiver
A Colleen Bawn, a lady's blush, a cocktail, or a flash of
   lightning
Juleps, smashes, sangarees, or else a corpse reviver.'

The song climaxes with his consuming the lot.

These can mostly be 'translated', whether or not they were really available on this side of the Pond. *Cocktail* (the word may be common, its etymology is still unresolved and may reflect the *cocked* or docked *tails* of horses considered inferior to full-on thoroughbreds, thus a mixed drink was similarly *déclassé*) and *julep* (from the Spanish *julepe* and ultimately the Persian *golâb*, rose-water) are standard English. *Sangaree* was properly spiced wine, diluted with water (ultimately Spain's *sangria*) in slang meaning not a drink but a drinking bout. The *locomotive* was a winter drink made of Burgundy, curaçao, egg yolks, honey and cloves all heated together; the *stone fence* or *stone-wall* was either whisky or some other spirit mixed with cider or ginger-beer and brandy (whether the effect of the 'wall' was to stop you in your tracks, or perhaps to fall on you, is unresolved); a *whiskey skin* was any mixed drink that contained a large proportion of whisky. The *rattlesnake* presumably 'bit' the drinker (and had a 'sting in its tail') while the *renovator* and *pick-me-up* mimicked the corpse reviver.

A *smile*, *fancy smile* or *private smile* either promoted a smile through the sheer pleasure of its consumption or represented the 'smile' that was formed by lips open for drinking; it covered any drink, though whisky was the usual, and was found in *do a smile*, have a drink, and the invitation, *will you try a smile?* A *smiler*, logically, was a drinker, as well as a form of shandygaff, a mixture of beer and ginger beer or stout and lemonade. A *flash of lightning* (see further below) began life in London as a glass of gin, but with its synonyms *blue lightning*, *lightning juice* and *liquid lightning*, for Americans it represented whisky or any form of cheap, strong liquor. *Smash*, from brandy-smash, was iced brandy and water.

Pink drinks, being seen as 'girly', attracted female names.

Thus the *lady's* or *maiden's blush* (occasionally *maiden's prayers*) which involved either port and lemonade or, in Australia, ginger beer and raspberry cordial. Australia added the *barmaid's blush* which is ginger beer or rum plus raspberry cordial. It can also be a cocktail based on champagne or, again, the British favourite port and lemon. Unlisted, but contemporary, was *flesh-and-blood*, a loose approximation of the colours of the drinks, composed of equal measures of port and brandy.

Last in the lyrics, *Colleen Bawn*. Slang knows no liquorous definition. The name, the anglicised version of Irish *cailínbán*, the white or fair woman, was used for the heroine of the opera 'The Lily of Killarney', first produced in 1862 at the Royal English Opera, Covent Garden, London. It was quickly adopted by rhyming slang and means a *horn*, an erection. This may suggest some sniggering link to *cock-tail*, but then again, perhaps not.

Still musical, and a century on, we meet *spodiodi* or *bolly-olly*, defined by Jack Kerouac as 'a shot of port wine, a shot of whiskey and a shot of port wine', the sweet port playing the role of a 'jacket' for the whisky. The port tended to be cheap, and the whisky whatever generic version the bar was selling. The drink was much consumed by jazz musicians and beatniks and in 1949 inspired Stick McGhee's song 'Drinkin' Wine Spo-Dee-O-Dee.' McGhee's Wikipedia entry suggests that the original lyric ran 'Drinkin' wine motherfucker, drinkin' wine!'

The young may lack finesse, but they know what they want. Obliteration. There are ways of achieving this, borne out in the names of the juvenile cocktails. *Rocket fuel*, a New Zealand mix which blends alcohol and a soft drink in a plastic bottle; the intent is presumably for the weak one to hide the strong. *Snakebite* began life as cheap but potent whisky and moved on to the modern mix of cider and lager; it can also mean a 'cocktail' of heroin and morphine. (The wider-ranging *cider-and* is any form of mixed drink in which the basic constituent is cider.) An *anaconda* is a mixture of strong beer and rough cider or scrumpy. Less in-your-face, even euphemistic, is the frat boys' *party juice*, a cocktail of liquids including an unspecified alcohol content, typically served at fraternity parties.

Given the variety of ingredients, it is hard to isolate flavours, but a number of slang's favourites must have been notably sweet. Thus the *bishop*, supposedly an episcopal delight, a mixture of wine and water, topped off by a roasted orange. Australia's *Madame Bishop* combined port, sugar and nutmeg, but the suggested link to an Australian hotel-keeper is probably specious. *Cherry-bounce*, named for its effects, was either cherry brandy or brandy mixed with sugar; *blackjack* was rum sweetened with molasses (as well as very strong black coffee, again plus molasses, or illegally distilled whisky). The earliest blackjack, around 1600, was a vessel for liquor (either for holding it or for drinking from) which was made of waxed leather coated on its outside with tar or pitch.

Flip or *phlip*, both based on standard English *flip*, to whip up, was a mixture of beer and spirit sweetened with sugar into which one plunged a red-hot iron; *hot tiger*, an Oxford University speciality, mixed hot spiced ale and sherry (*tiger's milk*, however is illicitly distilled whiskey). *Humpty-dumpty* was another hot drink (despite the suggestion of falling, from walls or elsewhere, the name is based on the 'humping together' of the two liquors) made of ale and brandy boiled together. *Bumbo*, possibly based on Italian children's use of *bombo* for drink, is brandy, sugar and water while *rumbo*, logically, substitutes rum for the brandy. Still with brandy one finds *hotpot*, a hot drink made of ale and brandy, and *conny wobble*, eggs and brandy beaten up together. This cries out for an etymology but *cony*, a fool, hardly fits (nor does a standard English *cony*, a rabbit), while *collywobbles*, feelings of tension, fear or sickness, was coined a century later. *Callibogus* similarly demands a concrete origin; once again, this mix of rum and spruce beer defies the researcher.

Beer, already found in a number of mixtures, has other terms, mostly negative. *Balderdash*, long since used to mean nonsense, was once any adulterated or mixed drink, typically milk and beer, beer and wine, brandy and mineral water, which, while duly consumed, was generally considered unpleasant. All senses come from the sixteenth-century *balderdash*, frothy water. The origin of this appears to be Scandinavian, whether in Danish *balder*, noise or clatter, Norwegian *bjaldra*, to speak indistinctly, or Icelandic *baldras*, to make a clatter. The *dash* comes from Danish *daske*, to slap or flap. The Welsh *baldorddus*, noisy, from *baldordd*, idle, noisy talk, chatter, may also play a role. An alternative etymology has been suggested (and backed up by a sixteenth-century reference to 'barbers balderdash') as coming from the froth and foam made by barbers in *dashing* their *balls* (spherical pieces of soap) backwards and forwards in hot water.

Bilgewater is a straight steal from standard English *bilgewater*, the foul water that collects in a vessel's bilges. For slang it means thin beer and beyond that any thin, tasteless drink, alcoholic or otherwise, although a mid-nineteenth-century example only denotes a mixed drink, not a weak one. Francis Grose offered three ingredients: 'half common ale, mixed with stale and double beer'; it sounds unappetising. Another lexicographer, Hotten has *heavy wet* and defines it as 'malt liquor, because the more a man drinks of it, the heavier and more stupid he becomes'; it can also mean a heavy drinking bout, a mixture of porter and beer (also *heavy cheer*) and non-alcoholically, a downpour, a rainstorm.

It is arguable as to whether the drinks that were produced during America's 1920s temperance experiment, Prohibition, best remembered for its institutionalisation of organised crime, strictly qualify as 'mixed'. On the other hand, their constituents were rarely what they claimed, e.g. 'whiskey'. *Bathtub hooch* reflected the bathtub in which it was supposedly made (though it may also have tasted like dirty bathwater) and *hooch* had begun life as *hoochinoo*, an alcoholic liquor made by Alaskan Indians, especially the Hoochinoo people. Hooch survived prohibition: it can just mean liquor, even the good stuff, which at the time was known as *the quill* (from the *pure quill*, which had meant something flawless since the 1880s) or *the real A.V.*, that is ante-Volstead: before Prohibition's legal launch, the Volstead Act of 1920. Otherwise there was *coffin varnish*, alcohol's equivalent to tobacco's *coffin nail*, or *monkey swill*. A *camouflage cocktail* was any mix that might hide the poor-quality liquor of the era. Or there was *cougar juice,* which has been part-adopted by US skiers in 'Cougar Milk', a blend of condensed milk, rum, nutmeg and boiling water, originally known as 'moose milk'. *Two-and-over* suggests a drink of which after two shots the drinker collapses; a 'cousin', perhaps of *block-and-fall*, very strong and usually adulterated liquor sold, usually to African Americans, in *block and fall joints:* 'you'd get a shock, walk a block and fall in the gutter' as the critic and historian Luc Sante has put it. At which point the local vultures stripped your pockets.

Prison, supposedly free of all intoxicants, is of course a veritable liquor store of home-brews. On the top shelf stands *pruno*, which suggests a one-time base of prunes, and which 'classic prison drink' is described thus in the prisoner's dictionary, *The Other Side of the Wall* (2000): 'It is made by putting fruit juice, fruit, fruit peelings in a plastic bag with bread and/or sugar. The yeast in the bread along with the sugar helps ferment the fruit juice, fruit, or peelings. The plastic bag is usually placed down the toilet and secured so that it is not detected.' Other prison creations include *julep*, the contents of which are unlikely to be those in the term that originated it, the (*mint*) *julep*, 'a mixture of brandy, whisky, or other spirit, with sugar and ice and some flavouring, usually mint.' Other vegetable-based concoctions include *spud juice* (potatoes), *silo*, *shinny* and New Zealand's *hokonui*.

Slang's shelves are weighed down with tempting bottles, but we can't open them all. Reluctantly, we must pass over beer, whisky and wine, but of all the major liquors, gin might be said to the most innately slangy. Like modern-day drugs, gin in its eighteenth-century heyday was not just a drink, but a whole culture, closely knit to degeneracy, excess, poverty and the moral panics that the fantasies about such things tend to create. It was not simply *mother's ruin* (a term that for all Hogarth's celebrated drawing of Gin Lane, with its gin-soaked mother blearily watching her baby tumble from her arms, is not recorded before 1917) but badged as the collapse of an entire society. Its drinkers were as addicted as junkies.

> Queen Gin: Oh! what is this that runs so cold about me?
> A dram!—a dram!—a large one or I die.
> 'Tis vain [*drinks hastily*]
> O, O, Farewell [*dies*]
> Mob: What, dead drunk or dead in earnest?
> Finale of *The Deposing of Queen Gin, with the Ruin of the Duke of Rum, Marquee de Nantz and the Lord Sugarcane, &c.* by Jack Juniper

Those were the days, eh? Gin in parliament (with a much-reviled act which engendered those lines; *nantz* by the way being brandy, from Nantes), gin on stage, gin in ballads, gin in the press and of course gin in Hogarth's Gin Lane – the one with the poxed drab, the falling baby, the skeletal lush, the collapsing house, the run-down pawnbrokers and similar snapshots of Merrie England. And gin wasn't even gin. Not as mixed with tonic at the *cockers-p.* or as turns up in your over-priced 'Shove-Me-Up-Against-the-Wall-Rip-My-Clothes-Off-Sod-That-You're-Too-Pissed-to-Get-It-Up' down Ayia Napa. No. Gin was genever, which was Dutch for juniper and thus en-slanged as *Hollands* or the *Dutch drop* or *Geneva* (even if that is in France) and a heavy drinker was *taking his drops* or *reading Geneva print*.

Nor was that all. Far from it. It was *Old Tom* which memorialised Thomas Norris, who was employed at Hodges' distillery and who opened a gin palace in Great Russell Street, Covent Garden. It was *daffy*, not because that was its effect (though it was) but from Daffy's Elixir which was otherwise a proprietary remedy popularly merchandised as 'the soothing syrup'. It could also be *duffy*, which also stood for a quarter-pint measure, or it was *deady*, again nodding to its effects, but this time from a distiller, one D. Deady of Sol's Row off Tottenham Court Road. Tom and Jerry, in *Life in London*, went East to debauch at All Max, which not only punned on the West End's fashionable Almacks but played with *max* or *old max*, which meant gin. A *max-ken* sold the stuff and the drunken clientele were *maxy*.

It was transparent; it came in colours: blue or white; some saw it as a form of textile. The first led to *brilliant*, which was raw and undiluted (*raw* was another name), and *clear crystal* and thence *flash* or *strike of lightning* or *thunder and lightning* (which added bitters, but came also to mean treacle and clotted cream and the flaming brandy that decks the Christmas pudding) and *strikefire*.

Transparency gave *see-through* which moved on to whiteness, and asking for *white port* or *white wine* in the wrong tavern might not get what you expected. The 'port' and 'wine' were meant to be euphemisms, so was the later *twankay* or *twankey* which in tea-trade jargon meant green tea. It might lie behind the name of pantomime dame Widow Twankey who first appeared in *Aladdin* in 1861, portraying the hero's mother and running a Chinese laundry in what was still called Peking. *Bunter's tea* referred to the *bunter*, a run-down old whore or a female rag-scavenger.

It could be *true blue* or *light blue* and a century on *bluestone* which in standard English means copper sulphate or even sulphuric acid. The textiles suggested smoothness and were coloured as well: *blue* or *white ribbin*, i.e. ribbon, which played on the earlier *blue* or *white tape* (which might have been underpinned by *taphouse*) which could also be *red tape* (though 'red' in drinks was usually brandy), and *white velvet* or *satin* (later appropriated by Sir Robert Burnett as a trade name). A *yard of satin* or of *tape* was a glassful. The main blue was *blue ruin*, which had the same effect on *mother*, though another synonym was *mother's milk*, as were *cold cream* and *cream of the valley*.

Less appealing was *rag water*, so called as Captain Grose explained because 'these [are] liquors seldom failing to reduce those that drink them to rags'. Not that one might always boast even a rag: *stark-* or *staff-naked* suggested raw alcohol, 'unclothed' in congeners or mixers, not to mention the poverty of its drinkers. *Strip-me-down-naked* was synonymous. Some saw it as a universal panacea: *meat-drink-washing-and-lodging*.

The effects provide a regular flow of imagery: *busthead*, *crank* (which mixed gin with water and 'cranked you up'), *kick in the guts*, *roll-me-in-the-kennel* (a *kennel* being a gutter), *gunpowder* (you head 'went off with a bang'), *heartsease*, *kill-grief* (but also *kill-cobbler* which suggests a professional propensity), *tittery*, which in dialect meant tottering along on the verge of collapse, and *wind* which 'caught your breath'. *Diddle* was another one that meant unsteadiness, and the *diddle-cove* or *-spinner* was the landlord of a *diddle-ken*. Then there was the simply uncompromising: *ruin*, *misery* or *poverty*, though *royal poverty* suggested that at least for a while you would 'feel like a king'. Much later came South Africa's *Queen's tears*, a Zulu term back-referring to the tears Queen Victoria supposedly shed after her troops' defeat at Isandhlwana in 1879.

As in the martini (not to mention the camp if defunct *English martini* wherein tea is mixed with gin), gin works as an ingredient. There's the *dog's nose* (like the animal's nose, the drink is black): beer warmed nearly to boiling, sugar, ginger and gin or wormwood (the basis of absinthe); absent wormwood, substitute brandy. It also referred to an alcoholic whose preferred tipple is whisky. Another gin-and-wormwood combo was *purl* (possibly linked to standard *purl*, a rill or whirl of water) which used the dog's nose ingredients plus sugar and ginger. It was a popular morning pick-me-up and a cut-down version, *early purl* simply heated beer with gin. So popular was the combination that there were *purl-shops*, specialising in the drink, which were run by *purl-men*.

Gin and beer could also be *huckle-my-buff* or *-butt* which uses dialect's *huckle*, to jog along, thus making it literally 'jog my skin' or 'my buttocks'. Sometimes eggs and brandy were included (though the gin was then left out). *Piss quick* – either from its resemblance to urine or the fact that it made the drinker do exactly what its name suggested – is gin mixed with marmalade topped up with boiling water. *Twist* blends brandy and gin.

Ever-popular was *hot*, described by George Parker in his London guide *Life's Painter of Variegated Characters in Public and Private Life* (1789) as 'a mixed kind of liquor, of beer and gin, with egg, sugar and nutmeg'. He added that it was 'drank mostly in night-houses, but when drank in a morning, it is called flannel'. Like the material *flannel* 'kept you warm' and if you were *wrapt in warm flannel* you'd had too much. An older name, which underpinned flannel, had been *lambswool*. And for the really desperate, there was *alls*, which came either from *all nations*, as in 'flags of . . .', or more basically 'all the leftovers'. (Up the market Victorian wine merchants talked of *omnes*, Latin for 'all', the odds and ends of various wines.) Either way it consisted of the dregs collected from the overflow from the pouring taps, the ends of spirit bottles and similar leavings; it was sold cheap in gin shops where female customers, misogynists claimed, were particular devotees.

A cocktail composed of gin and ice, with a little sugar and a trace of water was a *monkey-chaser*; a *steel bottom* (perhaps from the need for such a lining to one's stomach to drink such a thing) was a cocktail of gin and wine; *mahogany*, from the colour, blended either gin and treacle or brandy and water; finally *bitter-gatter* mixed beer (gatter, from Romani *gatter*, water) and gin.

By 1736 the gin craze, boosted by unlicensed production and heavy duties on imported spirits, proved too much: Parliament passed the Gin Act, adding high taxes to what had been a poor man's tipple. The drinkers rioted. The tax was removed in 1742 but the spirit was in decline. Further legislation in 1751, which limited sales, was a law too far.

> 'Ye link and shoe boys clubb a tear,
> Ye basket-women join;
> Grubb-street, pour forth a stream of brine,
> Ye porters hang your heads and pine;
> All, all are damn'd to rot-gut beer.'
>
>   Timothy Scrub 'Desolation, or, The Fall of Gin' 1736

Now for something not really all that different. The tone is lowered, refinement a far-off chimera. Let us talk slang's tipple of choice, the blue, the blushful *cru argotois*, let us talk *meths*. In formal terms, denatured alcohol, or ethanol with unpleasant additives that in theory, but theory remains a good way from practice, stop you knocking it back.

> O for a beaker full of the warm South,
> Full of the true, the blushful Hippocrene,
> With beaded bubbles winking at the brim.
> And purple-stainèd mouth;
> That I might drink, and leave the world unseen.

This is taken from Keats' 'Ode to Nightingale'. Seemingly irrelevant but the poet got two things spot-on: the geography and, or nearly, the colour. Because while the chilly north, i.e. the UK, seems reticent in its naming of this ethanol/methanol mix, the warm and Southern lands of Australia, New Zealand and South Africa are far more creative. And denatured alcohol, thanks to those nasty extras, is very often purple, or at least a variety of muted violet.

It can be very simple: the simple *meths* itself, otherwise found as *meth* (not to be confused with über-speed methedrine) and *metha*. But, and perhaps here we owe something to its effects, there are other possibilities. The slang lexicon has swallowed the lot.

Australasia's contribution is marked upon its own map. There is *bush champagne*, defined as a pannikin of methylated spirits mixed with river water and a spoonful of *sal volatile* (the latter being better known as smelling salts). An alternative is the similarly constituted *Northern Territory champagne*. The salts give it that larky fizz. There is *bidgee*, from the Murrum*bidgee* River, and presumably those drunkards who frequent its banks, and the urban *Fitzroy cocktail*, celebrating a suburb of Melbourne. Decant methylated spirits as preferred, and add some form of mixer to mediate the taste. Meths could also be *round the world for a dollar*, with alternative prices listed as *threepence, fourpence* or *ninepence*. In all cases the 'trip' was provoked by meths, or a very cheap but almost equally potent wine.

Other terms from the lucky country have included *Jessie's Dream* and *Johnny Gee*. Jessie is lost to etymologists but generic Johnny is seen as 'gee-ing up' the drinker. So too does *jump-about*. Then there has been *fix bayonets*, a New Zealand term from World War I, a meths and orange juice mix used as a form of Dutch courage; *lunatic soup* or *broth* (which also denotes cheap red wine); World War II's *fong* or *fong-eye*, underpinned perhaps by Australia's ongoing terror of the so-called Yellow Peril. *Goom* is attributed to the Jagara language of Queensland, in which *goom*, less intoxicatingly, means simply water; *bombo*, which can be meths or cheap wine or a combination of the two, 'knocks one out'. *Atom-bombo*, of the late 1940s, simply puns on the drink and the recently empowered weapon. The *white lady*, otherwise a cocktail composed of two parts of dry gin, one of orange liqueur and one of lemon juice, can also, context permitting, be plain meths as well. *Steam* is another meths-and-wine cocktail, while *steamboats* rejects the wine and adds tea – Chinese, Indian or even Australia's own *post-and-rail* – to the ethanol base.

South Africa's standout term is *vlam*, from the Afrikaans for flame, but there are a variety of others: *ai-ai* (a mispronunciation of 'A.A.': nothing to do with temperance but 'absolute alcohol'), *queer stuff, mix, fly machine* (presumably from the effect of the drink) and *speed trap*. The meths drinker is a *spiritsuiper*, literally a 'spirit swiller'. But if these are relatively few, the country makes up with its accentuation of colour.

There is *bloutrein* (sometimes Englished as *blue train*), a dubious tribute to the Blue Train, a luxury passenger train running between Cape Town and Pretoria; those who drink meths are seen as boarding the 'fast train' to death. Slower but considered equally sure is *blouperd*, using Afrikaans *perd*, a horse. There is *blue ocean* and *die blou*, i.e. the blue. There is also, from New Zealand, the *blue lady* and from Australia *pink-eye*. A rare exception to the usual 'blues' is *Red Lizzie*, which dilutes the methylated spirits with cheap port.

There is Ireland's *blow* or *blowhard*, and *chat*, all apparently from the garrulousness that meths drinking can promote. *Feke*, meaning fake, and thus representing 'fake alcohol', was a favourite of the Thirties; drinkers usually added it to beer. If the meths was diluted with water it was known as *milk*, since the pure alcohol became cloudy.

America's best-known synonym is *canned heat*, or the proprietary *Sterno* (as in the original 'Sterno-Inferno' alcohol burner); its drinkers were the *canned heater* and *canned-heat stiff*. *Jack* is another US term and has been extended to cover a variety of illicitly distilled liquors, e.g. *tater jack* (potatoes), *prune jack* and *raisin jack*. There is also *jake*, which doubled as Jamaica ginger, an alcoholic but still legal high much favoured during Prohibition. The legs of habitual consumers became paralysed, leaving them *jake-legged*. Finally, fittingly, there is *finish*. Which, so it would appear, does to the drinker exactly what it promises on the label.

Pulp Diction: 'A roscoe coughed'

Horse and carriage? Once upon a time. Love and marriage? If you say so. Slang and crime. Now there's the union made in heaven. It's there at the beginning, in the first glossaries of the language of beggars, it's there in ballads, in so-called confessions and memoirs, in plays and novels, in newspaper sensation, in police procedurals, in noir, in TV and movies, in fanfic.

But it has never been there the way it was in pulp. The downmarket monthly million-sellers that dominated the news-stands before World War II. The opposite of *slicks*. Wood-pulp stock, lurid covers and mainly geared to working-class men instead of something shiny aimed at middle-class women. Born in the Twenties, reached their peak in the Thirties and Forties, and screwed in the Fifties, like much else in US popular culture, by the new juggernaut: TV. A theme for every market so long as it was down: military pulps, scifi pulps, mystery pulps, adventure pulps, sports pulps, western pulps, softcore pulps, romantic pulps (for the girls) and crime and detective pulps. A working-class market needed working-class language and every flavour of pulp dipped its toe into slang, but nothing used it, nothing needed it like the crim and detective pulps.

You might argue, and I do, on the basis of truffling out slang from all sorts of sources, that the books, short stories, and TV and movie scripts that can be grouped as 'pulp' or in the case of the visual stuff, *noir*, are the only example of a wholly slang-led cultural form. Slang had always been among the driving forces of various criminal tales – in fact or fiction, it was vital for authenticity, even if not everyone got it right – but pulp took things to another level. More than characterisation – minimal at best – or plot – sketchy if resolutely sensational – language was what drew people to the pulps and delineated what they were being offered. In a word, slang. And in two: hard-boiled, rough-edged, two-fisted . . . above all, tough slang. If the fictional likes of Dan Turner or Flashgun Casey might be seen as possessing a personality, it was that which they, or at least their creators projected in their conversation. Even Philip Marlowe, for all that his creator Raymond Chandler would philosophise about mean streets and the type of men who chose to walk them, showed his style in his speech.

Before we go on, to explore the vocabulary, let us have a look at pulp itself.

The use of wood pulp as the basis of paper-making is an invention of the mid-nineteenth century. Prior to that modern paper had been based on rags and other fibres, ever since the process had been discovered in China, around 105 CE. The move to wood pulp had been attempted in the later eighteenth century, but without success. Then, in 1844, two men, one American, the other German, succeeded in making the theory practice. Using the same processes, but substituting wood fibres for those of rags, they created a revolution in paper-making. Couple that to another novelty, the rotary printing press, plus the century's expansion of mass literacy, and the possibilities of profitable, mass-produced popular literature – whether fiction, non-fiction or as seen in the vast range of new newspapers and magazines – were infinite.

Pulp had one drawback; produced cheaply, it made for a cheap and ultimately ephemeral product. It was acidic, which meant that in time the pages would first yellow, then crumble to the touch. Publishers of upmarket books and magazines would still opt for rag-based paper, and charge accordingly, but the mass market made no such demands. Like the jerry-built housing that underpinned the growth of the great cities of the industrialised west, and which would house the readers of these new pulp-based media, it was form not content that counted. The future was not on the agenda.

The writer's work is not usually identified with the material on which it is produced. Who, other than book dealers and their customers, cared what the words were printed on. In magazine terms there was pulp or there was what the US called *slicks* and the UK *glossies*, high-end magazines – typically those devoted to women's fashion – printed on shiny stock. And even then, the reference was to the smooth, shiny surface rather than the underlying production process. Not quite digital vs dead-tree, but certainly disposable vs at least potentially longer-term.

Pulp would describe the magazine, the writer and what he or occasionally she wrote. The word was not congratulatory, but at best descriptive. The first one, Munsey's relaunch of *Argosy Magazine*, was geared to boys' adventure fiction and general information (not dissimilar to the UK's non-pulp *Boy's Own Paper*) and appeared in 1896. It offered 192 pages on untrimmed paper, with no illustrations, and, remarkably given what was to come, that meant a words-only cover too. But it was a hit: the first issue sold in the thousands, and by the start of the twentieth century sales were around half a million each month. It survived until 1978. The bandwagon rolled; other publishers would combine cheap paper, less than stellar writers paid less than stellar fees, and the mass production of steam-driven presses to feed a hungry market. The covers might be slick – in terms of paper, anyway, and unlike the pioneer, now wonderfully colourful – but the rest of the content, in every sense, was pure pulp. Usually 128 untrimmed pages, seven inches wide by ten inches high and a half an inch thick. Today such magazines have become collectors' items: back then they were built for immediate, exciting satisfaction. Like the tales they featured, and the language they were told in, they were never meant to last.

Slang's first recorded glossaries came from 'civilians' trying to make sense of what criminals were saying and criminal slang has been central to the vocabulary for half a millennium. The pulps exploited that vocabulary, but also set about creating it. Readers didn't expect standard English, they wanted rough, tough, and vivid. A tough guy used tough terminology. It was as vital to the story as James Bond's brand-names. Sometimes it got a little absurd: the nearest some of the words came to the real-life street was sitting on a newsstand between lurid covers, but no matter. It was all part of the atmosphere. Like the stereotypes of the world it aimed to portray it was terse, urgent, in your face. It wasn't invariably new, but what mattered was that it never cracked wise. Nothing fancy. Like the writing, no time to think. It was all action. No three-dollar words. Big on crisp synonymy: who would settle for one description when there were so many more to create. If the essence was guns and gals, cops and robbers, then you needed a good range of alternatives to spice up the basic story. Did villains and PIs really talk like this?

Most likely not, but that wasn't the point. In any case, as the spread of lines from movies such as the *Godfather* series or *Goodfellas* have made clear, the underworld isn't above taking a few tips from its fictional peers.

To discover pulp diction, let's take a look at the vocabulary used by one of the pulpiest of them all, Robert Leslie Bellem. This is the opening of 'Dead Heat' published in *Hollywood Detective* in January 1944.

I reached for the doorknob of Linda LaMarre's dressing room on the Altamount lot. Before I could turn it I heard a gurgling screech from inside, followed by a heavy thud. I yanked the portal open, catapulted over the threshold. Then I froze as I lamped the gorgeous LaMarre cupcake writhing on the floor. Her squirms reminded me of a gaffed eel on a hot rock. I knew she was a goner the instant I hung the focus on her glazing glims, her bluish-purple mush, her protruding tongue. A guy doesn't have to be a doctor to recognize the symptoms of suffocation. The quail on the carpet was obviously passing to her reward; and not from natural causes, either.

He was born in 1896. Or maybe 1904. He died in 1968 but so did John Steinbeck and Upton Sinclair not to mention Bobby Kennedy and Martin Luther King, and who was going to notice? He was called Robert Leslie Bellem but if there was a cheque on offer he'd answer to Ellery Watson Calder, Harley L. Court, Walt Bruce, John Grange, Nelson Kent, Kenneth A. Nelson, Jerome Severs Perry and Harcourt Weems. He wrote a million words a year, around three thousand stories in all, plus maybe seventy comic book scripts and when all that was through he moved into TV. There were even a pair of novels, but what he did best was pulp. He wrote for something called Culture Publications that specialised in 'spicy' titles which, by mid-century standards meant sexy: *Spicy Detective*, *Spicy Adventure*, *Spicy Western* and *Spicy Mystery*. He had various series characters but the one the readers loved was Dan Turner. The private dick. Bellem launched Turner in *Spicy Detective* with 'Murder By Proxy' in 1934 and finished off with 'Murder Wears Makeup' sixteen years on. There was a lot of murder in the titles. That and 'death', 'corpse', killer', and 'bump-off'. Art it wasn't. Turner moved on: in 1942 Bellem quit the Spicy stable and gave him a mag of his own: *Dan Turner, Hollywood Detective*. Then dropped the moniker and made it *Hollywood Detective*. They all sold.

It was such crime sheets, ranging from *Black Mask* (the first and best) to such as *Double-Action Detective*, *Detective Fiction Weekly*, and, inevitably, *Spicy Detective*, with dozens more on the newsies' racks, that remain the most celebrated of the genre. Hammett started there, on *Black Mask* (which, at least for a while, was what H.L. Mencken edited when he wasn't running *The Smart Set* or writing *The American Language*); Chandler too, and a whole bunch of others. But those two were the big boys and when they could they quit the pulps and started on novels and movies and as the best of breed were allowed to qualify as literature.

Most didn't, and didn't want to. Most hacks were more like Bellem, or Joe Archibald, who knocked out tales of his hen-pecked sad sack PI Willie Klump, the 'Hawkeye Hawkshaw' and bumbling 'president of the Hawkeye Detective Agency' (as well as the Dizzy Duo: 'Snooty Piper and Scoop Binney, those two newshawk scalawags' and several others). If Bellem's prose got unintentional laughs through its excess, Archibald played strictly for yuks. Either way he could knock it out week after week (after the pulps died he carried on with prototype YA titles: sports-themed books for boys and teens). You get the flavour from this ad for a bunch of 'classic Willie Klump Tales':

'BIRD CAGEY: A Fowl in the Hand May Be Worth Two in the Hedge, But Willie Klump Goes After Two Jailbirds with One Grindstone! ALIBI BYE: When Lady Luck Knocks On Willie Klump's Door, the Ingrate Detective Checks Up On Her Fingerprints. DOG COLLARED: When Willie Sees Red and Battles Saboteurs who Threaten the Navy Yard, He Wins the Fur-Lined Pooch for Sleuthing!'

Tongue well in cheek, puns aforethought: Archibald's stories were much the same.

It was a publishers' paradise. You could play one word a dozen ways and slap them each on a cover: *All Detective, Crack Detective, Double-Action Detective, Detective Fiction Weekly, Headquarters Detective, Lone Wolf Detective, Romantic Detective, Sure-Fire Detective, Ten Detective Aces, Thrilling Detective, Vice Squad Detective.*

Between them they put together a new star: the hard-boiled dick. The *eye*. The *shamus*. The *private operator*. Superstars like Hammett's Continental Op and Chandler's Philip Marlowe, and near-peers (but never quite near enough) like Flashgun Casey (from George Harmon Coxe) or Race Williams (from Carroll John Daley) and lesser players (in celebrity if not output) such as C.S. Montanye and Thomas Thursday. The public couldn't get enough. Voyeurs really, reading the pulps, watching the movies: *Public Enemy, White Heat, Scarface* and the rest, usually products of the Warners Brothers lot. Guns, girls, glamour and what the mob, at least on pulp paper, would call *geetus*, which was money. Maybe not aspirational, like the slicks, but definitely day-dreams. The underworld, as ever, looked a lot sexier than the daily grind. One pulp title billed itself as *Racket and Gangster Stories*. No one bitched. The penny-a-liners just had to remember to toss in a moral ending.

Bellem took it to the limit. Slang in excelsis. Synonyms like a thesaurus. Tough guy: tough terminology. Looking back, maybe he was parodying the whole form. You weren't an investigator but a *private dick, pry, skulk* or *snoop*. There were even hat-tips to culture: *Hawkshaw* and *Sherlock*. You met women, had women (none of Chandler's squirming, euphemistic 'erotic as a stallion' for Dan: no limp-wristed *gazooks, jessies* or *she-males* – though confusingly a *she-male* can also be all-woman – invited to his spartan *shebang*). You called them *chicks, cookies, cupcakes, cuties, dames, muffins, tomatoes* and *dishes, dolls, janes, numbers, patoot-ies, tricks, twists, wrens, frails, tails* and *quails*. As ever, when slang meets women, the emphasis was on food or birds.

Linguistically at least, Bellem was a *tit-man* (though the term isn't known before 1960): *glims* wide open he *lamps* a range of *bonbons* ('voluptuous'), *doo-dads* ('full, rounded'), *tidbits* ('perk-ily mounded'), *half-melons* ('heaving, panting, ripe') and *thingumabobs* ('jiggling like mounds of aspic in an earthquake'), but merely *gams, pins* or *stems* for legs (and he elaborates on none of them). Of course there was nothing extreme. Like what Turner called the *galloping snapshots* or *tintypes* even at the spicy end where the illustrations – with a regular nipple count and plenty of flesh: hot stuff for the period – were probably the sexiest aspect of the story, the pulps exerted their own self-censoring version of Hollywood's Hays Code. S.J. Perelman, who penned scripts for the Marx Brothers and called his journalism *feuille-tons*, wrote up Turner for the *New Yorker*. Bellem's boy was 'the apotheosis of all private detectives' and Perelman paired (or as he put it 'juxtaposed') 'the steely automatic' with 'the frilly pantie'. But while Turner might enjoy the occasional *hook-up* (long before today's relaunch of the term), and a pair of cute *stems* or a flash of lingerie has him *ga-ga*, he always shut the door (or cut the narrative) right there.

This stuff jostled with much more respectable material on the news-stands so self-censorship ran through the text. Obscenity was out, so too blasphemy and even the milder oaths. Turner beats 'the bejunior' out of some luckless victim, 'Pal . . .' says another, 'Pal, my elbow' demurs our hero. Others fall 'end' or 'neck over appetite'. Nonsense is 'sheepdip'.

Other pleasures? The occasional *cokey* or *hophead* might *hit the hype* with a bit of *nose candy* but such were not Turner's drugs of choice. Philip Marlowe was equally squeamish and like Marlowe and any other PI, Dan was a hard liquor man. You *belted the bottle, bent the elbow, inhaled* and *irrigated*. You downed *jolts, slugs* and *snootfuls* of *giggle-juice* or *grog, jiggers of joy-water* and *jorums of skee* (*skee* being whisky, a *jorum* was an eighteenth-century punch-bowl). Occasionally someone slipped you a *mickey finn* (from an 1890s Chicago bartender who supposedly picked up the recipe from voodoo operators in New Orleans). You got *oiled, stinko, wacked, fried* (*to your hat, to the gills, to the tonsils*), *drunker than a fiddler's bitch* or *so bottled you couldn't hit the side-walk with a handful of soybeans*. Of course you smoked: *coffin nails* or *wheezers* which you never merely lit, but *torched* or *fired*.

Back at work it was all about the money, which was *chips, fish, geetus, gravy, cabbage, greenery* or *salad, kopecks, marbles, pelf, iron men, spondulicks, moola* and *ducats*. Guns were *cannons, gats, rods* or *rodneys, peashooters, persuaders, roscoes* and *equalisers*. Guns that fired *slugs* but mainly *lead* or *lead pills* and gave the unfortu-nate target *lead poisoning* or a *lead supper*. Guns that didn't simply shoot, but *burned, cracked, whopped, squibbed, coughed* and *yapped.* And didn't kill but *beefed, biffed, blipped, bopped, belted, browned, bumped* and *butched* and that was just the Bs. If you held back a little there was fisticuffs and you doled out *knuckle medicine* or *knuckle tonic.* The dead had *croaked* (murder was *croakery*) and *cashed in their chips,* unless they did it themselves, which was *the Dutch act.*

Off on another case you drove to the *wigwam, igloo, tepee, stash* or *shebang* in your *go-cart, go-buggy, jitney, jalopy, heap, bucket, chariot, wheels, tub, kettle, hack, skate* or *sled.* When the *flatheads, gendarmes, harness bulls* and *slewfoots* (Irish to a man) came in, late as ever and if you'd left the *ginzos, grifters, bimbos, bozos, slobs, bohunks, apes, gorillas, slugs, tough boys, bruisers, muggs, strongarms* and *jibones* alive, they took them off to the *bastille,* the *gow,* the *slammer* or the *big house.* (If not, they'd need the *meat basket,* which took the body to the morgue.) Later, when they got the *juice,* they'd *cook* in the *smokehouse,* astride the *sizzle sofa.*

If Bellem represents one extreme, he and his fellow-pulpsters had no monopoly. We are talking pulp, but paradoxically one of the great exploiters of gangland language never met that downmarket medium. Damon Runyon wrote strictly for the slicks.

In January 1934 W.J. Funk, of the dictionary publisher Funk and Wagnalls, offered his list of the 'ten modern Americans who have done most to keep American jargon alive'. His candidates included Sime Silverman, editor of the 'show business bible' *Variety,* which boasted a lingo all of its own, the cartoonist 'TAD' (Theodore Aloysius) Dorgan, regularly credited with many more coinages than he actually achieved, mid-West humourist George Ade who wrote best-selling 'Fables in Slang', sports journo-turned-short story writer Ring Lardner, the Broadway showbiz columnist and one-time vaudeville hoofer Walter Winchell, and Winchell's best buddy, another ex-sports-writer, Damon Runyon.

Runyon (1880–1946), in a phrase, is what happened when pulp hit the slicks. In terms of linguistic creativity and his influence on slang – as much in his popularisation as in his coinages – from the point of view of *Black Mask* or even *Spicy Detective*, Damon Runyon is the one that got away. By any standards – the big city backdrop, the low-life 'Guys and Dolls' who peopled his tales, the slang they gave them – he seemed a natural for the pulps. In the event they never crossed his mind.

Unlike his pal the gossip-monger Walter Winchell, who made a career from sucking up to the FBI's paranoid, homophobic, cross-dressing, Red-baiting boss J. Edgar Hoover, Runyon, who arrived in New York in 1910 and was one of a number who would parlay sports journalism into something much more substantial, came at the low-life from a very different angle.

Winchell was a law and order groupie. Runyon seemed to sympathise with the gangsters and their molls. And if he made a career from fictionalising their antics, it was not as an amateur policeman, though he wrote up a number of major trials including that of Bruno Hauptmann, the Linbergh baby kidnapper, and of an old pal, Al Capone. And towards the end, unable to speak after treatment for throat cancer, he toured the night-time city alongside his friend Winchell, tracking down underworld action via Winchell's police radio.

He was a big gambler and moved regularly in those less than legitimate circles. His best friend was Dutch Schultz's accountant, Otto 'Abbadabba' Berman who died in 1935 in the same burst of machine-gun bullets as did his boss. Runyon put him into his stories as 'Regret, the horse player'. He put Winchell in too, as the newspaper scribe 'Waldo Winchester'.

The first story of what would be known as the 'Guys and Dolls' of Broadway appeared in 1929. The tale runs that Runyon, with his knowledge of gangland, was told to write about the assassination that year of 'Mr Big' Arnold Rothstein. He dried but turned for rescue to a fictional take, writing: 'Only a rank sucker will think of taking two peeks at Dave the Dude's doll, because while Dave may stand for the first peek, figuring it is a mistake, it is a sure thing he will get sored up at the second peek, and Dave the Dude is certainly not a man to have sored up at you.' The *New York American*, the tabloid for which he wrote on baseball and boxing, bought the story for $800.

There would be eighty more and they would be published in high-selling and high-paying magazines like *Cosmopolitan*, *Colliers* and the *Saturday Evening Post* where you might also find such literary superstars as Hemingway or Scott Fitzgerald. They were printed, predictably, on slick stock. Runyon's characters may have walked out of the hard-boiled section of the pulp magazines, but they would never be bracketed with even the best of them. Apart from the sheer quality of the writing, Runyon's robbers and good-time girls were paradoxically soft-boiled. Hearts were invariably golden (even if the usual possessor of such an organ, the whore, was absent). Their creator claimed that his basic plot was that of the fairy-tale Cinderella. And although there is a good deal of violence and not a few murders, the stories do have a fairy-tale element. They are perhaps fables, although the reader has to work out the moral for themselves. The good may not always win, but the bad always get their deserts. There is sentiment in Runyon's Broadway as well as sensation. Runyon celebrated the underworld, but his mobsters were strictly for those who bought the slicks. Like the middle-class readers who revelled in the canting terms that Dickens put into *Oliver Twist*, but tut-tutted over those who actually used them, Runyon's readers found his stories as near real-life villainy as they wished to go. The middle classes wouldn't read *Black Mask*, even when Hammett or Chandler were on the cover; they did take *Cosmopolitan* and the *SEP*.

Readers did not turn to Runyon for his plots, even if several of them became movies and one the regularly revived musical *Guys and Dolls*. Runyon was about language and while many observers swore that Runyon was making it up as he went along, it wasn't so: the bulk of that language was well established, whether within the underworld or elsewhere. His works can be mined for over a thousand terms, and while there are occasions on which he tinkers, typically by adding suffixes (*-eroo*, *-aroo*, *-ola*, and *-us*), or tweaking an established slang term with a variant synonym (e.g. *Francesca* for *fanny*), Runyon's slang is sound. Terms such as *bim, collar, cut up old touches, duke, ear-ie, flogger, keister, moxie, potatoes, roscoe, scratch* and *yard* were all established part of the speech-worlds in which he moved. Even the seemingly *echt*-Runyon *ever-loving* (usually applied, ironically or otherwise, to a wife) was two decades old. That didn't disqualify him from originality: the *old ackama-rackus, walk-about money*, an *umbrella* (a useless boxer who 'folds up') and *zillionaire* plus around 250 more were all his own work.

Bellem may have shared far more of his vocabulary with the rest of the pulp crew (for instance over 120 terms with Chandler) but there were places where he and Runyon overlapped. *Deal them off the arm* (to wait tables), *behind the eight ball* (in trouble), *crush out* (to escape), *elly-bay* (backslang for the stomach), *lamster* (an escapee), *the shorts* (poverty), *sconce* (the head), *yard* ($100) and maybe thirty more.

A recent critic, Adam Gopnik, has compared Runyon's use of language to that of another star of the slicks, P.G. Wodehouse, who also revelled in slang, whether such Edwardianisms as *oojah-cum-spiff* or *rannygazoo*, or the monosyllables of American low-life. For Gopnik, 'Like Wodehouse, [. . .] Runyon inherited a comedy of morals and turned it into a comedy of sounds, language playing for its own sake.'

Bellem used language for a simpler reason: to pay the bills. Runyon, an artist, lives on, Bellem, the hack, is quite invisible. Let him have the last words:

Ordinarily I'm opposed to dames wearing trousers, but this doll was different. She was a tall and luscious red-haired tomato in a sleekly tailored emerald slack suit that made you want to howl like a wolf when you saw how it stressed her willowy curves, and her chiseled mush was just as gorgeous as her contours. She came drifting into the Trocambo on the Sunset Strip while I was inhaling supper, and the instant I lamped her I lost my appetite for fried chicken. She was that kind of cookie; she sent you. And after you'd been sent you had the feeling that you didn't want to come back, ever.

Tell Me a Story: Proper Names

THE TRUTH, FRUSTRATING as ever, is that the bulk of slang, some 75 per cent or even more, is based on standard English. No elaborate coinages, no revolutionary groundbreaking inventions, nothing plucked all new and shiny from the air. Or pretty much not so. What so much of slang is about is manipulating those well-known words: playing and punning, twisting and tweaking, turning inside out and round about. *Dog* may have two hundred-plus uses in slang, but in the end they all go back to those well-known three letters (and to make things worse, a check with the etymologists shows that we don't actually know where d-o-g comes from itself. Nor c-a-t either). As noted, slang's vocabulary comes mainly from the exploitation and recycling of slang's themes. Thus the multiple synonyms of so many.

However, and we should definitely be grateful that this is so in a book entitled *The Stories of Slang*, there are exceptions. Sometimes there is a word, though usually some kind of phrase, that comes with a built-in tale. Whether that tale is true, well, that is, as they say, another story.

Drunk, drink and drunkards are among slang's central pillars. The founding father, *booze*, albeit as *bouse*, turns up in the first-ever slang glossary, penned around 1535, and is still hanging in, backed by around forty compounds (*booze artist, booze hound, booze gob, boozologist, boozery . . .*). It comes either from Dutch (*buizen*) or German (*bausen*), which meant to drink to excess. The *OED*'s first use is *c.*1300, but this may only refer to a drinking vessel, rather than its contents (the Dutch term is also rooted in *buise,* a large drinking vessel). Either way, the term really came on stream when co-opted by the sixteenth century's criminal canting crew.

Stories, however, tend to accumulate round drunk, the adjective rather than the noun. Much depends on comparison, i.e. those to whom, as, *bouyant* yet *scuttered,* we *pull a Daniel Boone* or *make indentures with our legs* (which referred to the drunkard's stumbling path, supposedly reminiscent of the custom of indenting the top edges of legal documents) we seem to resemble. In many cases slang takes on the animal, bird or insect role: drunk as a *bat,* a *boiled owl,* a *coon* (though this may be a racial slur), a *cootie,* a *dog,* a *fish,* a *fly,* a *fowl,* a *hog, sow, swine* or *pig,* a *jaybird,* a *monkey,* a *mouse* or *rat,* a *skunk in a trunk* or a *tick.* Whether any of these are exceptional tipplers in nature is unlikely. No matter: slang has little time for detail. As for the humans, it's a matter of stereotyping: contenders include a *bastard,* a *beggar,* a *besom* (an old woman rather than a broom), a *bowdow* (possibly a misconstruction of Bordeaux and thus a nod to its vintners), a *brewer's fart,* a *cook,* an *emperor,* a *fiddler,* a *Gosport fiddler* or indeed a *fiddler's bitch,* as *forty,* as a *little red wagon* or a *wheelbarrow,* a *log,* a *loon,* a *lord,* a *peep,* a *Perraner,* a *piper,* a *poet,* a *rolling fart,* a *sailor,* a *tapster* (the nearest we come to publican), or a *top.*

If none of these, at least as recorded, offers a story then others do. Let us start with *Davy's* or *David's sow.* According to the *Lexicon Balatronicum,* a slang dictionary of 1811, it went like this:

'One David Lloyd, a Welchman, who kept an alehouse at Hereford, had a living sow with six legs, which was greatly resorted to by the curious; he had also a wife much addicted to drunkenness, for which he used sometimes to give her due correction. One day David's wife having taken a cup too much, and being fearful of the consequences, turned out the sow, and lay down to sleep herself sober in the stye. A company coming in to see the sow, David ushered them into the stye, exclaiming, there is a sow for you! did any of you ever see such another? all the while supposing the sow had really been there; to which some of the company, seeing the state the woman was in, replied, it was the drunkenest sow they had ever beheld; whence the woman was ever after called *David's sow*.'

From misogyny, one slang staple, we turn to another, racism. In this case the exemplary *lushington* is one *Cooter*, also known as *Cootie Brown*. There are two versions. In the first we find Cooter living on the line that, in the US Civil War, divided North and South. This apparently made him eligible for the draft whichever side's recruiting sergeant came calling. Cooter's solution: to get drunk and stay drunk, thus rendering himself militarily useless for the duration. And so he did, with his story living on long after him. If that seems barely feasible, how about this? Cooter Brown was mixed race; half Cherokee, half African American. He was also all misanthropist, wholly drunk, and he too, though living far from the border in a shack in Lousiana, was unfortunate enough to encounter the Civil War. Given the situation he carefully dressed as a Cherokee and was as such considered a free man. Yankees and Johnny-Rebs both came to call, invariably found him drunk and shared his bottles. Cooter survived the war but not long after his shack caught fire and burned to the ground. There was no sign of its owner's remains. Popular wisdom had it that so sodden with alcohol was the old man that he had simply evaporated in the flames. *Drunk as cooter brown* remains his memorial.

Then, still souse-shaming, we have *Chloe*. Why *drunk as Chloe*? In truth, who knows. But again, there are theories. Given the phrase turns up in Australia, it may well be a back-handed reference to a notorious painting, *Chloé* (painted in 1875) which, having been rejected in 1883 by the Melbourne National Gallery – not only naked, she was also French and actually named Marie – had been bought by the city's well-known Young and Jackson Hotel, where it became a point of attraction for many visitors, especially soldiers on R and R. However, back in 1789, in a poem 'The Bunter's Christening', we meet a variety of low-lifes: 'muzzy Tom', 'sneaking Snip, the boozer' (and presumably tailor, since *snip* was slang's term for the occupation), 'blear-ey'd Ciss' . . . and 'dust-cart Chloe'. An excellent thrash ensues to wet the baby's head and the poem ends thus:

> For supper, Joey stood,
> To treat these curious cronies;
> A bullock's melt, hog's maw
> Sheep's heads, and stale polonies:
> And then they swill'd gin-hot,
> Until blind drunk as Chloe.

Which gives us our final comparison: *drunk as a polony*. The simple interpretation of polony, as consumed by Chloe and pals, is a Bologna sausage. Such a sausage, like a drunk, cannot stand upright and polony, to underline the image, can also mean a fool. Thus the link. However there is an alternative. French slang once gave *soul comme un Polonnais*, drunk as a Pole, a comparison that supposedly mocked the Polish-French Maréchal de Saxe, a great tippler.

Let us stay in Australia. And indeed at the bar. If that great but generally unloved tradition the *six o'clock swill* (the pubs shut at that time, you had to drink hard and fast for the brief period that followed five o'clock knocking-off time at work) is long gone, another, the *shout*, remains in place. Like the UK's *round*, the shout means you buy drinks for your mates, and on occasion the entire bar. But the shout is perhaps even more ritualistic. It's not just a matter of missing one's round, but down in *Godzone*, nature abhors the solitary boozer. He even has a name: a *Jimmy Woodser* (and very occasionally *Jack Smithers*), applied both to the drinker and the miserable, lonely glass he's gazing into. It is not a much-loved state. As a newspaper versifier put it in 1916:

When I 'as a 'Jimmy Woodser' on my own,
'Twas like someone shook the meat an' left the bone,
The bloomin' flavour's left the beer,
An' there isn't 'arf the cheer.
It's like torking to yerself upon the 'phone

As ever, there are rival etymologies. One ties him to an eponymous and 'solitary Briton' (yes, the whingeing pom, as ever), no friend of shouting, whose egregious lack of sociability was the subject of the poem 'Jimmy Wood', by B.H.T. Boake, published in *The Bulletin* on 7 May 1892. It wasn't that he disliked drink: 'His "put away" for liquid was abnormal' (his tipple being 'unsweetened gin, most moderately watered') but 'he viewed this "shouting" mania with disgust, / As being generosity perverted' and 'vowed a vow to put all "shouting" down'. There are four-teen quadruplets, we can't have them all, but the bottom line was that Jimmy drank himself to death. The shout, however, remained undaunted.

So that's 1892. The problem is that in 1926 a correspondent of the *Brisbane Courier* offered his own take. This was from 1860. According to his story, around that date two rival pub-licans, John Ward and James Woods, had hotels [i.e. pubs] on the opposite corners of York and Market streets in Sydney. 'Mr. Woods, in the course of business, refused to serve the female section of his customers, as by their habits they were giving his "house" a bad name, and they perforce transferred their libations to the opposition; hence the term "Johnny Warders". Mr. Woods, having got rid of the women, had then for his customers the aforesaid barrowmen, gardeners, and casual hands and shoppers from the markets, and as the majority of these individuals, not being overburdened with wealth, usually drank by themselves, the term applied to them, and subsequently, even to the present day, given to "lone drinkers", was "Jimmy Woodsers".' Perhaps, but *Johnny Warder*, at least as recorded, means not 'woman' but 'drunken layabout' (indeed its first recorded use features a female complainant, loath to join such figures) and it was those who made their way to John Ward's *boozorium*.

Enough of Australia, at least for now. Clerkenwell lies just north-east of the City of London. The area, just beyond the city walls, was the first suburb, and with its errant population, focused on Turnmill (sometimes Turnbull) Street running along-side the Fleet River (now Farringdon Road), once celebrated as the home of whores and villainy. Shakespeare's Falstaff mentions it, as did many contemporary playwrights and the nine-teenth-century sociologist James Greenwood, keen to set a story against the slums, used it in a novel. It gained, of course, a slang nickname: *Jack Adams' Parish*, and *Jack Adams* alone and used generically, meant a fool.

For once we have an undisputed back-story. Jack Adams was indeed a fool, a professional one, and in time made himself over as an astrologer and fortune-teller. Fortunes were apparently graded: the more pay the more play and a five-guinea prognostication was far more positive than a five-shilling one (logical enough given the wealth of one who could afford the former sum). He was sufficiently well known to bestow his name on a dance: 'Do you know Jack Adams' Parish', which was still popular in the 1770s. In 1663 he brought out *Jack Adams his perpetual almanack with astrological rules and instructions, directing to an exact knowledge of all future things till the morrow after doomsday. Together with his rare art of fortune-telling, and interpretation of dreams . . . A work much desired, and by a strange accident preserved, and now published for the illumination of posterity.* Sold exclusively 'by the Ginger-Bred-Woman in Clarkenwell-Green' it carried the warning: 'If you do refuse to buy / You'll shew yourself more fool than I'.

The first use of *all my eye and Betty Martin* emerged in 1780 (*all my eye* had been there since 1728). Other versions include *all in my eye and Betty, all my eye and Elizabeth Martin, my eye and Peggy Martin*, and *oh Betty Martin, that's my eye*. Whatever the format *Betty Martin* herself continues to be a source of controversy. Eric Partridge suspected that she was a late-eighteenth-century London character and that no record of her exists other than this catchphrase. Other slang collectors – Jon Bee and John Camden Hotten – both refer to the alleged Latin prayer, *Ora pro mihi, beate Martine* ('Pray for me blessed Martin'), i.e. St Martin of Tours, the patron saint of publicans and reformed drunkards. It has yet to be found in any version of the liturgy. Writing in 1914, Dr L.A. Waddell suggests another Latinism, *O mihi Britomartis* ('O bring help to me, Britomartis'), referring to the tutelary goddess of Crete. Most likely, and predating Partridge, is the idea proposed in Charles Lee's *Memoirs* (1805), that there had once been 'an abandoned woman called Grace', who, in the late eighteenth century, married a Mr Martin. She became notorious as *Betty Martin*, and *all my eye* was apparently among her favourite phrases.

Buckley comes up twice in slang's phraseology. There is the nineteenth century's question *Who struck Buckley?* and the dismissive Australianism *Buckley's chance*, coined in the 1890s and still going strong.

The former is defined by John Camden Hotten as 'a common phrase used to irritate Irishmen'. Setting aside the justification of such irritation, Hotten went on to explain it thus: 'The story is that an Englishman having struck an Irishman named Buckley, the latter made a great outcry, and one of his friends rushed forth screaming, "Who struck Buckley?" "I did," said the Englishman, preparing for the apparently inevitable combat. "Then," said the ferocious Hibernian, after a careful investigation of the other's thews and sinews, "then, sarve him right."' This form of equivocation seems to lie behind all Buckley-pertinent anecdotes: the violence, the sympathetic supporter, the judicious assessment of the assailant and the substitution of valour by discretion. The *Spectator*, in 1912, replaced the Irishman with an unfortunate junior boy at a public school and used it to critique Parliament's failure to offer any more than empty bombast – and certainly no gunboats – when the horrors of the Belgian treatment of their Congolese subjects was revealed. A year later one Boris Sidis, writing about 'The Psychology of

Laughter', resurrected the centrality of the Emerald Isle: in this case the sympathetic speaker was 'a peasant, undersized but wrathful, and with his shillelagh grasped threateningly in his hand . . . going about the fair asking, "Who struck Buckley?"' and again, on encountering 'a stalwart and dangerous man,' swiftly backed down: 'Well, afther all perhaps Buckley desarved it.'

Australian *Buckley's*, often amplified as *Buckley's chance*, *hope* or *show*, has elicited a wide range of theories. Of these, which (quite erroneously) include the Yindjibarndi verb *bucklee*, to initiate an Aborigine boy, especially by circumcision, the best hopes lie with William *Buckley* (1780–1856), an escaped convict (known as 'the wild white man') who spent thirty-two years living with Aborigines in South Victoria; or a pun on the name of defunct firm *Buckley and Nunn* (founded by Mars Buckley and Crumpton Nunn in 1851) which states that one has two chances: 'Buckley and Nunn', i.e. none. The main problem with William was that the phrase doesn't turn up until nearly forty years after his death, and in any case, whatever the vagaries of his life – both before and after his return to 'civilisation' – chance, whether bad or indeed good doesn't seem to come into it. The journal *Ozwords* (produced by the *Australian National Dictionary*) deals with the whole topic in its October 2000 edition (available online). Suffice it to say that their conclusion is that Buckley and Nunn, providers of the pun, are the most likely originators.

Ireland offers *Johnny Wet-bread*, a teasing rather than aggressive term of mockery. Johnny existed – he was a well-known Dublin beggar who, bereft of alternatives, moistened his bread in the city's fountains. Unlike most street people he has a memorial, albeit shared. It is to be found on a plaque at the city's Coombe Maternity Hospital on Cork Street, where his name joins those of other city characters: Stab the Basher, Damn the Weather, and Nancy Needle Balls.

The last of these has sadly not, despite the undoubted poten-tial, entered the slang lists. As we know, slang is too often a man-made vocabulary. However we do have the historically proven Mrs Phillips, she of *Mrs Phillips's ware*, condoms. Captain Grose explains: 'These machines were long prepared and sold by a matron of the name of Phillips, at the Green Canister, in Half-moon Street, in the Strand. That good lady, having acquired a fortune, retired from business, but learning that the town was not well served by her successors, she, out of a patriotic zeal for the public welfare, returned to her occupation . . . in the year 1776.' Whether – grandmother, great-aunt? – she was related to Mrs Phillips, that brothel-keeper who, in the mid-nineteenth century, ran a house specialising in flagellation at 11 Upper Belgrave Place in Pimlico, is alas unknown.

Nor are such women who exist strictly 'real'. Sometimes they have been appropriated by men: typically *Mrs Hand* and *Mrs Palm* (first name *Patsy*) both of whom are blessed with *five daughters* (or sometimes *sisters*) who represent the hand, as used for masturbation (for further details see **The Body: Only Man is Vile**).

Other generic 'women' include a variety of Misses and Missuses. Examples include the overdressed socialite *Miss Lizzie Tish*, the well-built and noisy *Miss Big Stockings*, the unpopular *Miss Fitch*, who rhymes with *bitch*, flouncing *Miss Nancy* who is not in fact a girl but a gay young man, opulent *Miss van Neck*, known for a magnificent cleavage and minatory *Miss Placed Confidence*, a mid-nineteenth-century term for venereal disease. *Mrs Evans* and *Mrs Fubbs* are both (literal) cats, and *Mrs Fubbs' parlour*, pushing the whole *pussy* thing that distance further, is the vagina. *Mrs Jones' counting house* is a lavatory and *Mrs Greenfields* sleeping in the open air. The one area where men do not trespass is, predictably, menstruation. Among its many euphemisms are the punning *Aunt Flo*, *Auntie Jane* and sanguine *Aunt Rose*, *Grandma George* and *Granny Grunts*, *Monica*; quite how *Charlie* and *Tommy* join the party is unknown, but so they do.

One last woman is *Kathleen Mavourneen*. The name, which comes from the song 'Kathleen Mavourneen', written in 1837 and meaning, in Gaelic 'Kathleen my beloved', was initially popular in the US but its slang uses have been Australian and focus on the chorus which runs 'It may be for years, it may be forever,' and is defined variously as an indeterminate period of time, an indeterminate prison sentence, an habitual criminal (who may be serving the former), a promise (usually in the context of a loan, which most likely will remain outstanding; business jargon uses the name for any defaulting debtor) and an Australian swagman's pack (better known as a *bluey*) which he may carry for a lifetime. Finally there is the *Kathleen Mavourneen system*, Australia's name for hire purchase.

The better-known term is *tell it to the Marines (the sailors won't believe it)!* which plays on the true salt's contempt for the half-sailors, half-soldiers who once sailed alongside him, but slang has also come up with an equivalent: *tell it to* (or *save it for*, or *that'll do for*) *Sweeney!* Both work as a dismissive exclamation of disbelief in a previous far-fetched statement. The Sweeney version seems to have emerged in the 1920s. It was likely popularised by a silent movie of that name, released in 1927 and starring funnyman Chester Conklin, but US researcher Barry Popik has it a few years earlier, first used in an advertisement for the New York *Daily News*, first appearing in August 1922: 'Tell it to Sweeney! (The Stuyvesants will understand.)' The *Daily*

News being a devotedly blue-collar paper, it picked Sweeney – a classic Irish name, alongside Riley, Kelsey or Kilroy, all of whom play their own slang roles – and set it against the Stuyvesants, a name and family long established among the city's aristocracy. However, the phrase can be pushed back a little further: to the 1910 musical *The Yankee Girl*, which featured the song 'Tell it to Sweeney'. There was even an ad, used a year earlier, which suggested to New Yorkers that 'If you have any harness trouble tell it to SWEENEY, the leading harness maker' but this may be coincidental. Quite unconnected, Sweeney can also mean a barber, from the fictional *Sweeney Todd*, the 'demon barber' of Fleet Street, who sold 'golopshious' pies made from the flesh of those he had murdered.

Further violence links to *Morgan Rattler*, which comes from dialect and was used around 1890 to describe a hard or reckless fighter and thence a good boxer; outside pugilism it simply meant an outstanding example. But its original use came a century earlier: some form of stick with a knob of lead at one or both ends; unlike the rigid police truncheon, the stick itself was flexible, made of bamboo or metal and especially favoured as the garrotters' weapon of choice. It could and sometimes did kill. All of which leads to its use in slang: the penis. Whether this under-pinned its adoption as the name of a popular fiddle tune is unknown, but there was a song 'Morgan Rattler' included in *Chap Book Songs* around 1790 which ran: 'At night with the girls he still is a flatterer, / They never seem coy, but tremble for joy, / When they get a taste of his Morgan Rattler.' Terry Pratchett fans will recall the popular Discworld ditty 'A wizard's staff has a knob on the end'.

Animals have already cropped up as similes for drunk humans; they also boast some names on their own account. There is *Mrs*

Astor's pet (or *plush*) *horse*, a US term for an over-made-up or overdressed person, Mrs William Backhouse Astor Jr. (neé Caroline Schermerhorn) being the immensely rich doyenne of New York society (a.k.a. the '400', that being the maximum number that could fit comfortably into her ballroom). Another horse, this time all-equine is *Phar Lap*, which meant 'flash of lightning', and remains Australia's most famous racehorse, since its glory days in the 1930s. In slang it means (heavy-handedly) a very slow person and (gruesomely) a wild dog, with its hair burnt off, trussed up and cooked in the ashes. The *phar lap gallop* is (perhaps anomalously) a foxtrot.

Ireland provides a number of creatures that stand for humans who are happy to befriend whoever turns up, and will go 'a little way with everyone'. Presumably the journey was once literal; the figurative has wholly replaced it. What we don't know, frustratingly, is the background of any of these affectionate if less than wholly loyal creatures: *Lanna* or *Alanna Macree's dog*, *Lanty MacHale's goat* (he had a *dog* as well), *Larry McHale's dog*, *Billy Harran's dog*, *Dolan's ass*, and *O'Brien's dog*. All must have sprung from some local character, none bothered to explain to the wider world. Nor did *Paddy Ward's pig*, a lazy person, constantly relaxing in the face of work; *Goodyer's pig*, which was constantly in or causing trouble, *Joe Heath's mare*, a hard worker, expanded into the phrase *like Joe Heath's mare*, exerting oneself or behaving in an excited manner.

We have better luck with *all on one side like Lord Thomond's cocks*, a phrase that denotes a group of people who appear to be united but are, in fact, more likely to quarrel. There was a late-eighteenth-century Lord Thomond, an Irish peer, there were a group of cocks – bred for fighting and the gambling that went with the cockpit – and there was a cock-feeder, one James

O'Brien, who foolishly confined a number of his lordship's cocks, due to fight the next day for a considerable sum, all in the same room. Stereotyped for the story as a stupid Irishman, he supposedly believed that since they were all 'on the same side', they would not squabble. He was wrong, and the valuable cocks destroyed each other.

Too many of slang's proper names offer no clues as to their origin, although most suggest some kind of lost anecdote. Some, e.g. *Charlie Prescott* (or *Billy Prescot, Colonel Prescott, Jim(my)* or *John Prescott*) for waistcoat or *Dan Tucker* for butter are rhyming slang and there are dozens of similar examples which can be drawn from most of the format's two-hundred-year history: *Germaine Greer* or *Britney Spears*, beer, *Posh and Becks*, sex, *Harry Randle*, candle, *Nervo and Knox*, the pox and on it goes. But the names are mere conveniences, they rarely if ever link to their meaning, they are there for assonance not anecdote.

Some names, on the other hand, beg for a story. The US south-west's *Charlie Taylor*, syrup or molasses into which bacon or ham fat has been poured; the mid-nineteenth-century UK's *Jerry Lynch*, a poor-quality pickled pig's head reserved for sale in slum butchers; *make a Judy (Fitzsimmons) of oneself*, to be a fool, to make an idiot of oneself; *Ned Stokes*, the four of spades; *Tom Brown*, a name for cribbage and *Tom Bray's bilk*, laying out the ace and deuce when playing that game; *not for Joe* (nor *for Joseph*), by no means, not on any account; a *Salamanca wedding*, the marriage of an old man to a (rich) young woman; *Joe McGee*, a stupid, unreliable person; *Lady Dacre's wine*, gin, but which Lady Dacre? *Mickey T*, a woman who pursues powerful and/or wealthy men and spurns the rest; *Kennedy*, a poker; *Johnny O'Brien*, a freight train or one of its boxcars; being a *passenger on the Cape Ann stage* or *talking to Jamie Moore*, drunk, and the exclamation *in* (or *off*) *you go says Bob Munro*. Even *Roscoe* or *John Roscoe*, so widely used for a handgun, has no known origin. There are others. Slang, frustratingly, remains careless of such tales and they may beg, but we do not receive.

It is not just these. Slang has a number of what might be termed known unknowns: how well we know the words, how little chance we have of eliciting a concrete etymology. The words and phrases that defy all explanation: *the whole nine yards* is an exemplar. *OK* was another but that has long since been explained. To conclude let us take one more, focused on a name, and still defying explanation.

Although the *OED* states that 'None of the several colourful explanations of the origin of the expression is authenticated by contemporary printed evidence,' *gone for a Burton* remains one of the most tantalising slang expressions, Britain's version of America's *OK*, as it were, and for all the *OED's* self-denial, a trawl through the possibilities is simply too tempting to resist.

There is no argument as regards what the phrase, used invariably in the past tense (*gone for a Burton*), meant: initially, as recorded during World War II and specifically amongst RAF pilots, it was dead, killed either during some sortie or in a dogfight; latterly, post-1941, it came to mean missing, whether in the air or not. Although there are some claims for its existence during World War I, when Burton was supposedly derived from an elision of the words 'burnt 'un' (the fate of many young aviators), most lexicographers, including Partridge, an expert on every aspect of 1914–18 slang, opt for the following conflict and the magisterial *OED* offers no citation before that from the *New Statesman*, dated August 1941. From thereon in, all is confusion.

Partridge in the 7th edition of the *Dictionary of Slang and Unconventional English*, and Paul Beale in the 8th, suggest, but sadly fail to prove any of four alternatives. There is a euphemism: going for a glass of Burton ale; there is Burton-on-Trent as rhyming slang for *went*, as in 'went west' (though this has other possible origins); there is the fact, at least among beer cognoscenti, that Burton ale is heavy, as is a burning aircraft as it crashes to the ground; finally a reference to the suits made by the ready-to-wear tailor Montague Burton. This ties in neatly with descriptions of coffins as *wooden overcoats, kimonos* and the like, but would conclusively disqualify any World War I origins, since Burtons had yet to appear on the High Street. To confound the whole issue even further, during World War II the RAF used a number of billiard halls, invariably sited above Burton shops, as medical centres. Those who attended such centres had 'gone for a Burton'; the black joke was that such treatment was more likely to kill than cure.

Other suggestions, vouchsafed by correspondents to BBC Radio 4's *Enquire Within* brought up the large-scale inter-war advertising campaign for Burton's Ales (which, pace Partridge, were apparently not that heavy). The campaign featured on posters 'several scenes depicting a Burton Ale house in the background and a tableau in the foreground where a principal character was obviously missing. An example is a broken-down car, bonnet up, distraught lady standing beside it, male character disappearing up the road towards the pub.' The copy line for this and similar pictures was 'He's gone for a Burton'. Only after the advertising campaign was it picked up by participants in the military one.

A second correspondent noted that Montague Burton's halls were used for morse aptitude tests, not medical checkups, and *going for a Burton* meant failing such a test, 'made,' he noted 'more difficult by open windows and passing trams.' It was also claimed that the *burton* came from seafarers' jargon, referring to the stowing of a barrel athwart rather than fore-and-aft. Such stowage was notoriously unsafe in a rough sea, and a rolling barrel could be a genuine threat to a sailor deputed to tackle it. Thus this going for a Burton meant risking death.

All have a certain feasibility, none suggest an absolute. Like so much slang etymology, anecdotal or otherwise, we must reject Eric Partridge's premise 'something is always better than nothing' and go instead, and however reluctantly, with Anatoly Liberman of the *OED*: 'better no etymology at all than a wrong one'. The case rests.

Nudge-Nudge, Wink-Wink: The Pun

THE PUN. A play on words that works because the words sound similar. The word itself defies origins, though some plump for the Italian *punctilio*, which meant variously a trifling point, a quibble, and any minute detail of action or behaviour. Linguists, possibly nearer the mark, call it *paronomasia*, which goes back to the Greek παρονομάζειν, which means 'to alter slightly in naming'.

It seems to have exercised the greats. Some love it: the pun is 'among the smaller excellencies of lively conversation' (James Boswell, Samuel Johnson's biographer), or 'an art of harmonious jingling upon words, which, passing in at the ears, excites a titillary motion in those parts; and this, being conveyed by the animal spirits into the muscles of the face, raises the cockles of the heart' (Jonathan Swift, he of *Gulliver's Travels* and much besides). Some do not: to pun is, 'to torture one poor word ten thousand ways' (John Dryden, the poet), or simply 'the lowest form of wit' (the celebrity pianist Oscar Levant, along with dozens of others who set puns even lower than the usual sarcasm). True, the reduction of the rape of some unfortunate laundresses by a mentally challenged escapist to 'Nut screws washers and bolts' may lack much charm in a less linguistically tolerant world. Yet Shakespeare loves them (see **Carry on Barding, or, Much**

Ado About Pistol's Cock), and more recently we have the Marx Brothers ('Love flies out the door when money comes innuendo') while fans of Patrick O'Brian's navy novels will recall an elaborate, and recurring scenario which permits his seaborne heroes, with rotting stores in mind, to opt for 'the lesser of two weevils'.

No matter. Slang loves a pun. There are times when, just as one despairs of finding a term that might not be labelled 'derogatory', every example seems to demand the note: 'No pun intended'. Except for the many that do. My database lists nearly 750 terms that use the form. Their frequency underlines the role of wit in slang. No, Virginia, it isn't just those words Mummy would rather you didn't know and which you and your friends doubtless trill across the playground. Puns also represent a side of slang that makes one wonder: just who coined this stuff? On the whole slang's punning takes it beyond the usual themes. There's an element of creativity here that one doesn't need to search out in the usual equation of fucking with 'man hits woman' or insanity with 'not all there'.

Let us start at the beginning. Or at least with the oldest recording of slang's punning. The *green gown*: which looks to standard English *green*, with its figurative sense of innocence and the literal images of the countryside and the green stains that come from rolling on the grass. Usually linked to *getting* or *giving* the definition is sexual play, usually assuming intercourse, performed out of doors; as B.E.'s dictionary of 1698 puts it: 'a throwing of young Lasses on the Grass and Kissing them'. *Kiss*, of course, like the double-defined French *baiser*, could also mean full-on sex, and led in turn to puns. Thus in *The Parliament of Women* (1646) one 'Dorcas Do-little' declares, 'My husband is a Gamester and as he games abroad, so I play at home; if he bee at bowles and kisse the Mistris, I can for recreation play at rubbers with his man.' *Gamester* (a gambler but equally a womaniser) and *game* (sport in every sense), *bowls* (or *balls*), *kiss the mistress*, *play at rubbers* (which doesn't just mean a game, nor indeed to rub, but also promoting one's own interests) . . . like certain scenes in Shakespeare, it's a prototype *Carry On* script.

But when slang meets sex, the sniggering of *Carry On* movies is often the default setting. The whole *play at* thing: *play at brangle, bouncy-bouncy, buttock, hot cockles, leapfrog, mumble-peg, prick the garter, pully-hauly, put in all, stuble my naggie, tops and bottoms, top sawyer, where the Jack takes Ace* (that's the *black ace*, the pubic hair-girt vagina). Or *dance*: *bobb-in-jo* (Bob being the penis or as verb, to fuck, and thus perhaps *in* Joan), the *blanket hornpipe*, the *buttock jig*, the *married man's cotillion*, the *matrimonial polka* (could that also be *poke her*?), and plays on such real-life country whirligigs as *Sallinger's round*, the *shaking of the sheets* and *Barnaby*. Where do we stop? Take one tiny example, there's *needle* (and its coeval, *sew*). OK: the needle is the penis, except that you can *thread* it, and that lets it gender-bend as the vagina. A *needlewoman* is a whore, *needlework*, sexual intercourse and to *pick a needle without an eye* (which needle is useless) is used of a young woman who marries a man, knowing that he'll offer little joy in the sack.

On it goes; the *navel engagement*, and still seaborne, the *light frigate*, a prostitute who is both 'light' on her heels, and offering to 'frig it'; *hare* (hair) *pie*, which can of course be *eaten*, *hairyfordshire*, whence one can visit, although slang seems to have missed a trick with the possibilities of 'going down into the country'. A *bit on the fork* which blends all those feminised *bits* (of *muslin*, of *melon* . . .) with *fork*, the crotch; the *netherlands* and *furbelow*, both 'down there', *Bushey Park*, the *bush* or pubic hair, the *agreeable ruts of life*, the *breakfast of champions*, which one *eats* and signifies cunnilingus and leads to that abecedarists' friend, the *cunning-linguist*. And to stretch a point, there's the *cunt-hat*, nothing sexual, merely a derby (America's name for the bowler), but it's 'often felt'.

It's not all sex. Slang's themes range further. There is, for instance, *mad*. Or 'intellect impaired' as might prefer the politically pure in heart. Pun-based terms include *crackerbox* (playing on biscuits and *crackers/cracked*), *gonzo*, which looks like a blend of the old hipster-era *gone* and *crazo* but apparently started life as a play on the military attribute *gung-ho*, the eccentric 'sweetmeats' *nutbar*, *nutcake* and *nut roll* (all based like many other 'mad' words on *nut*: the head [see **The Body: Only Man is Vile**]); *brain salad surgery*, however, requires no operating theatre, it simply puns on *head*, oral sex.

However, slang's all-purpose synonym for eccentricity, to whatever degree, is 'not all there', or as a popular term has it *Dagenham*, which as London tube users will know is 'two stops on from Barking' (*barking mad* that is, howling at the moon). Still underground, *one stop short of East Ham* is Barking itself. The *member for Barkshire*, however, is merely suffering from a nasty cough. 'Not all there' melds into 'not getting there' and 'not amounting to' and phrases using *short of . . .* are multitudinous. There's *a couple of chips short of . . .* , whether the punning chips are of the silicone, chocolate, potato or even gambling variety, and those things missing include: . . . a *computer*, . . . a *cookie*, . . . an *order*, . . . a *complete circuit*, . . . a *casino bet*, . . . a *butty*, or . . . a *happy meal* (which may also lack its *French fries*). Other variations give us *wafers short of a communion*, *tacos short of a combination plate*, *a few spring rolls short of a banquet*, *tinnies short of a slab*, and a sliding scale of *snags* (or *chops*) that have failed to make it to the *barbie*.

Keeping it thematic, homosexuality, and in particular what the standard dictionaries term sodomy, is always good for a (coarse, stereotyped, homophobic) laugh. One barely needs proceed beyond the *back door* (or *passage* or *avenue*): there is the *gentleman* (or the *usher*) *of the back door*, the *backdoor bandit, kicker, man, gentleman* and *merchant*; there is *backdoor action* and *backdoor work* whereby one cops it up the back door or *goes in* or *up the back door*. All such pleasures unified as *bestial backsliding*, a synonym for homosexuality that combines physical distaste with pulpit moralising. Enough? Not yet. Still punning away we meet the *backgammoner*, the *breechloader*, the *navigator of the windward passage*, one who is *behind with the rent* (which also rhymes with *bent*), the *rear-end loader* and noted by Francis Grose who eventually chose not to include it, the *invader of the rear settlements* (which, more bluntly, he termed simply an *a—e man*). None of which even touches on what was once termed the *browning family* or *brown pipe engineers* and all the colour-coded crudity that introduced (not to mention a few byways via *Marmite* and other colour-indicative trade names).

One last theme for the road: drinking. What do we find? The *bottle baby*, not an infant, merely an alcoholic tramp whose excesses, possibly including drinking *dehorn*, adulterated alcohol that does nothing for the libido (the *horn*, geddit?), have reduced him to that state; the *hoisting engineer* (from *hoist*, to lower) who is *canned, chateaued* (everyday *shattered*, but on at least a *cru bourgeois*), *elevated, petrified* . . .

Some pun occasionally, while others seemed hard-wired to the task. Francis Grose, antiquary, militia captain and the Samuel Johnson of slang from 1785 (the first edition of his *Classical Dictionary of the Vulgar Tongue*), boasted well over 150 examples. There was the *gentleman of* (*the*) *three ins* (or indeed *inns*): 'In

Debt, in Gaol, and in danger of remaining there for Life: or, in Gaol, Indicted, & in danger of being hanged in Chains.' There was his antithesis, the *gentleman of three* (or *four*) *outs*: without money, without wit, and without manners: some add another out, i.e. without credit. Variations on this latter, essayed by the Newgate novelists Lord Lytton in *Paul Clifford* (with its grand guignol opener: 'It was a dark and stormy night . . .') and Harrison Ainsworth in *Rookwood*, his pot-boiling tale of high-wayman Dick Turpin, suggest respectively that the properties lacking are 'out of pocket, out of elbows, and out of credit' or 'shoes, stockings and shirt'.

But this barely scrapes the surface. The Captain, a splendid figure from whom butchers, overawed by his corpulence, would beg for his sponsorship, desperate to tell clients that it was their beef that had transformed into his, had much more to offer. There was the *burning shame*, 'a lighted candle stuck into the parts of a woman, certainly not intended by nature for a candle-stick' (primly reinterpreted by Grose's successor Pierce Egan as 'a nightwatchman placed at the door of a brothel, holding a lantern, even in daylight, to deter people from wandering in and out') and a *Catamaran*, defined as 'an Old Scraggy Woman; from a kind of float made of spars and yards lashed together, for saving persons ship-wrecked' and seemingly knitting together *cat*, the old woman, and *catamaran*, a *fireship* (a slang term for a clapped whore) or *catamaran*, an ill-tempered person.

Grose, who like his contemporaries would not have under-stood the concept, did not do political correctness. The prostitute was a *bobtail* (playing variously with *rabbit/coney/cunny*, *bob*, 'go up and down' and *tail*, both buttocks and vagina, and the idea of a horse which gave a good 'ride'), *Miss Laycock* (also *Gammar Laycock*, *Lady Laycock*, *Mrs Laycock* and *Nancy Laycock* who may, though it is not indicated in examples, have been gay), a *public ledger* ('like that paper, she is open to all parties'), or an *Athanasian wench*, which punned on the Athanasian Creed, which begins with the words 'quicumque vult' (Latin for 'whoever wants' and was itself a synonym for whore) and defined by the Captain as 'a forward girl, ready to oblige every man that shall ask her'. Her vagina, 'the stock in trade of a prostitute, because fairly entered', was *custom house goods*. It might also be *Mr Thingstable*, 'a ludicrous affectation of delicacy in avoiding the pronunciation of the first syllable in the title of that officer, which in sound has some similarity to an indecent monosyllable'. Or there were the blasphemous and anti-papist, if quasi-accurate jokes on *mother of all saints, all souls, St Patrick* or *St Paul*. Then there was the *butcher's dog*, defined as a married man, and attributed to the fact that both can 'lie by the beef without touching it'. But maybe that's simply ageist: as Middleton and Rowley put it in their play *Old Law* (1656): 'a piece of old beefe will serve to breakfast, yet a man would be glad of a Chicken to supper'. *Chicken* as a young woman is thus old, and the sense of cowardice emerges at the same time, but the modern usage, an underage boy or girl, is a nineteenth-century coinage.

A *Cambridge fortune*, punning on two supposed staples of the Cambridgeshire countryside, referred to a woman who possesses nothing material of her own but 'a wind mill and a water mill', i.e. she can talk and urinate but nothing else, and without money must rely for attraction on her personal charms alone. Finally the gross, to pun on the name of its first collector, *make a coffee-house out of a woman's cunt*. This reference to the popularity of coffee-houses as social centres, rather than places for eating and drinking, was defined as performing coitus interruptus, i.e. 'to go in and out and spend nothing'. The alternative term rendered the vagina 'a lobster-kettle': it is hard to suggest why, unless it played on *lobster*, a soldier, and the idea of the kettle as both wet and hot.

From sex, as ever, to violence, in this case as urged by the law. A man unashamedly of his era, Grose was not squeamish when it came to judicial executions. The gallows was the *deadly never-green* or the *anodyne necklace*, which played on health-care's equivalent, a form of medicinal amulet, peddled by charlatans and especially popular earlier in the century; based on the original definition of *anodyne* as soothing pain, in this context that of a misspent life, the phrase is thus a pun on 'painkiller'. Similarly medicinal was the *morning drop*, the execution itself, which paired *drop*, a popular form of medicine, and the fall through the gallows' trapdoor.

The moment of hanging was a *hearty choke* (with *caper sauce*), playing with the vegetable, the gurgling victim (before the drop snapped necks one literally choked to death) and the 'capering' legs of the expiring hanged. To die was to *go to Ratisbon* (or more aggressively, 'Rot-His-Bone') which played on the religious colloquy or Diet of Ratisbon. One who is imprisoned in the stocks or pillory was a *babe in the wood*; to be hanged in chains was to *keep an ironmonger's shop* (either *by the side of the common* or *where the sheriff sets up*). Hanging, like sex, was keen on *dancing*: there was *dance on air*, or *on nothing* (*in a hempen cravat*), *dance the Newgate* or *Tyburn horpipe*, *dance at Tuck 'em Fair* (to *tuck up* was to kill), *dance at the sheriff's ball and loll out one's tongue at the company*, and *dance at Beilby's ball*, an elaborate concept which, failing an actual sheriff named Beilby, played either with that legal mecca the Old *Bailey*, or the *bilbo*, a long iron bar, furnished with sliding shackles to confine the ankles of prisoners and a lock by which to fix one end of the bar to the floor or ground. *Bilbo* comes from the Spanish town of Bilbao, where these fetters were invented. Such *dancing* accompanied the pre-drop gallows, when the victim choked to death rather than suffering an instantly broken neck; sometimes one's friends rushed to pull on those dancing legs, intent on speeding the inevitable.

The drop, whereby two hinged panels fell away beneath the villain's feet, brought in *go off with the fall of the leaf* which punned on the drop's hinged 'leaves' and the dead leaves that fall from a natural, rather than judicial 'tree'. Grose aside, judicial execution was awash with black humour, for instance the gallows was the *tree that bears fruit all the year round* or the *government signpost*, presumably directing the hanged individual to hell; to mount it was to *climb three trees without a ladder*. The noose, name-checking the execution ground of Tyburn, near modern Paddington, gave a Tyburn *tippet* or *pickadill*, that same form of stiff collar, originally Spanish, that would, in the following century, give a name to the London thoroughfare Piccadilly. The *Tyburn tiffany* took its name from a transparent gauze muslin, often used as a woman's headcover.

Executions aside, Grose's puns were all pretty wince-worthy: *master of the rolls*, a baker; *marinated*, transported to Botany Bay, *book-keeper*, one who fails to return borrowed books, *figure-dancer*, a forger who specialises in altering the figures on banknotes (a real figure-dancer performed in a dance that offered representations of famous historical events), the *king of Spain's trumpeter*, a donkey (i.e. 'Don Key'), a *parson*, a signpost (the clergyman supposedly 'sets people in the right way'), *manoeuvre the apostles*, to manipulate one's accounts to pay off one debt while incurring another and thus a pun on the popular phrase 'rob Peter to pay Paul'. Finally, *two stone underweight* or *wanting*: a eunuch, bereft of his testicles or *stones*.

Slang's sex-related puns were hardly limited to a single lexicographer. Elsewhere a *finishing academy* or *finishing school* meant a brothel, with 'finishing' meaning coming to orgasm; other educational brothels included the *boarding school*, the *pushing school* (*push* meaning to fuck), *cavaulting school* (another play on 'ride'), the *college*, the *dancing school*, the *topping school* and the *seminary* (with its extra wink at 'semen'). There was the *solicitor general*, the penis and the *receiver general*, a prostitute who 'receives' such lovers as pay their money. She was also the *deadly nightshade*, the *guinea hen* (her price) and, if rich, drove around in a carriage nicknamed a *loose box* (in standard use, a stall in which a horse can move around freely). More recently she has been a *garden tool*, i.e a *ho*(*e*).

To round off the puns, a few taken at random. *Grand Central Station* was the scarred arm of a long-term heroin user; such an arm was covered in *tracks*. A *growler* was a form of four-wheeled cab and punned on another vehicle, the two-wheeled *sulky*, though it may have referred to the stereotypically poor temper of the driver. *Understandings* were either boots, shoes or legs. The *republic of letters* (usually hymning the world of literature and coined for standard use, albeit originally French, by Pierre Bayle in 1664) was the post office. Australia's *ornythorhynchus*, in slang a creditor, was properly the duck-billed platypus, and the pun was on 'a beast with a bill'. Australia also has the elaborate *Wallaby Bob's cousin*, which means exhausted or worn out. Why? Well, Wallaby Bob's cousin is (*Kanga*) *Roo Ted*, and *rooted*, an all-purpose substitute for *fucked*, means exhausted. America offered *Kelsey's nuts*, which mixed *nuts*, the very best, with the nuts and bolts that were the product of the Kelsey Wheel

Company, founded in 1910 to produce automobile wheels. There was *kidney pie*, flattery, humbug, deceit and based on the verb to *kid*, to fool or tease. *All holiday at Peckham*, playing on *peck*, food, meant that things were all over and beyond redemption, while another game with food gave a general phrase of encouragement *don't let your meat loaf*, which used slang's *meat*, the penis and *loaf*, to loiter.

Now 'ere's a funny thing . . . : Catchphrases

Today, digitised, we call them *memes*, and distribute them through social media. Based on a single image, that for whatever reason latches on to the brain, they have names that, at least as listed by Wikipedia but perhaps beyond those of us over twenty, everyone recalls – The Most Interesting Man in the World, Condescending Willy Wonka, Success Kid, Be Like Bill, Grumpy Cat – and their success is noted in the millions of home-brewed variations they inspire.

Pre-meme, but very much the same even if technology restricted it to words, and some individual, usually celebrated, was necessary to set it in motion, was the *catchphrase*, a form of lexical rather than visual earworm, which is one of a number of terms – *catch-cry, catch-idea, catch-sound* – all of which intend to 'catch the eye, ear or fancy'.

The *OED* suggests a first recorded use for *catchphrase* of 'ante 1850', and its second, in 1856, is already taking the judgemental high ground, suggesting that 'Catch phrases of this kind are sufficient to satisfy the simple.' The phrase in question is sadly left uncited, but the 'satisfaction of the simple', one might propose, has lain at the heart of the term, and its thousands of popular variations, ever since.

According to Eric Partridge's *Dictionary of Catch Phrases*

(1977, 1985) the use of these snappy references – sometimes a whole line, often literally no more than a phrase or even single word – has existed since the sixteenth century. Who knows: perhaps the great jesters capered before their lords and masters armed not merely with the obligatory stick-borne bladder, cap and bells, but with a much-loved one-liner, guaranteed to set the aristocratic audience giggling on cue. Perhaps, but the 'modern' catchphrase is very much tied into mass popular entertainment, and that means the music halls of the nineteenth and early-to-mid-twentieth century and the radio and TV shows (and even soaps: the Internet offers a 'Dictionary of Catchphrases used on Coronation Street') that have taken their place.

They don't even have to be spoken, or not out loud. Sherlock Holmes' 'Elementary, my dear Watson' definitely qualifies (for all that he never actually voiced the line in print); and Conan Doyle's best-selling detective, of course, was a 'popular entertainer', in his way. Or Hercule Poirot, with his 'little grey cells'. These phrasal trademarks qualify too. But the halls, the radio comedies, and latterly the sit-coms and quiz-shows, are the catchphrase's true home and it is from them that the examples that follow almost invariably spring.

Not just earworm, the catchphrase is essentially a verbal autograph. It 'catches the ear' but simultaneously comes over as a tiny but highly focused biography. What you hear is what you get. Usually this serves to announce, in shorthand as it were, the nature of the comic character, if not the actual comedian, on display. Hear Arthur Askey's 'Hello playmates', Max Bygraves' 'I wanna tell you a story . . .', Flanagan and Allen's 'Oi-Oi!', Hylda Baker's 'She knows y'know', or Billy Cotton's 'Wakey-wakey!' and you knew exactly what was in store. On it goes, Ali G. offers 'Is it 'cos I is black', Arabella Weir 'Does my bum look big in this?', Catherine Tate 'Does my face looked bovvered?'. Like a verbal/aural comfort blanket (or, the cynical might prefer, some Pavlovian bell) the catchphrase settles the audience down, ready for comfort and delight.

Sometimes they're all too real. George Formby Senior's regular on-stage declaration, 'Coughing well tonight' was grimly true. The 'Wigan Nightingale' died, first collapsing onstage like a good trouper, of TB. Of course, they're not obligatory: the Marx Brothers had no such easy identifiers; but at the same time their three distinct personas, evolving from three racial stereotypes (Jewish, Irish and Italian; the generally unfunny Zeppo presumably played the WASP) are 'catchphrases' in themselves. On other occasions it can extend to an entire vocabulary. The ageing chorus boys 'Julian' and 'Sandy' (Hugh Paddick and Kenneth Williams) of radio's *Round the Horne* turned a century-old theatrical jargon (the Italian-cum-Romani Polari), with its *bona* and *naff*, *thews* and *lallies*, *omipalones* and *lucoddies* into what might be seen as the biggest catchphrase of the lot.

Like the song (comic and/or sentimental) that as if by law once concluded every comic's act, a catchphrase came with the job. The songs are largely gone (though Victoria Wood refused to let go, and Morecambe and Wise's sign-off 'Give me sunshine' was as much a catchphrase in itself as the oft-repeated 'You can't see the join') but the need for the instant identification provided so conveniently by the catchphrase soldiers on. That they are as likely to spring from a quiz show ('Come on down!', 'Nice to see you, to see you nice'; 'Bernie, the bolt', 'Shut that door' and 'You'll like this, not a lot') as from a performance says as much about the contemporary role of the old-style 'variety' comic as the development of the phrases he or she uses. Sitcoms are equally productive. *Dad's Army* was especially so: 'You stupid boy', 'They don't like it up 'em', 'We're doomed, all doomed', among others, but most of the great ones have something to offer. *Till Death Us Do Part* ('Silly moo'), *Are You Being Served* ('I'm free'), *Blackadder* ('I have a cunning plan . . .'), *Only Fools and Horses* ('Luvvly jubbly'), *Steptoe and Son* ('You dirty old man'), *One Foot in the Grave* ('I don't believe it'). Then there are shows like *Monty Python* ('And now for something completely different') or even cartoons such as *The Simpsons* ('Eat my shorts') or *South Park* ('They killed Kenny'). The list is long, the pantheon ever expanding. But expand it does. Every one – and there are hundreds necessarily unreprised here – a winner, yet paradoxically deracinated in chilly print. What's so funny? the uninitiated might justifiably enquire, but for those who do know, what a panorama of delights they each and all unleash.

The quiz shows and sitcoms, music-hall stars, radio and TV comics all use catchphrases, but on the whole they remain an adjunct to the greater performance. Two shows, fifty years apart, seem obsessed by the things: Tommy Handley's 1940s' *ITMA* ('It's That Man Again') in which the very title was a catchphrase, and Paul Whitehouse's late 1990s *Fast Show*. *ITMA* was awash with 'characters' and every one proclaimed their identificatory line: 'After you Claude.' 'No, after *you*, Cecil.' (the pair of ultra-chirpy broker's men); 'It's being so cheerful keeps me going' (Mona Lott); 'Don't forget the diver' (culled from a real-life unfortunate, plying his trade at New Brighton pier-head); 'Can I do you now, sir?' (Mrs. Mopp). *ITMA*, following its own title, also produced the acronymic catchphrase, most obviously TTFN (subsequently appropriated by radio's Jimmy Young): 'ta-ta for now'. But if *ITMA*'s catchphrases were, so to speak, 'serious', then the *Fast Show*'s vast selection were far more ironic, a post-modern take on the whole thing that's best summed up by Whitehouse's cod-variety star Arthur Atkinson. His catchphrases, 'How queer' and 'Have you seen my washboard missus?' their absolute humourlessness followed invariably by the shot of an hysterical audience (apparently a genuine piece of music hall footage) dealt neatly and cruelly with the whole tradition. But even so, the *Fast Show*'s phrases rushed into the language: 'Suits you, sir'; 'Scorchio'; 'Which is nice'; 'This week I be mostly eating . . . ,' 'I'll get me coat' and the rest. People, stubbornly, simply didn't get the joke. Or not the right one.

The mass of catchphrases are innately ephemeral. Tied to a show or a specific individual they live a relatively brief albeit definitely merry life, massively popular, on, it seems, every lip, only to vanish before the next crop of amusements. Like fashionable slang, they age too quickly for long-term retention. Take Harry Enfield's 'Loadsamoney', once omnivocalised, now a historical curiosity, the leitmotif of the Thatcher years.

You didn't need modern media. The mid-nineteenth century was catchphrase heaven. Among them 'all serene', 'go it you cripples (crutches are cheap)!', 'Jim along Josey', 'do you see any green in my eye?', 'who shot the dog?' and 'not in these boots'. The origins were various but they sprang mainly from the music hall and from popular plays. Some, however, had no obvious origin. Such was *bender!* which appears in 1812 and in effect meant *bullshit!* As defined in James Hardy Vaux's *Vocabulary of the Flash Language* it was 'an ironical word used in conversation by flash people; as where one party affirms or professes any thing which the other believes to be false or insincere, the latter expresses his incredulity by exclaiming *bender!* or, if one asks another to do any act which the latter considers unreasonable or impracticable, he replies, O yes, I'll do it – bender; meaning, by the addition of the last word, that, in fact, he will do no such thing.' An ancestor for modernity's *not*. By 1835 bender has become *over the bender*, which apparently reflected a tradition that a declaration made over the (left) elbow as distinct from not over it need not be held sacred. The Victorians also used *over the left*, i.e. pointing with one's right thumb over one's left shoulder, implying disbelief.

Charles Mackay's classic sociological study, *Memoirs of Extraordinary Popular Delusions* (1841) was especially interested in the phenomenon of catchphrases. Aside from Partridge's Dictionary, his study represents the great single concentration of the type. Mackay (1814–89) was a poet and journalist, who mixed such posts as that of the *Times'* special correspondent during the American Civil War with the writing of song lyrics and of a wide variety of books, many on London or the English countryside. *Memoirs* deals with a variety of such delusions – among them religious relics, witch and tulip manias, the crusades and economic 'bubbles' – and in volume II turns to 'Popular Follies in Great Cities'. These, it transpires, are catchphrases, which are 'repeated with delight, and received with laughter, by men with hard hands and dirty faces—by saucy butcher lads and errand-boys—by loose women—by hackney coachmen, cabriolet drivers, and idle fellows who loiter at the corners of streets.' He also notes that each one 'seems applicable to every circumstance, and is the universal answer to every question; in short, it is the favourite slang phrase of the day, a phrase that, while its brief season of popularity lasts, throws a dash of fun and frolicsomeness over the existence of squalid poverty and ill-requited labour, and gives them reason to laugh as well as their more fortunate fellows in a higher stage of society. London is peculiarly fertile in this sort of phrases, which spring up suddenly, no one knows exactly in what spot, and pervade the whole population in a few hours, no one knows how.'

His earliest example 'though but a monosyllable, it was a phrase in itself' was *quoz*, which dated back to the 1790s. It seemed to have come from *quiz*, an eccentric person or an odd-looking thing, and itself from Latin *quis*, who. As the *New Vocal Enchantress* put it in 1791: 'Hey for buckish words, for phrases we've a passion / [. . .] / All have had their day, but now must yield to *quoz*.' Like many such phrases he noted, *quoz* multi-tasked. It was all down to the user. 'When vulgar wit wished to mark its incredulity, and raise a laugh at the same time, there was no resource so sure as this popular piece of slang. When a man was asked a favour which he did not choose to grant, he marked his sense of the suitor's unparalleled presumption by exclaiming *Quoz!* When a mischievous urchin wished to annoy a passenger, and create mirth for his comrades, he looked him in the face, and cried out *Quoz!* and the exclamation never failed in its object. When a disputant was desirous of throwing a doubt upon the veracity of his opponent, and getting summarily rid of an argument which he could not overturn, he uttered the word *Quoz*, with a contemptuous curl of his lip and an impatient shrug of his shoulders.'

After quoz another monosyllable: *walker!* which worked as did *bender!* as an all-purpose teasing, dismissive exclamation which 'was uttered with a peculiar drawl upon the first syllable, a sharp turn upon the last'. It was short-lived, maybe three months, but served 'to answer all questions. In the course of time the latter word alone became the favourite', and 'if a lively servant girl was importuned for a kiss by a fellow she did not care about, she cocked her little nose, and cried "Walker!" If a dustman asked his friend for the loan of a shilling, and his friend was either unable or unwilling to accommodate him, the probable answer he would receive was, "Walker!" If a drunken man was reeling about the streets, and a boy pulled his coat-tails, or a man knocked his hat over his eyes to make fun of him, the joke was always accompanied by the same exclamation.'

Walker! shortened the slightly earlier *Hookey walker!* which otherwise functioned similarly. It came, said Jon Bee in 1823, from one John Walker, 'an outdoor clerk' at a firm in Cheapside; Walker had a hooked or crooked nose and was used by the 'nobs of the firm' to spy on his fellow employees. Those upon whom he spied naturally declared that his reports were nonsense and since they outnumbered him, they tended to prevail. Bee added that the word was accompanied by a gesture: 'a significant upliftment of the hand and a crooking of the forefinger that [meant that] what is said is a lie, or is to be taken contrariwise'.

Bee's slang-collecting successor, Hotten, suggested 'a person named Walker, an aquiline-nosed Jew' (this was an assumption based on a stereotype: nose aside, he came from Westmorland and seems wholly English) who exhibited an orrery 'the Eidoranion' along which he would *take a sight*, which action, when used in slang, was the equivalent of a dismissive gesture. It was explained as a gesture of derision, made by placing the thumb on the tip of one's nose and spreading out the fingers like a fan; thus the *double sight*, the same gesture, intensified by joining the tip of the little finger to the thumb of the other hand, which in turn has its fingers extended fanwise. Failing all that dexterity, *Walker!* was attributed to a magistrate named Walker, complete with the requisite nose.

Mackay also offered *bad hat*, which he links to a London election in the borough of Southwark, c.1838, in which one of the candidates was well known as a hat-maker. As he campaigned he would single out any voter whose hat fell beneath the highest standards and declare: 'What a shocking bad hat you have got, call at my warehouse and you shall have a new one.' On the day of the election, as he gave his final speech, his opponents urged a hostile crowd to drown him out by chanting: 'What a shocking bad hat!' The phrase, first in its entirety, then reduced to 'bad hat', survived through the nineteenth century though it gradually declined through the first half of the twentieth. An alternative etymology attributes the phrase to the Duke of Wellington, who on his first visit to the Peers' Gallery of the House of Commons remarked, on looking down on the members of the Reform Parliament: 'I never saw so many shocking bad hats in my life.'

Used as a cry of delight, triumph or defiance *Flare up (and join the union)!* had a solid background. It referred to the fires that accompanied the Reform Riots of 1832, notably, as Mackay noted, in Bristol which 'was nearly half burned by the infuriated populace'. The flames were said to have *flared up* in the devoted city. Whether there was anything peculiarly captivating in the sound, or in the idea of these words, is hard to say; but whatever was the reason, it tickled the mob fancy mightily, and drove all other slang out of the field before it. The phrase was hugely popular: 'It answered all questions, settled all disputes, was applied to all persons, all things, and all circumstances, and became suddenly the most comprehensive phrase in the English language.'

Mackay also included *Jim Crow,* which is better known in its twentieth-century incarnation as an adjective used to indicate racist laws. The name is found in an old Kentucky plantation song with the chorus 'Jump Jim Crow' and was hugely popularised when the 'black face' entertainer Thomas Dartmouth Rice performed it in Louisville in 1828. It crossed the Atlantic, along with Rice, who sang it at London's Adelphi theatre in 1836, in a 'farcical Burletta' [i.e. short comic opera] entitled 'A Flight to America, or, Twelve Hours in New York'. The lexicographer Schele De Vere, writing in 1871, saw it as pure Americana: 'We have no ballad and no song that can be called American. The nearest approach [. . .] was the dramatic song Jim Crow, brought out about the year 1835 by an enthusiastic Yankee on the boards of a theatre in New York; it created a sensation, for it was new in form and conception, and no doubt rendered still more attractive by the strange guise in which it was presented. [. . .] For a time this African inroad drove nearly every other song from the publisher's store and the drawing-room.'

Mackay was not amused, and termed it 'a vile song'. Rice 'sang his verses in appropriate costume, with grotesque gesticulations, and a sudden whirl of his body at the close of each verse. It took the taste of the town immediately, and for months the ears of orderly people were stunned by the senseless chorus – "Turn about and wheel about, / And do just so— / Turn about and wheel about, / And jump, Jim Crow".'

There he goes with his eye out! (which could also take the female 'she' and 'her') was one of a number of exclamations aimed at such passers-by as the speaker found amusing. Mackay was unimpressed, and termed the phrase 'most preposterous. Who invented it, how it arose, or where it was first heard, are alike unknown. Nothing about it is certain, but that for months it was the slang par excellence of the Londoners, and afforded them a vast gratification. "There he goes with his eye out!" or "There she goes with her eye out!" [. . .] was in the mouth of everybody who knew the town. The sober part of the community were as much puzzled by this unaccountable saying as the vulgar were delighted with it. The wise thought it very foolish, but the many thought it very funny, and the idle amused themselves by chalking it upon walls, or scribbling it upon monuments.'

Similar shouts were framed as questions. *Does your mother know you're out?* 'was the provoking query addressed to young men of more than reasonable swagger, who smoked cigars in the streets, and wore false whiskers to look irresistible'. In other words, young men who claimed the affectations of manhood without having earned them by age. It was much used by women who wished to counter an impertinent male gaze, and many a leering youngster was 'reduced at once into his natural insignificance by the mere utterance of this phrase'.

Still with mum, we find *Has your mother sold her mangle?* (a foretaste of the later, and inescapably if unquantifiably suggestive if not exactly obscene *How's your mother off for dripping?* a phrase that some claim is the correct response to the traditional Cockney greeting *Wotcher cock*). The mangle can be extended by 'and bought a piano' or the query: 'does your mother keep a mangle?' This 'impertinent and not universally apposite query' gained, in Mackay's words, only a 'brief career', being 'not of that boisterous and cordial kind which ensures a long continuance of favour'. Its problem, he felt, was that you couldn't use it to old people, whose mothers had long passed on.

Seemingly simple was *who are you?* which was delivered aggressively and met with an equally aggressive response, 'who are *you?*' Whether this led to fights is not recorded. Mackay told how 'this new favourite, like a mushroom, seems to have sprung up in a night, or, like a frog in Cheapside, to have come down in a sudden shower. One day it was unheard, unknown, uninvented; the next it pervaded London. Every alley resounded with it; every highway was musical with it.' A multipurpose line, it applied to anything the speaker wished.

MLE: A Speech of Many Colours

To CONCLUDE, AND to bring us to what passes for slang's current cutting edge, a story about immigration and its triumph. It is about young black Britons, their language, and the changes that language has wrought on the larger world. Not the whole world, but that of their contemporaries, irrespective of colour. It is not about the black slang that comes from America and has been increasingly important throughout the twentieth century, although that variety will play a part. And just as Black-America's powerful role in world-wide popular culture, notably through music, helped spread that slang, then popular culture, again spearheaded by music, plays its part in this British phenomenon.

To go forward, we must first look back.

In 2006, barely ten years ago, those who follow such interests in the nation's media might have seen, emerging as if from nowhere, that the speech of London, that eternal linguistic melting-pot, had been augmented by a new ingredient. An extra verbal spice, born as such things tend to be in the tropics – or at least their proxy reincarnations in such immigrant-dense areas as Bow and Brixton. It came with a name: *Jafaikan*, which seemed to be a journalistic invention, which neat and punning blend combined the proper name *Jamaican* and the dismissive adjective *fake*. The *Guardian*, hot on the multi-culti bandwagon, referenced television's Ali G. and offered readers the chance to 'learn jafaikan in two minutes', and in the way of half a millennium's slang expositors, offered both a short glossary and a few sample sentences: 'You lookin buff in dem low batties. Dey's sick man. Me. I'm just jammin wid me bruds. Dis me yard, innit? Is nang, you get me? No? What ends you from then?'

It was left to the estimable Michael Quinion, the Oxford etymologist behind the website *World Wide Words* to make a little sense. Jafaikan did not refer to a language or a youth dialect but was a London slang term used by working-class black teens to deride their middle-class, though equally black peers, posing, just like the equivalent white *wiggas*, *wannabes* and *waspafarians*, as hardcore proles, all the way from Trenchtown with a Rasta tam, waist-length dreads and a spliff-ful of sensimilia. The earliest recorded example of the word was just two years earlier.

There was, certainly, a form of language, but it had quite another name. Quinion explained that 'a team of linguists are investigating this emerging speech form. They prefer the neutral term Multicultural London English (MLE).' He quoted Professor Paul Kerswill, who had noted that 'A clear new vernacular is emerging in inner London, linking ethnicities, and forging shared identities – often around music like rap, hip-hop, grime or bangra.' There were certain changes in pronunciation, notably the shortening of traditional London vowel sounds, and the diminished stress of the Cockney's trademark, the glottal stop. It also appeared that MLE was overtaking the last 'new' London language: Estuary English, itself a mix of standard English and traditional Cockney pronunciation and vocabulary, and spoken by an older generation as their rejection of 'pure' cockney.

The Jafaikan bubble, being pretty much a journalistic

invention, duly burst. MLE did not. It took root, strengthened and spread. At the moment it is the default speech of young Londoners and it may be that since the young grow older and take their speech patterns with them, it may move beyond the current identification with a single generation.

MLE, in language terms, is just one more way-station in the progress of London speech. It may still be relatively new, and created by a young, black population, but it is a logical extension rather than an anomaly. Londoners have always spoken multiculturally. Standard English is a mongrel tongue, as is the counter-language, slang. The three hundred languages now spoken in London's schools represent a relatively modern development, but immigrants – one may start with the last invaders, the Normans of 1066, or go back to Angles, Saxons and after them Danes – have always played a role in forming first England, then Britain and its language.

The city had known a tiny black population for centuries, but it had been primarily imported either as servants or, occasionally, as flesh-and-blood souvenirs of distant lands, brought home by explorers and paraded before gawping Londoners. They can be seen in Hogarth's illustrations and in grander paintings. Dr Johnson's black servant Francis Barber was well known to the great man's friends, and Johnson's main inheritor. Francis Grose, in his *Classical Dictionary of the Vulgar Tongue* (1785) noted a few 'negroe' terms, although these were from the plantations. In a Cruikshank illustration for Pearce Egan's *Life in London* (1821) where Tom and Jerry, slumming in an East End gin shop, meet Black Sal, resplendent in her spotted yellow skirt, five of the gin shop's dozen customers (plus one babe-in-arms) are black. Compared to the major immigrant arrivals – Irish, Jews – the numbers remained limited, but by 1919 black Britons existed in large enough numbers to inspire the country's first race riots, focused on ports where a black population, abandoning the ships they had crewed, had accumulated and expanded. The real turning point, and the arrival of a substantial number of what would become Black Britons, came after World War II.

After that war successive governments began looking outside England for new workers to help the steadily improving economy of the 1950s which could no longer be serviced by the indigenous population. They began recruiting in the Commonwealth, notably in the islands of the West Indies, and found that the black populations were more than willing to make the journey. They barely needed the alluring government invitations. England was 'the mother country', many of them spoke its language, worshipped in the same church, experienced the same education. Home life was often hard and even the skilled and the middle class saw England as a land of opportunity.

They did not, as yet, impinge on English speech. If they spoke slang, which for most listeners would in any case have been hard to distinguish from island patois, they kept it to themselves. For the first decade it was a mainly male society, and without women there were no children and without children far less cross-cultural mixing. Such immigrant narratives as the Trinidadian Samuel Selvon's *The Lonely Londoners* (1956), which did offer their language, remained rare and looked inward. If Selvon uses slang terms, such as *boldface*, to pose as braver than one is, *old-talk*, to gossip or *kiff-kiff*, first-rate, over half are island-based, and there is no sense that the whites with whom his characters worked and sometimes socialised picked them up. The better-known Colin MacInnes, another immigrant but white and Australian, while embracing the culture, especially in *City of*

Spades (1957), gives no particular linguistic insights (although he seems to be the first to print the insult *raasclat*, literally 'arse-cloth' and thus a sanitary towel). Nor is MacInnes' *Absolute Beginners* (1959), while focused squarely on a much poorer, multicultural Notting Hill than today's wealthy ghetto, and reaching its climax in the race riots of 1959, especially revelatory. MacInnes offers around two hundred terms, but there is no real sense of an especially youthful, let alone black lexis.

A decade later there was little sense of change. Black slang had arrived in the UK, but it was very much African-American. The lexis of the urban ghetto had undoubtedly infiltrated, even dominated the language of first beats and then hippies. But hippie slang – *heavy, outasight, uptight, cool* – whether it realised or not, was a direct decsendant of an established African-American lexis and filtered through America's mainly white 'counter-culture'. There was no discernible Caribbean input.

Only with the early-Seventies' appearance of reggae, spear-headed by Bob Marley, did a new variety of black slang start to gain a foothold. Anyone who knew Marley's lyrics soon knew *Babylon*, the Rastaman term for the police in particular and the 'downpressing' Western society in general. Other terms would follow, even if they still sounded absurd on white lips, typically Marley's use of Rastafarianisms such as *I and I* (me) and the adjectives *dread* or *irie* (both meaning excellent). The work of the Brixton-based poet Linton Kwesi Johnson, appearing in the late Seventies, revealed more terms – among them *juke*, to stab, *mauger*, thin (from French *maigre*), *yout*, both a young man and a generic for the increasingly disaffected community of young working-class Black Britons – but it was Johnson's heavily accented delivery that was as potent an indicator of the arena in which he worked as was his vocabulary. The races, even those who were educated in the same schools, remained in parallel. Punks enjoyed black music; ironically so did the overtly racist skinheads who had picked up on Jamaica-made ska and bluebeat in the Sixties. The dreadlocked Don Letts – whose father had been a celebrated sound-system operator – was a favourite punk DJ, but there was no sense of linguistic blending.

Such moments are always hard to pin down, and nothing in language, even slang, happens 'overnight'. The concept was yet to emerge, let alone the name, but if there is a moment when MLE, even in embryo, seems to be emerging, then it comes in 1985, with the release of the record 'Cockney Translation' by black British dancehall DJ Smiley Culture. His birth name was David Emmanuel, he was the son of a Jamaican father and Guyanese mother, and born in Stockwell, next door to the black centre of Brixton in South London. On one level it was what the music business sidelined as a novelty song, the lyrics laying out a bilingual glossary of words used by young Cockney tearaways and their black peers.

For instance:

Say cockney *fire shooter*, We *bus' gun*
Cockney say *tea leaf*, We say *sticks man*
You know dem have *wedge* while we have *corn*
Say cockney say be *first*, *my son*! We just say *Gwan*!

Smiley Culture was perhaps the first songwriter to put black and white slang in the same place. Yet there is still no suggestion of crossover. His whole point is difference, and as the singer pointed out, 'Cockney Translation' was meant as a social tourist guide, even a survival mechanism.

In an essay in 1955 Colin MacInnes had coined the phrase 'Young England, Half-English'. The young England in question had been the pop singer Tommy Steele and his fans; the other 'half' was America. A music-hall fan with a romantic view of what constituted popular entertainment, MacInnes was lamenting American influence, but unconsciously and with quite a different focus, the phrase was prescient. American influence would only increase, but what would form MLE was a blurring between the two varieties of English young: native white and immigrant black. In *Cut 'n' Mix: Culture, Identity and Caribbean Music,* the social commentator Dick Hebdige suggested that 'In some parts of Britain, West Indian patois has become *the* public language of inner-city youths, irrespective of their racial origin,' and wondered whether 'Perhaps there is another nation being formed for the future beyond the boundaries of race. If that nation can't yet be visualised, then it can perhaps be heard in the rhythms of the airwaves, in the beat that binds together histories, cultures, new identities.'

Black was *cool* (even if that word seemed to have started off at Eton, the most elite of all British schools). A knowledge was desirable and if one couldn't change race, then one could learn the necessary language. If the Eighties and even more the Nineties offered London's white speakers a way into blackness, it was via what the linguists called code-switching. Not between class but between colour. A switch that was encouraged not so much by homegrown music, but by the new and increasingly powerful agency of what began as hip-hop and moved on, as what had begun as disco-originated party music transformed into something far angrier – not to mention slangier – with the advent of gangsta rap. The source, in common with that of most slang since World War II, was America.

Kanye West, as yet to move beyond his role as a highly success-ful rap star and talking in 2006, described the white man's fascination with black speech as 'diction addiction' and joked that there should be an obligatory moratorium of twelve months before white teens were allowed to start using the ghetto's latest coinages. It was far too late. Nothing epitomised the white incor-poration of this black culture more than the character Ali G. created by the white, Jewish, Cambridge-educated UK comedian Sacha Baron Cohen. Ali G., the 'voice of da yoof', came not from the mean ghetto streets but from the dormitory town of Staines, outside London. The character, self-styled leader of the 'West Staines Massive', debuted on TV in 1998; eventually there would be a movie. The joke was that he saw himself as black, dressing like a rapper, brandishing gang signs and speaking accordingly. His scripts were seeded with the ogligatory clichés: *big up yaself, booyaka, for real, punanny, chill, batty boy, respect, wa'g'waan* and most ironically, *keep it real*. The references, despite *batty-boy* (a homosexual) and *punanny* (the vagina), both staples of Jamican sexual 'slackness', and the greeting *wa'g'waan*, looked to the States.

MLE, however, is innately British, and fundamentally London, although it has been suggested that in other cities, where the immigrant community arrived from areas other than the Caribbean, there is a sprinkling of terms that reflect those origins, typically the appearance of Somali terms in Cardiff. The language of the Caribbean, and particularly of Jamaica, remains central. Smiley Culture notwithstanding, its more immediate roots lie in the language of a wholly British creation: grime, a musical style that appeared, at least for the wider public, in 2002. Like other youth slangs, music, or more properly the lyrics that accompany it has provided the primary impulsion for its adop-tion. If MLE has had a single driving engine, then this is it.

Grime, most easily, if inaccurately, described as British hip-hop or British rap draws on a variety of roots. There is rap itself, of course, but more locally there is UK garage (pronounced 'garridge') and West Indian dancehall. It came out of East London, particularly Bow, E8 – an area that was regularly name-checked in its early lyrics – and was initially promoted via the flourishing world of pirate radio stations, often broadcasting a mere few hours per week on kit thrown together in tower-block apartments and just as quickly dismantled before the police arrived. It enjoyed various names: 8-bar (which referred to the verse patterns) and Nu Shape (with more complex 16- and 32-bar patterns). It could also be Dark Garage, Sub-Lo, One-Step or Esky or Eskibeat (with a nod to slang's veteran term 'cool') which blended in dance and electro styles and was created by Wiley (Richard Cowie), who alongside Dizzee Rascal (Dylan Mills) – perhaps the most successful of all its stars, and now a far more mainstream performer – was the first to move the form from the underground to a wider audience.

Grime remained underground for fifteen years. Where American rap conquered the world, following in a succession of black-driven musics, grime seemed too insular, too London. Too *grimy*. As of 2016 that may have changed. That year's Mercury Prize (for best album in the UK and Ireland) was won by one of the style's best-known stars, Skepta (Joseph Junior Adenuga) who to the alleged horror of millions locked into their protracted mourning, pipped the late David Bowie to this particular post. Grime, so long a friendless, grubby Cinderella, appeared to have met its Prince Charming. Its fifteen minutes of fame seemed finally to have arrived.

Like all slangs MLE is not a language as such, other than in the very broadbrush definition of its being a form of communication. It has no grammatical rules, and again like slang, is essentially a vocabulary. It need not be the sole slang in a given context. A lyric from Skinnyman (Alexander Holland; Leeds-born, but north London raised), 'Little Man' (2004), set in prison, mixes MLE – *parro, feds, blud* – with terms such as *lockdown, hang up* and *sweatbox*, that are strictly prison-orginated (and all Americanisms).

It may be poised to move beyond its limits, but compared with the world-conquering juggernaut of mainstream rap, grime has remained a niche creation, still not so far removed from the hand-distributed tapes and on-on-one DJ 'battles' that typified its early incarnation. It is very much home-grown, not least in its rejection or at least side-stepping of the celebration of *bling* that typifies its American cousin. There is no concept of 'ghetto fabulous'. The lyrics underline the problems of life – unemployment, police harassment, gang warfare, racial prejudice. The overriding emotion, as punk's Sex Pistols put it thirty years before, is 'no future'. It has been described as music put together by the young for themselves. It uses their language, which means MLE.

Breaking down the MLE lexis, the primary strands are Jamaican speech, rap and Cockney. In addition there is a strong showing from contemporary black and white youth coinages. My own database offers around 250 terms, which is representative rather than comprehensive, and as with all slang new material keeps appearing, even if it tends to focus on the usual thematic suspects. Even within slang, it represents a reasonably narrow spectrum. The preoccupations of young men: money (but less overt self-congratulation than touted in America), drugs, girls, friends and enemies, insults, violence and weapons, music and its performance, clothes, the police. There are certain phrases – *allow it* (as in let it pass, forget it), *true dat, all good, get me?* – but few abstracts other than terms that can be loosely qualifed as good and bad. On the whole emotions are absent. This is neither praiseworthy nor reprehensible: it is very much according to slang's long-established paradigm, within a further subset delineated by rap/grime. It is the world of the *street*, the world of article-less *road*, a self-defensive, cover-your-arse, all-against-all existence. Grime lyrics reflect what the white performer Skinnyman neatly expressed as 'a council estate of mind'.

Aggression, whether or not it leads to actual violence, seems to play the largest part, followed by sex, or at least the assessment of young women, and by money and drugs. The aggression may be a pose, and like rap, grime's lyrics are filled with exaggeration and boasting, but it is inescapable and as retailed by the young writers is based on lived experience on the street. One's default mode is the *screwface*, which dates to 1970s Jamaica. Bob Marley's *Talkin' Blues* (1974) tells how he has been 'down on the rock so long / I seem to wear a permanent screw' and in 1973 his band, the Wailers, released a track called 'Screwface'. It was explained as 'the custom of grimacing fiercely in order to unsettle nighttime bush-whackers who preyed on those caught in shantytown'.

Insults include *wasteman* (plus *wastewoman, wastegash* or plain *waste*) which suggests a waste of time or space, *pussyhole* (i.e. *cunt*), *poomplex* or the long-established *clown, joker, snake* (which as a verb means *cheat*) and *dickhead*. A *shower* or *shower-man* is a show-off though there is a positive definition: a success. *Fascio*, from Jamaica, is specifically a male homosexual, but can be used more widely, in the same way as gay. The term is either an elision of 'fuck ass' or linked to Jamaican *fas, fassy*, dirty. There is *chief*, which seems to play on the stereotyping of Native Americans as stupid, and works as a verb, meaning to insult or humiliate. Other terms for insult include *burn*, *bury*, *brush* or *rip* which has meant infuriate in Australia since the 1940s and the long-established *cuss*. To *dis*, which is seen as a coinage of the 1980s but can be found as long ago as 1905, and then in Australia, is to disrespect. *Beef*, which goes back to the late nineteenth century and is probably rooted in an even earlier form, the cry of *hot beef!* or stop thief!, is an argument. One can be *boyed* (treated like a child) or *had up*, *hotted*, and if one loses one's temper one *switches*. Negatives, whether for people, objects or experiences offer *bait*, *dark*, *raw*, *deadout*, *wack* (a rap staple), *faastie*, probably from *fuss* though its Jamaican origins may include Surinam Creole *fiesti*, nasty, *swag*, *deep*. To be *begging* is to be talking nonsense, which can be *fuckery*, *air*, *jokes* or *far*, with its implication that something is figuratively too far away or too much of a hassle to consider. The sycophant is *up on your balls* while an irritating person is *up in your hair*.

All of which remains verbal. Real violence, up to and including murder, has its own vocabulary. A gang rival is a *pagan*, which suggests a certain religious faith in one's own side, or *opp*, as in opponent or opposition. Armed gang warfare is the punning *armshouse*, and a gun can be a *biscuit* (one of many terms that also means penis, though the link to gun is unstated; perhaps one 'snaps' them both), a *bucky* (thus *buck*, to shoot and *bucked*, shot), a *gat* (from the *Gatling* gun and coined in 1897) and a *skeng*, which covers knives too; a knife is a *bora*, i.e. 'borer'. The origins of skeng are unknown, but Caribbean English *skengay*, a form of music in which the guitar sounds are seen as mimicking those of gunfire, has been suggested. Bullets are *corn* (whether from a resemblance to an ear of corn or because they are scattered), while a gun that has been used in a (fatal) shooting is *haunted*. To shoot is to *light up* (the flash, but the phrase has meant attack or beat since 1970), to *lick off* (from *lick*, to hit), to *spray* (i.e with shots), to *burst* and to *bust a cap* (found in 1866, but dormant for the next century). Perhaps the key word is *merk* or *murk*, which can mean to murder, but also to beat figuratively, i.e. surpass, to humiliate or to act aggressively. *Merked* can also mean very drunk, while *merky* is aggressive, which can also be *act-up*. The etymology is arguable: some opt for *murky*, dark, while others, claiming the spelling to be *merc*, link it to a gun-for-hire mercenary though this spelling is not recorded in MLE or rap. To fight or beat up is to *scuff, beat, rush* or *work* (a weaker use of the 1970s *put in work*, to go out killing). To rob is to *jack*, from *hijack*, and a *jacker* a robber and *jack move* a wild, foolish, eccentric move or type of behaviour; a *rudeboy* a young gansgter, a *mashman* a thug and *ninja*, tough. A core term is *stoush*, variously defined as arrogant or stuck-up and which seems to come from ostentatious, by way of slang's *stocious* which also means stuck-up, but also well-dressed and stylish, and physically attractive. (It does not, despite appearances, have links to Australia's *stoush*, a fight or to hit, which comes from the dialect *stashie*, a quarrel or, an uproar.)

This is a language of young men and there is no suggestion that their attitudes to women have moved on from slang's inevitable sexism. Women exist as sex objects, or worse, fail to make that cut. There is the usual double-standard and what is defined as 'promiscuous' is only what the boys want to believe. To have sex is to *wok* or *wuk* (from the older *work* and which like *fuck* enjoys an echoic sense of flesh slapping flesh), to *knock boots*, *beat, hit the sack* (from the 1930s and less excitingly simply go to bed) or *juice*, and *juice up* means to excite while *jiggy* means 'hot to trot'. If sensible one wears a *hat*, from America's *jimmy hat*, a condom (the *jimmy* being the penis as is the *bone*). Intercourse is *lash*, yet another example of slang's essential definition of the act: man hits woman. Attractive girls include the *beanie* (from 'keen as a bean'?) and *four-by-four*, and sexy or attractive brings in *gritty*, *tromp*, *choong*, *criss* (i.e. crisp), *trueing*, with suggestions of faithfulness, *buff* and *fly*. *Fine*, equally attractive, has been used since the 1930s, but can be found as far back as the early eighteenth century.

There is the much-publicised *on fleek*, which as simple *fleek* emerged around 2000 to mean admirable, but came into its own as a phrase in 2014. Perhaps its greatest importance is that unlike so much slang, we can trace its origins to a specific moment: a Vine video produced by an American girl, Peaches Monroe, and uploaded to the Internet on 21 June 2014. What was *on fleek* was her carefully groomed eyebrows, but the term quickly expanded to mean, as long as it was positive, whatever the user wished.

Booty (literally the buttocks) or *brud* mean a girl, usually seen sexually but not invariably; the root is *breed* and *breeded up* means pregnant. The same goes for *tings*, i.e. 'things' and less than congratulatory (and *thing* has been used to sidestep direct references to both vagina and penis for centuries). Definitely sexual are the *link* and the *live blanket*, both seeing the girl as a partner in intercourse, when one is *on the link*, and to *wife* is to have a sexual relationship. *Gash* has meant females (including prostitutes) since the 1910s, but can be found as a crudely physical description of the vagina from the 1780s. Unequivocally critical are *junz*, *yat* or *yatty*, *sket* or *sketel* (perhaps from *skittle*, which 'falls over easily' and was the nickname of Catherine 'Skittles' Walters, mistress of Edward VII, Louis Napoleon and several other grandees), all of whom are condemned as promiscuous, *pancoot* (perhaps from the Caribbean *pan cart*, a wheelbarrow, i.e. something large and inelegant) is simply ugly. *Shyst* is promiscuous and aggressive with it, perhaps the word we need is 'independent', though the origins may lie in *feisty*.

Yet in the end it's a man's world and the philosophy is rap's *MOB*: Money Over Bitches, i.e. profit before sex. There are no great innovations. *Cabbage* (green and thus reminiscent of dollar bills, and once pound notes) dates from 1903, *chips* from 1836 and *paper* from 1786. *Doe* is simply a respelt *dough* and thus 170 years old, and while *queen heads* refers to Elizabeth II, *queen's pictures* was used for her great-great-grandmother, Victoria and long before her, Queen Anne. *Cheese* has enjoyed something of a relaunch, but it emerges in Australia before 1860; it may be a play on the older *bread*. *Notes* (since the 1850s) and *sterling* play on standard uses and the high-value £50 note is a *pinkie* or a *red one*. Making money is *flossing* and *blowing up* while enjoying it is *rolling* and *balling*. Perhaps the most recent terms are *Gs*, although that has signified $1000 since 1928 and *grand*, which it abbreviates is twenty years older, and *wong*. Yet even this is an antique: wong cut *wonga* and wonga looks back to the late nineteenth-century Romani *wangur*, coal (thus the *wongar-camming mush*, a miser, i.e. 'one who loves coal'), which puns on slang's much older *cole*, money (1591), which in turn misspells the fuel and plays on the equivalence of money and life's vital staples. Money must be earned, legitimately otherwise: one *hustles*, *grinds* and *struggles*. None are new, simply practicable.

Selling drugs is one of the ways. Drugs have been interwoven with every youth culture since the beatniks and show no signs of going away. Marijuana, with its links to Jamaica-born Rastafarianism, is the default, but there is cocaine, especially as crack, and heroin and the general term for drugs is *food*. The vocabulary is wide and constantly changing; this selection is simply culled from a number of lyrics. Marijuana is *loud* (a notably strong variety), *head* (usually used of the consumer), *draw* (as in *drawing* on a pipe or cigarette), *grade, score* (used since the 1950s as a purchase of drugs) and *weed* (from the 1920s, the first recorded use is Caribbean). One's personal supply is a *persy* or *percy* and an ounce is an *aussie*. To roll a joint is to *bill* or *build* it, and to smoke it is to *blaze*. To be *burse, lean* or *lick-up* is to be seriously stoned. Crack can be *cheese* or *white* and heroin *brown*. To deal is to *slang*, from *sling*, or to *shot*, thus the *shotter*, the dealer and the *shotting game*: drug dealing.

Which leads, or usually, to the police: the *beast*, the *feds, po-po*, who conduct an *obbo* (observation) then swoop to *shift, nab* or *pull you up*. Po-po comes straight from rap, and feds is an unashamed steal from the US where the term was orginally restricted to the FBI and dates to the 1920s. *Nab* is even older, first recorded in 1681.

It is not all violence and if you have enemies there should be friends. People with whom you can *post up* and *cotch, chill, chat shit* and *kick back*, in other words, relax. *Mandem* and *g(y)aldem, manaman* and *mans, bredrin, fam, bruvs, black, blad* and *bloods* and *Bs*. Or *cuz*, from the States. People who you greet not with a screwface but with the query *what a gwarn?* or *whaa gwaan?* a Jamaicanised elision of 'what's going on?' A boss is a *don*, while junior members are *youngers, pickneys* and *yute* or *yout*. *Street* and *road*, the arenas of 'real' life, have been noted. Other environments include the *hood*, i.e neighbourhood and borrowed from the States, *ends* (a development of the long-established duopoly of London's East and West), and *crib* (coined as a slang term in 1597), *gates* and *yard* (one's home).

And for topics of conversation, there's always clothes, which seem primarily to be trainers: *creps, kicks, sneaks* and occasionally *boogers*. Jewellery is *ice* (formerly the province of old-school robbers) or *chops* (presumbly from *choparita*, as mentioned by Smiley Culture). Clothes in general are *garms* and *threads,* and can be *bad taste* or *moist acting*, which are not compliments. To wear something is to *bust, push* or most popularly *rock it*. There is music, which gives *spit*, to perform a song, *snapper*, a lyricist (with a possibly connection to black America's *snaps*, instant repartee and a descendant of the word-playing street exchanges known as *the dozens*), *rinse*, to play a record (and to have sex) and *shutdown*, which means a success.

Even slang must move beyond simply description. There are value judgements. Good. And bad. For the former MLE offers *long, nang* (coined in the Caribbean in 1902 and from Mende *nyanga*, showing off), *blatant, sick* and *grimey* (continuing slang's age-old use of 'bad' things to mean their opposite), *heavy* (once a hippie favourite), *cushty* (from Romani *kushto, kushti*, good and widely popularised by the 1980s BBC TV series *Only Fools and Horses*), *dapper* and *safe*, which also works as a greeting, as does *easy*. Feeling good is to be *on smash* and *on this ting*. For the latter there is *peak*, defined as very bad, though it is popularly used to mean extreme, to the greatest possible extent. *Mad,* used as adjective or adverb, suggests literal or figurative plenty as does bare, which comes from the Bajan *bare*, meaning nothing but, i.e. plenty. Used negatively *long* is overly complicated, boring, difficult or time-consuming and may be linked to the illiterates' online abbreviation of choice: tl;dr.

This is, it must be re-stressed, merely representative. The themes do seem pretty much to cover the available waterfront, but the words themselves are only a sample. Nor are these the only words and phrases available to MLE speakers. London,

Jamaica, New York and elsewhere can offer much more and the offer is fully accepted.

A couple of last thoughts. Although MLE was touted as something new, its arrival was surely quite logical. The all-male immigrant society of the Fifties had long been replaced; children and grandchildren were now living in the UK and, certainly as regarded the working class, were being schooled with their white contemporaries. It was hardly surprising that there would be an increasing overlap in the way that both races spoke. In addition there has been the allure of black culture, seen and indeed promoted by those who merchandise 'urban style' as de facto rebellious, 'hard', more masculine, more 'sexy'. The novelty, if there is one, is the adoption of MLE by an increasing section of the white middle class, but again, one can see this in the previous popularity of Estuary English. The terror of being perceived as elitist, let alone 'posh', holds serious power among those whose credo is 'authenticity'. In the local context of the East End, whose latest 'immigrants', in the wake of the artists of the Nineties, have turned out to be the gentrifying and well-off white middle classes, it is perhaps unsurprising that these new 'East Enders' have opted to take on the predominant linguistic coloration.

MLE surely exists, but it may be dangerous to isolate and simplify, however much this may suit the media. Slang is a long-established form of language, half a millennium old at least, and MLE is simply the latest version, a development and not a sidetrack let alone parallel creation. MLE is the name that has been given to the current set of words that for the last few years are those that fulfil the role of 'youth slang', mainly as sourced within the confines of London. That the slang was originally black and has crossed both race and class (not merely to whites but, given the current demographics, also to Asians) is not a wholly new phenomenon: it was there, whether the users noticed it or not, in the middle-class adoption by the beats then hippies of black American slang in the 1960s. The difference there, again because of demographics, is simply that we now have a substantial young native-born black population, whose slang production is strengthened by their fulfilling the primary role of social outsiders / 'cool' rebels. This has created a home-grown UK input that did not hitherto exist as much as anything because those who would provide the slang did not yet exist in the UK. So what we are seeing is a perfectly logical development. Perhaps the adoption of black speech sounds – phonology – is different, but then that seems to me to echo Mockney, where the sounds adopted were those of the white slang speakers again by a social group – the young white middle-class – who would never hitherto have used them.

There is also a final proviso, which is focused as much on the gatherers of slang as on the language itself. The baseline of contemporary slang, whether MLE or other, is its fissiparousness. Niche, as the slogan used to say, rules. If simple divisions such as 'American' and 'English' remind one of the days of four-channel terrestrial TV, the variety of modern slangs echoes that of cable and its seemingly infinite selection of choices. Slang differs from estate to estate and project to project, from postcode to postcode and from city to city.

Outside temporary labels and subsets, slang in its most broad-brush form remains a continuum. We have slang's themes and its users – the dispossessed, the marginal – in 1531 and have been seeing them one way or another ever since. The marginality is what counts, not the drugs, the clothes or the music. To an extent MLE exists because the media shone its light and lo! it was there. It may represent the latest form, at least in the UK, but it is still, just as is the succession of synonyms that form slang's evolving lexis, more of what we have already seen and, surely, a precursor of what is to come.

Index